Globalized urban precarity in Berlin and Abidjan

Manchester University Press

Globalized urban precarity in Berlin and Abidjan

Young men and the digital economy

Hannah Schilling

Manchester University Press

Published by Manchester University Press
Oxford Road, Manchester M13 9PL

www.manchesteruniversitypress.co.uk

British Library Cataloguing-in-Publication Data
A catalogue record for this book is available from the British Library

ISBN 978 1 5261 6209 0 hardback

First published 2023

Typeset by
New Best-set Typesetters Ltd

Contents

Preface and acknowledgements

This project would not have been possible without the many residents, airtime sellers and riders amongst them, in Abidjan and Berlin whom I met during my fieldwork in both cities. The encounters were full of hospitality and I am grateful for learning so much through meeting every single one; and I thank them for showing me their worlds and their ways of making do and holding on. Particular thanks go to Stéphane, Eric, Darius & SII, Abidjan Lutte and Shalom International, who have been key to understanding Abidjan's everyday business and introduced me to so many others. Similarly in Berlin, many thanks go to Deliverunion and the people involved, who facilitated access for me to interview partners and gain deeper insights into the world of work as a rider.

Many people have informed my sociological thinking for this project, but certainly one of the most significant was Talja Blokland. She has supported my project in many ways, but particularly through inspiring conversations in which she showed me how to 'turn the glass' to give phenomena a new perspective. I learned much about theory in practice and doing critical sociology. Her relational sociology profoundly informs my work. I thank her for her encouragement throughout the research and writing process, and the valuable advice she gave to get a 'feel for the game' in academia.

The Urbanizing Faith project was a starting point from where this journey began. I thank the entire team for this exciting research collaboration, which drew me into urban sociology beyond Berlin and Paris and was a start for me to ask questions about how to work on urban theory from cities 'off the map'. Christine Hentschel and AbdouMaliq Simone were so much inspiration here – and I thank both of them for conversing, thinking together and giving

Contents

Preface and acknowledgements

This project would not have been possible without the many residents, airtime sellers and riders amongst them, in Abidjan and Berlin whom I met during my fieldwork in both cities. The encounters were full of hospitality and I am grateful for learning so much through meeting every single one; and I thank them for showing me their worlds and their ways of making do and holding on. Particular thanks go to Stéphane, Eric, Darius & SII, Abidjan Lutte and Shalom International, who have been key to understanding Abidjan's everyday business and introduced me to so many others. Similarly in Berlin, many thanks go to Deliverunion and the people involved, who facilitated access for me to interview partners and gain deeper insights into the world of work as a rider.

Many people have informed my sociological thinking for this project, but certainly one of the most significant was Talja Blokland. She has supported my project in many ways, but particularly through inspiring conversations in which she showed me how to 'turn the glass' to give phenomena a new perspective. I learned much about theory in practice and doing critical sociology. Her relational sociology profoundly informs my work. I thank her for her encouragement throughout the research and writing process, and the valuable advice she gave to get a 'feel for the game' in academia.

The Urbanizing Faith project was a starting point from where this journey began. I thank the entire team for this exciting research collaboration, which drew me into urban sociology beyond Berlin and Paris and was a start for me to ask questions about how to work on urban theory from cities 'off the map'. Christine Hentschel and AbdouMaliq Simone were so much inspiration here – and I thank both of them for conversing, thinking together and giving me the opportunity to learn from their imagination. For this project, AbdouMaliq's work on African cities laid an important ground for my fieldwork and research inquiry. I thank Christine for all the discussions we had throughout the process of developing my PhD, and her encouragement to think out of the box, and to make me feel that this project was valuable.

I am indebted to Ousmane Dembélé. Our research collaboration in the Urbanizing Faith project motivated me to continue learning about Abidjan. His knowledge of Abidjan as urban geographer, philosopher and entrepreneur was extremely valuable for developing the research project and doing the fieldwork. I am thankful for the many discussions we had in which he took the time to listen to my experiences in Abidjan and helped me to connect them to theoretical questions.

I thank Andreas Eckert for his important advice on literature and research perspectives from a global labour history, and his valuable comments on my research project. The Re:Work Kolleg with its lectures was an important place to help the project evolve, and I thank the team at Re:Work for providing me with infrastructure for a workshop related to my project.

I am grateful to the International Graduate Program Berlin-New York-Toronto (IGK) at the Center for Metropolitan Studies at Technical University Berlin, and thank in particular all my colleagues of the cohort 2015–18 for mutual support throughout the three years together. In particular I want to thank Katharina and Marlène for three amazing years as office neighbours! Daniel Tödt and Noa Ha have been wonderful tutors. The German Research Foundation (DFG) has provided generous financial support, without which my stays in Abidjan, and attendance at various international conferences and the summer school of *ECAS* in Cagliari would not have been possible. I would also like to thank the German Academic Scholarship Foundation for enabling me to visit the foundation's summer schools while doing my PhD, and its uncountable support on the way there.

In Abidjan, as in Berlin, many other researchers have helped towards the realization of this project. In Abidjan, I thank in particular the 'team Dembélé': Adou, Appolinaire, Awa, Dénise, Estelle, Fatou, Djama, Lydie, Marie-Hélène, Nadja, Priscille, Sabine, Safi, Sanata and all those names which are missed, but who belonged here. Many thanks to Daniel. And to Ronan, for showing me Brakaguhé.

Moreover, the team at the Laboratoire de sociologie économique et d'anthropologie des appartenances symboliques (LAASSE), directed by Prof. Roch Gnabéli, and including Laurent Bazin, has been important to me, offering a research centre to present and discuss my research project. At the Department of Geography (Institut de Géographie Tropicale, Abidjan), I thank in particular Mireille and Siriki. For the space in between Abidjan and Berlin, I want to express my sincere gratitude to Dominique, who has given me shelter for writing and thinking, and who contributed much to finding my way as a researcher from Europe in Abidjan.

In Berlin, I thank the team of the Urban and Regional Sociology Department at Humboldt Universität zu Berlin for their support and inspiring discussions around urban theory. In particular I would like to thank Daniela K. and Nina for commenting on later drafts of my writing. Another academic environment intellectually enriching for this research project was the NYLON-Einstein Circle, and I thank all members I met in these many years for the interdisciplinary dialogue, critical readings and peer-to-peer support. In particular, I would like to thank Hanna for her advice and for thinking together through informality. A special thanks goes to Daniela R., who was my friend and partner in crime during the numerous days passed at the library. My colleagues at the Lottum Street office helped me to continue writing and thinking in the difficult times of the pandemic, and I want to thank them for pizza and laughter, especially Nina.

My time at the Department of Political Sociology at Friedrich Schiller University in Jena as a postdoctoral researcher was very valuable to developing further theoretical discussions around work in the digital economy, and this book greatly benefitted from the conversations I had with Silke van Dyk and Stefanie Graefe on digital platform capitalism and 'voluntariness'. I thank all the members of the DFG research group 'Voluntariness', led by Jürgen Martschukat, for the inspiring discussions at workshops and group meetings.

Many thanks to Awa, Fatou, Adou and Sanata, as well as Josefine and Roman for their transcription work. Thank you to Fatin Abbas for the English proofreading and editing.

I would like to thank Tom Dark, my editor at Manchester University Press, for his assistance and patience in guiding me through the manuscript writing process. I would also like to thank my anonymous reviewers for their careful and helpful comments on my draft at different stages of the process.

This project has received funding from the German Research Foundation (DFG) in the context of a fellowship in the International Graduate Program Berlin-New York-Toronto (IGK) at the Center for Metropolitan Studies at Technical University Berlin (2015–18). The German Academic Scholarship Foundation (*Studienstiftung des deutschen Volkes*) supported the research project in the form of a scholarship (*ideelle Förderung*) that enabled me to participate in workshops and events for career development.

The conversations on which this book is built were held in French, German and English. The quotes in foreign languages are translated by the author into English. Where the original meaning is difficult to translate, expressions in the foreign language are maintained and included in brackets in the quotes, using *italics*. All quotes from interlocutors in the field(s) have been anonymized.

In transition: the making of urban livelihood

Sitting next to me in a hip bar-restaurant in Berlin, Tobias sipped his smoothie. His full, black hair was tamed by a thin hairband and his neon yellow tracksuit top went well with the colourful lights and artsy atmosphere at the bar. 'Berlin is *the* place to become an independent filmmaker; I dream of creating my own stories', he says enthusiastically. Tobias had moved to Berlin after he had failed his A-levels and quit school, since in his home town, he explained, 'there really wasn't anything going on. Only old people still live there.' Everything was different in Berlin though, and there are unexpected twists of fate. So far, instead of shooting films, Tobias had earned a living cycling around the city. He was a part-time bicycle courier at a start-up that delivered food to office workers and the homes of middle-class families. To him, it was just a temporary way to get by. 'Next month, I'll probably look for something else; maybe start some film projects for real.'

A couple of months earlier, I had encountered Marian, who was a similar age to Tobias, but made his living in Abidjan. When I met him the first time, he was sitting at a street corner in his neighbourhood, where he had set up a small table as a desk together with Alain, a friend on whom he relied to make the business work. They were both young men in their twenties who lived in Abidjan, Côte d'Ivoire's economic hub. Marian dreamed of joining public service, preferably as a police officer. For now, while waiting, he worked selling airtime to passers-by. A huge sun umbrella did its best to protect him from the sun and rain. The particular colour of the umbrella, branded with the logo of a telecommunications firm, distinguished him from all the other pedestrians and vendors on the street. Behind his desk, Marian wore a light-coloured shirt and denims, the look of a typical Abidjanese student, completed with glasses. He just had finished his A-levels, and had tried to pass the entrance exams for public service, in vain. So he spent the entire day here, six days a week, always available to refill SIM cards and provide on-site access for making phone calls. At least Marian liked to 'manage his things alone', and to be his own boss – this way, he was able to call it a day whenever he liked.[1]

Digital technologies enable new forms of work – tasks can be done remotely from confined offices at any time; services can be delivered on demand via platforms; electronic messages and calculations based on algorithms can replace personal assignment of tasks. Marian and Tobias are young urbanites who try to make ends meet with such new forms of work. They sell airtime[2] with their mobile phones and deliver food for online platforms with their bikes. Both jobs require working with mobile phones and on the basis of platform technologies, and were remunerated activities in the digital economy that attracted many young adults in the cities Abidjan and Berlin respectively in the 2010s.

In Berlin, food delivery is part of the 'gig economy' – that is, 'labour markets that are characterized by independent contracting that happens through, via, and on digital platforms' (Woodcock and Graham 2020, 2). This delivery work is paradigmatic for the digitally mediated contingent work, and central to it is a new type of firm: a platform that provides the 'infrastructure to intermediate between different user groups, by displaying monopoly tendencies driven by network effects, by employing cross-subsidization to draw in different user groups, and by having designed a core architecture that governs the interaction possibilities' (Woodcock and Graham 2020, 2). Riders like Tobias work on demand via an app to receive 'gigs': they 'log onto a smartphone app to receive single delivery jobs, automatically allocated by an algorithm' (Tassinari and Maccarrone 2017, 353). Their earnings are volatile. Some of the riders work as contractors.[3] And although some riders are employed and work for Germany's minimum wage,[4] their work is most often casual, and as such low-paid and offering few hours. Such 'gig-work' (Schmidt 2016) or geographically tethered gig work (Woodcock and Graham 2020, 2) is discussed as constituting new forms of precarization (Animento *et al.* 2017; Jan 2018; Ravenelle 2019; Scholz 2017).

In Abidjan, airtime sellers work as micro-entrepreneurs or in non-legally coded employment. The sale of airtime in Abidjan is discussed as constituting a new kind of informal work (Chéneau-Loquay 2004, 2010; Hamanys Broux de Ismael 2016; Loukou 2005, 2013a, 2013b; Ouédraogo 2010). The sale of airtime is not platform work, and as such is not a case of work of the gig economy in a narrow sense. The platform here doesn't play the same role as mediator between contractors and different user groups on the basis of algorithmic management. However, it similarly represents a case of casual, non-permanent piecework within the digital economy, with little job security and a lack of any options for career development.

It is in this sense that we can speak in both cases of 'gigs', that is 'casual, piecemeal work' (Woodcock and Graham 2020, 1), and of paradigmatic cases for a contemporary economic transformation in which 'work in many sectors is becoming temporary, unstable and patchworked. It entails workers spending less time at one job, a risk of time spent without income, workers undertaking more jobs (possibly at the same time), and unpaid time spent searching for tasks or gigs' (Woodcock and Graham 2020, 1). This work in the digital economy often comes along with precarious conditions: young urbanites like Marian and Tobias earn little, often not much more than half of the official minimum wage.[5] They work flexibly and in temporary contracts with few entitlements to social protection. This is why work as airtime seller and food delivery rider fit to what is commonly understood as precarious or informal work: it is characterized by flexibility, temporariness, low remuneration and few formal entitlements to social protection due to work status. Moreover, airtime sellers and delivery riders have to provide for their working tools, including bikes and mobile phones, on their own.

The following research asks how inequalities are reproduced in such new forms of work that emerge in digital transformations in contemporary cities. Working in instability is not necessarily marginalizing. This book wants to explain why it is that working in low-paid, temporary and poorly legally protected jobs makes it difficult for some youth to secure viable existences in transitions to adulthood. With this question, I shed light on the heterogeneity of livelihoods and positions of workers that are sometimes homogenized to a 'global precariat' (cf. Standing 2011). To understand the mechanisms that reproduce inequalities, I focus on the practices for making a living of urban youth who work in precarious conditions. How does a transitory precarity become enduring? What are the processes behind this? What is the role of work in these processes? To answer these questions, I study the making of a living of urban residents in Abidjan and Berlin, who are between 18 and 35 years old and make money in temporary, flexible and low-paid activities in digital economies. I work comparatively to advance our understanding of functional causes for the different distribution of economic security.

This book expands on the recent debate in sociology that seeks to connect the work on precarity by West European sociologists to debates on inequalities worldwide (for an overview see Köhler *et al.* 2017, 282f.). Here, informalization and precarization are the two concepts that are discussed in their commonalities (e.g. Breman and van der Linden 2014; Burchardt *et al.* 2013; Mayer-Ahuja 2012, 2017; Mosoetsa *et al.* 2016; Munck 2013). Building on this, I argue for a comparative analysis of precarious and informal work by looking at the two processes that both concepts capture: changes in legal regulation of work, or in the position of workers in relation to the state (law) (AlSayyad 2003; Castel 2003; Mayer-Ahuja 2013, 2012; Neilson and Rossiter 2008; Portes *et al.* 1989); and second, the (politics of) commodification of labour and labour power (Bazin 2014; Breman and van der Linden 2014; Marcelli *et al.* 2010; Paret 2016; Rekhviashvili 2015; Viti 2013; Williams and Nadin 2012). With that, this book neither adds another conceptual discussion on precarity and informality, nor does it compare airtime sellers and food delivery riders, looking at the differences and similarities of predefined dimensions of precarity/informality, as cases that stand for (national) economic contexts (see Barbier 2005 for the challenges of such comparison). Instead, I use the comparison of airtime distribution and platform food delivery as a means to identify common functional causes for the reproduction of inequalities in unstable work, that might vary between the two contexts, but can serve as analytical lenses beyond the particular case studies.

Work in the platform metropolis

This book sets out to explore in more depth the 'human relations of accumulation' within urban digital economies. In this way, it aims to contribute to urban theory (Buckley 2018, 2), by decentring its approach to class and to the 'metropolitan working class', and to study the position of labour within forms of accumulation taking place in cities (Buckley 2018, 4). Urban studies, not less than social sciences more generally, are trapped in a common idea about wage labour as the standard reference from which to think about work. A 'century of labouring man' (Standing 2002, quoted in Ferguson and Li 2018, 2) has turned a 'lifeway of what had been a small fraction of the population (the stabilized urban working class)' into the projected future of all (Ferguson and Li 2018, 2). Still today, the work outside of wage labour is mostly defined through what it is not. 'Indeed, the "proper job" has served for so long as a presumed norm or telos of "development" that we are too often left with a stunted and reactive set of categories and concepts for thinking about all the other ways in which people make their way in the world' (Ferguson and Li 2018, 1).

My analytical framework integrates a broader variety of ways in which labour and labour power can become commodified and can produce economic insecurities in urban livelihoods. Speaking of a global class is difficult (Breman 2013, 135). 'Workers of the world' (van der Linden 2008) have always existed under very diverse living conditions (Mezzadra 2012; Schilling *et al.* 2019; Scully 2016). With the ever-increasing visibility of non-standard forms of employment, the constitutive heterogeneity of work comes to the foreground, as well as the intersection of multiple categories of difference that define experiences of precarity (e.g. Castro Varela 2005; Jungwirth and Scherschel 2010; Manske and Pühl 2010; Nickel 2009 for the German debate). The 'populations subsisting outside of wage labour [can no longer be] characterised through notions of deviance and surplus; as informal workers, "dangerous classes" and "wasted lives" – as peoples without history or future' (Monteith 2020).

The digital economy, with its platform- and non-platform-mediated gig work, this book argues, is a particularly well suited site of economic practices to observe and study processes of institutionalizing work. We can see here how boundaries of work are negotiated. It is an area of work in which social relations around work should be made more visible in the debate, in order to fully understand how inequalities are reproduced in the precarious and informalized working conditions emerging here. In contexts in which much work is done at the margins of the market and the state, marginalization cannot be explained only by positioning actors in reference to formal labour markets or wage labour. It is necessary to undertake careful analysis of the 'shifting boundaries of market work' (Abbott 2005, 307). This is also necessary in regard to the notion of informal work, which is mostly discussed in relation to formal employment (e.g., Portes *et al.* 1989). Informalization is often equated with marketization (Marcelli *et al.* 2010, 23) and the informal economy as a sphere of entrepreneurialism outside of state regulation (e.g., de Soto 1989). A more nuanced analysis of how an 'informal economy' as such works and how inequalities are reproduced here is much needed (Viti 2013, 177; but see e.g. Lourenço-Lindell 2001; Neves and du Toit 2012). Informal economies are not only market exchanges or power-free community practices (Lourenço-Lindell 2001). I elaborate an analytical framework on economic practice, which accounts for more than market exchange and the rationality of a *homo economicus*, and acknowledges other sources of legitimation of economic practice than state law.

In the following research, I argue that the commonality between airtime selling and food delivery is that they are cases of commodification of labour and labour power which produce precarity for the making of livelihoods in youth transitions to adulthood. But rather than comparing them by class or as positioned in the labour market or the nation-state, I acknowledge the variety of commodifications and entanglement of forms of economic practice. Research on informalization and precarization has provided important insights into how precarious work conditions are the product of varieties of regulation of the economy and labour regimes, or of modes of governing that bring about new forms of subjectivation (AlSayyad 2003; Breman and van der Linden 2014; Freudenschuss 2013; Lorey 2010; Marchart 2013; Neilson and Rossiter 2008; Precarias a la deriva 2004; Rossiter and Neilson 2005; Slavnic 2010). This research illuminates structural conditions of precarities, but leaves opaque how the making of livelihood under these conditions is done in the everyday of urban residents, and how inequalities are reproduced in practice. Here, this book aims to contribute with a study of practices and an analysis of ways in which resources circulate between people, and actors organize resources in interactions with others. Adopting a relational approach to urban inequalities (Blokland 2012; Blokland *et al.* 2016), I conceive inequality as 'a relation between persons or sets of persons in which interaction generates greater advantages for one than for another ... Inequality results from unequal control over value-producing resources' (Tilly 2001, 365). At the focus is the organization of resources in social relations (cf. Blokland *et al.* 2016; Blokland and Savage 2008).

With a focus on social relations, we can explore the various forms of subsistence, sociality and hustle that make up urban economies. I draw attention to diverse socio-economic relations of people's working lives, their interdependencies and the ways in which they access resources through reciprocal and redistributive practices. Work exceeds the provision of material resources. Material activities of living are also important in their dimension for nurturing social being (Monteith 2020, quoting Melamed 2015, 84). Urban dwellers' making a living includes that they are 'making themselves living' (Ferguson and Li 2018, 13): 'Some of the most important sources of non-wage and non-farm livelihood today are bound up with the construction of persons and social relations' (Ferguson and Li 2018, 13). Work entails then not simply a quantum of labour, but 'instead entails the cultivation of relations of intimacy and sociality that are themselves part of one's whole personal and familial life' (Ferguson and Li 2018, 13).

To contextualize these new perspectives on work in the specific dynamics of the platform metropolis, we can learn from anthropological research in African societies. The latter trouble ideas of smooth technological change with their focus on infrastructure and their material and social elements, as well as their ruptures and 'hitches and fixes' (Archambault 2017, 28; Larkin 2013; see also, beyond Africa, Graham and Marvin 2002 on splintering urbanism). This scholarship shows how technology affects social and cultural life in societies outside of the North Atlantic core (Bruijn *et al.* 2009; Chéneau-Loquay 2012; De Broux 2016; Hahn and Kibora 2008; Kamga 2012; Kiyindou *et al.* 2015; Matlon 2014b; Pfaff 2010). Research points to mobile devices' symbolic capital and their usefulness in overcoming geographical limitations of knitting social ties. Also the recent interest in 'platforms' has opened up avenues for studying human relations of accumulation in cities. Coining the term 'platform urbanism', scholars here conceptualize socio-material and spatiotemporal relations that underpin, shape and emerge under platform businesses (Richardson 2018; Rodgers and Moore 2018;

Rossi 2019). This book, however, switches the focus from the technological devices and networks themselves, with all their forms of cultural appropriation, to the urban economic lives that unfold within the technological change termed digitalization. What meaning do people attach to work in platform-mediated services? To what extent do we see here a troubling of the idea of the centrality of work for organizing livelihood? What can we learn from this for the study of social inequalities in cities?

With these questions in mind, the making of livelihoods in gig economies turns less around the technological architecture of the work organization, but focuses more on the social relations during work and the negotiation of the symbolic meaning of gig work in the young residents' forms of sociality and their making do in diverse socio-economic relations. This perspective adds to research done in labour studies which situates gig work in new labour–capital relations and shows how technological tools are used to increase possibilities for control in hyper-flexible work contexts (Staab and Nachtwey 2016; Wood *et al.* 2019). At the same time, it complements urban studies' focus on the impact of technological change for economic growth and its political regulation in cities (cf. debate on 'smart cities': e.g. Drahokoupil and Piasna 2019; Jörg *et al.* 2016; Rossi and Di Bella 2017). That said, this research contributes on the one hand to urban studies' debate on the transformation of the urban through digital technologies, by bringing in insights from economic anthropology and global labour studies. On the other hand, my research is situated within the sociology of work and its discussion on the gig economy's repercussions on social inequalities. The lens of the urban can help here to integrate a wider range of socio-material infrastructures that make accumulation possible.

Coming of age in generic instability

By turning the making of a living into a question about 'making oneself living', questions about identity and belonging attached to work become central. Amidst all possible ways in which lives can become precarious, I focus on urban youth as a category that references to the 'structurally un-placed' (Ferguson and Li 2018,

14), those urban dwellers 'yet to become' (Simone 2004b). Their making do, their 'making themselves living', is a pressing question for youth. In my prism of social inequalities, I focus on inequalities in transitioning, or in other words inequalities in the life course. Information and communication technology (ICT) industries enter in a changing game of becoming adult, and as such represent tools to play, while at the same time they can turn into a trap of getting stuck in this game.

Being young in Abidjan is not an exception. Rather exceptional, however, is to have stable employment. While in Berlin youth unemployment is not as high as in many African cities, urban youth face similar challenges to making do in contexts of generic instability (Schilling *et al.* 2019). In what follows, I relate to each other the urban hustle of young people living in Berlin and Abidjan, in a way that allows us to start thinking through work in digital economies. Urban youth is often discussed in urban studies through the prism of the imagination of the exceptional, either in terms of innovation or the threat to the established order (e.g., Abbink and van Kessel 2005; Biaya 2000; Collignon and Diouf 2001; de Boeck and Honwana 2005; Diouf 2003; Skelton and Valentine 1998). Young urbanites' ordinary practices of making do have not yet been explored extensively in a comparative/global perspective, nor with a focus on the reproduction of inequalities among urban residents in their twenties (but see e.g. Ball *et al.* 2000; Hansen and Dalsgaard 2008; MacLeod 1995; Mains 2012).

Youth, as reference for the structurally unplaced, is experiencing a gap between expectations of progress and a reality of stagnation (e.g. Hansen 2005; Mains 2012; Masquelier 2005, 2019; Weiss 2009). What is happening in this gap? The existing work that studies the 'relationship between youth and work practices in urban contexts of resource scarcity' (Thieme 2018, 539) has used the notion of the 'hustle' and 'waithood' to describe the temporariness in which economic practices develop. 'Waiting is not absence of activity … waiting is not passive but entails forms of labour in/of time' (Bear 2014, quoted in Stasik *et al.* 2020, 2, 3). Hustling illustrates the reproduction of 'youth as a process of making do that negotiates the entanglements of crises and waiting, while moving towards the asymptotic horizons of "adulthood"' (Thieme 2018, 531). This complicates the idea of life stages and clear-cut phases of transitioning as 'thresholds to maturity' (Ungruhe and Esson 2017, 25), structured by linear time.

At the same time, even if youth as a concept works, it might work less as a category that speaks for a group of actors experiencing equally a 'precarious present across post-Fordist and post-colonial informal economies' (Thieme 2018, 532). When it comes to the social life of work, gendered expectations about 'a proper job' matter. As Raewyn Connell suggests, 'masculinity itself is deeply embedded in the social meaning of work' (McDowell 2003, 58). As Raewyn Connell suggests, '[d]efinitions of masculinity are deeply enmeshed in the history of institutions and economic structures' (Connell 1995, 29, quoted in McDowell 2003, 58). In this sense, gender roles are more than 'individual characteristics but ... they are constructed, defined and maintained in discourse and culture and sustained through institutional practices. Masculinities are, in other words, collective social practices' (McDowell 2003, 12).

This book looks at the struggles of making a living from the perspective of young men, living in predominantly lower middle- and working-class neighbourhoods in Berlin and Abidjan. It enquires how the performance of gender matters in their daily weaving of social existence, orienting choices and attachments to forms of income. Many of my interlocutors refer to aspirations for marriage, responsibility and to being in a position to give (see also Mains 2012; Matlon 2016; Ungruhe and Esson 2017, 25). However, rather than a book about the negotiation of new forms of masculinity and a diagnosis of the shifting 'roles in capitalism as workers and heads of households' (Matlon 2016), or men's shifting sense of self (McDowell 2003, 58), I start from young men's standpoints to work out how gender roles enable access to sites, spaces, social fields/networks, and how they enable flows of resources.

That said, I approach gender more in its performative dimension (Newell 2009). Newell shows, in his work on urban Abidjanese youth, how modern gender roles were enacted in a mutual knowledge about their illusion, or 'bluff' (2009). Male urban dwellers acted like a 'man', dressed in latest fashions and buying whatever women demanded. 'And it is this performance of masculine success that is important, not the actual "breadwinning" potential of the actor' (Newell 2009, 387). In the words of a relational sociologist, male youth interested me not so much for finding out 'who they are', what type of masculinity they embodied, but rather I used their standpoint to see how gender roles worked as bounded categories. '[T]heir boundaries [are] do[ing] crucial organizational work, and because categorical differences actually account for much of what ordinary observers take to be the result of variation in individual talent or effort' (McDowell 2003, 20, quoting Tilly 1999, 6). I look at youth struggles of coming of age as practices that aim at becoming a person of value, someone who has weight and who matters in their interdependent relations with others. Urban dwellers can change their roles; they can be perceived or perform as an 'adult' in one situation and as 'youth' in another, they can hide their economic successes in order to circumvent obligations to give, decide to go to an event or to call in sick, in their daily manoeuvres to make themselves living. It is in this acknowledging of improvisation and 'a city in the making' (Simone 2010), that I prefer to speak of practices of becoming a person of value, someone who has weight and who matters when weaving social interdependencies (cf. Ferguson 2015).

A comparative perspective for a global sociology of precarity

When I began this research in 2014, Abidjan was to me a blank spot on a map, far away. I travelled there to find the 'elsewhere' that Jennifer Robinson (2016) mobilizes to craft a more cosmopolitan urban theory which draws on a multiplicity of empirical standpoints for generating conceptual language. Integrating cities 'off the map' (Robinson 2002), this comparative project probes possibilities for a new way of relating urban places to each other and embedding this in an analytical project for a more global urban theory (McFarlane 2011; Robinson 2016; 2015; Simone and Pieterse 2017). What can we learn about sociality more in general, when we start in places where the majority of urban dwellers are making a living in what can be considered from the outside 'precarious conditions'?

The comparative analysis of young airtime sellers and food delivery riders serves to explore new connections and ways to relate urban contexts such as Abidjan and Berlin. Both cities are regional hubs that attract young people to invent themselves, and are places of cultural innovation and hubs of emerging digital economies. But this research does not compare these two cities as such, nor does it compare young urbanites' positions on the basis of measures of livelihoods, such as poverty rates, labour market statistics or GDPs – measures which easily sustain categorizations of Berlin as developed and Abidjan as underdeveloped settings. Instead, this research takes the two urban settings of Abidjan and Berlin as a starting point to develop a more 'cosmopolitan urban studies that situates its analysis in a greater diversity of experiences, including the experience of those places formerly off the map (of theory)' (Hentschel 2015, 79). In this, the book advances the debate on new forms of comparisons in urban studies (e.g. Heer 2019; Hentschel 2015; McFarlane 2010; Nijman 2007; Peck 2015; Robinson 2011). Exploring the way young airtime sellers in Abidjan and young food delivery riders in Berlin make ends meet, this book demonstrates the relevance of actors' capacity to improvise and to connect with others for organizing livelihood beyond stable employment (Simone 2004a; Simone and Pieterse 2017). For many youths today, the previous parameters according to which the horizons of adulthood could be reached – the investment into a master's degree or a professional qualification, for example – don't bring them anywhere. In such contexts of 'eroding maps of life' (Jeffrey 2010), the side job or the hustle on the side turn into a situational normalcy, a situation of permanent temporariness, in which instability is a shared condition rather than an exception. This book pays attention to such value making practices beyond the official capitals recognized in market/state operations, to show how within these interstices, urban precarities crystallize and social inequalities are reproduced.

Hence, thinking urban precarity through the comparative study of airtime sellers and food delivery riders is also a discussion about 'theory culture': I invite the reader to reflect on the 'ontological and epistemological framings that inform how the world is being debated, how knowledge is being produced and questioned'. It is a strategy that is not 'neutral but that seeks to unsettle and destabilize knowledge and theory as it is produced' (McFarlane 2010, 738). The airtime economy and the platform economy of food delivery are not sites that I consider as 'prototypical' for entire cities, nations or groups of workers, nor are they 'similar' as such – they have components that make them fruitful for comparison, for translating theories from one context to another and to ask how one context is 'thought through in reference to another' (McFarlane 2010, 734). This 'thinking cities through elsewhere' has been further conceptualized by Jennifer Robinson (2015), who invites us to begin conceptualizing 'anywhere, with any singularity, but always emerging through building connections with and identifying differentiations across other related instances' (Robinson 2015, 16).

Behind this plea for innovative conceptualization lies a fundamental rupture with forms of developmentalism and the idea of the global as a common frame of reference as to which cities can be positioned, ranked and clustered. City ranks based on the global city, as in the concept launched by Saskia Sassen (2001), or ranging cities as 'world cities', are such frameworks in which particular economic processes of globalization are left out and which thus invisibilize other forms of global entanglements and create cities 'off the map' (Robinson 2002). Instead, I take the ordinariness (Robinson 2006) of each urban context as a starting point and compare Abidjan and Berlin as cities 'off the map', which, despite and in all their ordinariness, teach us something about urban precarity in youth transitions in the digital era. With a focus on the ordinary, I also make a plea for a shift in perspective away from grounding relations between cities in the global North and South in imperialism, colonial entanglements and postcolonial dependencies. I see the danger here that analytic bifurcations would still persist and we 'may end up doing little else than turning colonialism or colonial discourse into a new "independent variable"' that explains differences (Go 2013, 39). Instead, I use postcolonial thought as a means to 'enable new lines of urban research and theory' and to shift from the postcolonial as an urban condition to the postcolonial as a 'critical, deconstructive methodology' (Roy 2011, 308). Postcolonial urbanism challenges the 'privileged link between modernity and certain kind of cities' (Robinson 2004, 709, quoted in Roy 2011, 309). African cities have often been described as 'an object "apart from the world", or as a failed and incomplete example of something else' (Mbembe and Nuttall 2004, 348) instead of seeing here how modernity and worldliness are 'intrinsically connected' (Nuttall and Mbembe 2008, 1).

Thinking through Abidjan and Berlin as 'ordinary cities' also overcomes a depiction of Abidjan as 'crisis', 'informality' and 'city of slums'. To write both cities into a global urban theory rewrites this narrative and reframes globalization as a 'set of processes that are refracted, splintered, and cracked' (Nuttall and Mbembe 2008, 5). Cities on the African continent have also 'attracted colonial and global capital', and today's 'fractured, colliding, and splintered orders of urban life' that characterize African cities might be characteristic for many cities around the world today (Nuttall and Mbembe 2008). In other words, I argue with Myers for the 'importance of conceptualizing with the global South-Southern intellectual thought, urban patterns, artistic expression, historical experiences, everyday urban life, and comparisons – when examining contemporary global urbanization and urbanism anywhere' (Myers 2020, 5). Especially when exploring lived experiences of precarity for urban youth, and when we want to understand urban life under generic instability (Schilling *et al.* 2019), starting from the global South is productive. Without ahistorizing and naturalizing life in 'Southern' urban settings, we can draw on an extensive urban scholarship that has theorized and given rich empirical accounts on the making of urban livelihoods under the radar, in a state of preparedness, making the most of a situation in contexts of scarcity (Bayat 2013; Simone 2004a, 2018, 2021). Current historical processes – and particularly the current digital era – thus seem to turn old margins into new frontiers: places 'where highly flexible, informal economies – of the kind now expanding everywhere have long thrived; ... where new idioms of work, time, and value take root, thus to alter planetary practices' (Comaroff and Comaroff 2012, 121). They locate 'the contemporary frontiers of capitalism ... in environments in which the protection of liberal democracy, the rule of law, and the labour contract are, at best, uneven' (Comaroff and Comaroff 2012, 125). In this sense, the 'Global South [may be] producing and exporting some ingenious modes of survival' (Comaroff and Comaroff 2012, 125). The global South is here not so much a geographical location, but rather a 'working concept, built around regions where a vulnerable majority of populations resides in conditions of comparable marginality' (Myers 2020, 2).[6]

Such a standpoint reflects also in the concrete research process and requires new starting points for theory building. I began conceptualizing economic practice from the study of the everyday of Abidjan's urban residents. From there, I developed analytical lenses to study the reproduction of inequalities in precarious work settings comparatively, in Berlin and in Abidjan. This way of crafting connections brings to the foreground the importance of relational work for the making of livelihood. It shows the limits of comparing formal labour positions and qualifications of young residents. These parameters alone can't explain the reproduction of inequalities. In other words, this book wants to expand explanations for reproducing inequalities through a study of practices in which resources are not exchanged as capitals with fixed and stable value (cf. Schilling *et al.* 2019). It asks: how are advantages maintained when institutionalized forms of capital are not the only ways to ensure social position, and no longer even provide a means for doing so? How do the deinstitutionalization of professional roles and the instability of rules operating at work make 'ambivalence' productive in power relations? What sociability do actors need to invest in and how do they build symbolic capital (i.e. reputation, prestige) to secure distributive outcomes, when access to employment positions and to the associated rights to welfare is difficult? I draw on economic sociologists and anthropologists (Bourdieu 1977, 2005; Guyer 2004, 1995; Hannerz 1980; Zelizer 2012) to show that the economic is constituted by way of social relations, and not only embedded in the social. Explaining the reproduction of inequalities in variegated processes of commodification of labour and labour power, hence, means not only identifying who depends most on market relations, but understanding how actors can accumulate privileges (or not) in their relational work of transactions of resources – transactions that encompass market transactions and are fed by very different cultural repertoires than the liberal credo (Münnich and Sachweh 2017, 12). Importantly, this project aims to contribute to a better understanding of when certain forms of transactions, as exchange, gift or compensation (Zelizer 1996), become legitimate, under what power relations these take place and how inequalities are reproduced in this relational work.

The chapters

Before we explore in more depth the lifeworlds of young men, we will contextualize their economic activities in the broader urban context of Abidjan and Berlin. To this end, the next chapter introduces the reader to the research design and the wider context of the young airtime sellers and food delivery riders at the heart of this book. Information and communication technologies have played an important role in restructuring Abidjan's urban economy since the 1990s. Subsequently, the use of mobile phones, data flows and mobile payment platforms have become an important aspect of the everyday lives of (young) urban dwellers, and constitutes a growing urban economic sector. Platform-based food delivery in Berlin is a recent form of work that emerged in the context of the gig economy. Abidjan's airtime economy and Berlin's platform food delivery constitute the two empirical cases studied in this book.

From there, Chapter 2 elucidates the book's conceptual devices. I begin with the rationale for the comparison: Abidjan and Berlin are not compared as urban sites, as such; rather, the research compares economic practices. This enables reconsideration of *how* work matters for reproducing socio-material (in)securities in relational mechanisms. Subsequently, I conceptualize work as economic practice and situate economic practices in social inequalities. More precisely, I am interested in three social mechanisms as entry points to study how inequalities get reproduced: social closure or opportunity hoarding, domination and exploitation. These three conceptual lenses structure the presentation of my findings, presented in the three subsequent chapters in which we delve into the young men's everyday life and making do as airtime sellers and food delivery riders.

The third chapter focuses on the symbolic value of the activities for the young men to construct status. It shows how in a context of apparent convenience and freedom, risks of enduring precarity result from processes of closure among workers. In both Berlin and Abidjan, young male workers were marginalized among their co-workers if they valued the activity as their main occupation rather than simply as a bridge or parallel activity. Situating the temporal work in the long term, the chapter concludes that official certificates and institutionalized cultural skills were differently meaningful in the two cases. In Berlin, they were functional elements in objectified mechanisms of social reproduction: for the urban youth in Berlin, presenting themselves to others as detached from work and celebrating flexibility concealed the importance of official qualifications for making a living. In Abidjan, official cultural resources and the pursuit of an economic activity served the investment in relationality – being and spending time with others – to gain 'wealth in people' (Guyer 1995; Vuarin 1994).

The fourth chapter analyses the airtime sellers' and delivery riders' relations to managers and dispatchers. In this way, the chapter decentres from the state as 'rule-maker' and having monopoly of symbolic and physical violence, to overcome dichotomous views on (in)formal spheres of work. Rather, I look at regulatory practices. Law-like arrangements get combined with personalized trust relations to organize relations of domination at work, which can put workers at risk of precarity. The comparative analysis points to the relevance of 'ideas of the state', i.e. how actors perceive and think of the state as a set of political practices (Abrams 1988). In Berlin, standardized rules represent official – or state – enunciations of authority. As such, actors share the belief in them as a legitimate reference against which work cooperation is organized. In Abidjan, the legitimacy of authority on the basis of personalized bonds reflects wider institutional normalcies in which actors see state institutions as institutions that utilize personal relations of domination as sources of authority.

The fifth chapter contextualizes the work in the wider social relations of care. In a work context in which companies exploit workers' labour but withdraw from any responsibility for risk, repair or recuperation, access to care is pivotal for understanding urban precarities. I decentre social security from the welfare state, and instead analyse care practices more broadly, either as kin, or in professionalized support relations, i.e. with state agents. The chapter compares the ways young men use the sale of airtime or food delivery as 'distributive labour' (Ferguson 2015), to be able to make claims on resources in support relations. The chapter shows variation in the ways in which kin and friendship ties are used to confront socio-material insecurities, and explains this by contextualizing how, historically, a particular separation of the public and domestic spheres has been institutionalized and used in mechanisms of secondary exploitation (Dörre and Haubner 2018).

The book's conclusion embeds the relevance of economies of symbolic goods within the debate on value making in the platform metropolis: capitalist accumulation extracts value from everyday life in cities. I argue that looking at the entanglement of economic practices makes it possible to see the implicit use of labour power, veiled in metaphors of a game, or of gifts, in urban digital economies.

Moreover, the digital transformation in cities challenges urban dwellers' opportunities for social reproduction. In a context of a permanent 'temporariness', the importance of work as a means to construct status, reputation, honour – of building person value – remains fundamental, even if not bound into long-term careers as self-accruing individuals. The urban youth at the centre of this research, and their longing to bring themselves into play (with others), working, searching and collaborating, show that work is more than making a living: in the end it is about making *oneself* living (Ferguson and Li 2018).

Notes

1 See Schilling 2017 for a similar vignette.
2 Airtime is communication credit for mobile telephony (data for the Internet, credit for phone calls or SMS messages).
3 To my knowledge, they got €5 per delivery (excluding all forms of bonus and tips).
4 The minimum wage in Germany is €8.50–9 per hour.
5 Airtime sellers' return is 4–6 per cent of the sum transferred for each transaction of airtime; as casual workers, their income often does not exceed €60 per month. This is two-thirds of the minimum wage in Côte d'Ivoire, which is 60,000 FCFA or €91.
6 The delineation originates 'in the so-called Brandt Line of the 1980s separating richer and poorer countries on the world map' (Myers 2020, 2). But the global South cannot be defined in substantive terms. 'The label bespeaks a relation, not a thing in or for itself. It is a labile signifier whose content is determined by everyday material and political processes. [... At the core,] its importance lies in [its reference to an] ex-centricity [an outside to Euro-America]' (Comaroff and Comaroff 2012, 127).

1

Crossing views: airtime selling in Abidjan and food delivery in Berlin

One day during my stay in Abidjan, I got the opportunity to present my research project at the German embassy, in an informal discussion round of German expats in Abidjan. The comparison of young precarious workers in Abidjan and Berlin created discomfort amongst my audience. In their feedback, they mainly emphasized the differences between the two contexts: the Ivorian state didn't provide protection for its young citizens at any comparable level to Germany's social welfare state. The demographics contrasted sharply between the two sites, too: underemployed youth was in a much more desperate situation in a country like Côte d'Ivoire, in which 77.7 per cent of the population is younger than 35 (MPJEJSC 2016, 12), and statistics measure unemployment as about 30.4 per cent among the population aged between 14 and 35 (MPJEJSC 2016, 13). In short, living conditions in Abidjan and Berlin were just too different to compare, commented my audience to my presentation at the German embassy.

This brief vignette of an informal conversation stands for many other discussions I had while presenting my research – and the remarks of my audience are plausible. Measuring official employment, and comparing labour law and welfare policies in Côte d'Ivoire and Germany, shows fundamental differences. In sociological literature, these differences have often been discussed in developmentalist terms, for example when comparing welfare regimes (i.e. for a critical overview [Wehr 2009]). When postcolonial and post-Fordist cities are brought into relation, or cities of the 'Global South and Global North', they are often related to each other through the idea that cities in the global South need to 'catch up' (Comaroff and Comaroff 2012, 114) – as places that lack expanded provision through welfare state institutions, and are inherently 'informally organized' – without clearly defining what this means. Also 'urban studies remains … caught up with an unfortunate history of categorization and developmentalism', in which cities are constructed as 'developed' and 'underdeveloped' (Comaroff and Comaroff 2012, 728). This chapter shows that the focus on practices and mechanisms has potential to overcome developmentalist frameworks of comparison. It lays out the methods with which I explored possible connections between livelihoods and introduces the two field sites in more detail, to embed the concrete everyday struggles of young men in Abidjan and Berlin in the broader historical context of each city.

The journey: travelling between Berlin and Abidjan

I got to know Abidjan as a guest of Dr Ousmane Dembélé, assistant professor in urban geography at the Université Félix Houphouët-Boigny, Abidjan. During several research stays in the city, which sum up to about a year in total, his household was my home, and from there I was able to go places and to meet urban youth at various sites in the city. I had worked with Abidjanese youth on questions of work and belonging in another research project together with Ousmane Dembélé,[1] and built on the knowledge gathered there to immerse myself in the lifeworlds of urban youth. I chose several entry points and anchors to meet young residents and to get familiar with the phenomenon of youth unemployment: most importantly, a friend I met in prior visits connected me with an acquaintance she had in one of the residential areas in Yopougon, built in the late 1980s as public housing projects for a rising urban middle class, developed by SICOGI[2] and SOGHEFIA.[3] Simon became my research assistant, and introduced me to the urban youth in this neighbourhood and its surroundings. To get a grasp of the field of activities in which young residents were involved in Abidjan, I began to hang around with youths and regularly visited several sites of youth activities. I started at a gambling spot in the residential area (see Schilling 2017), from which I created relations to other urban youths at a marketplace for technological devices and accessories related to mobile phones and the Internet, and youth involved in a drug scene. As well as the sites in Yopougon, I developed ties to a local youth association in another district, Koumassi. Through these encounters with youth, involved in drug selling, hair dressing, bar services or mobile phone sales, I got a sense about their local index of cultural hierarchies related to work: among others, airtime selling seemed to be an economic activity that was considered both informal and precarious – it was perceived as a temporary way to earn money and as a low-paid activity, and it was an activity that a lot of young men pursued in situations of waithood.

In other words, I constructed my field site (cf. Burrell 2009, 190) by seeking for entry points into the economic practices of young adults not formally employed, and by following them to places and sites indexed in interviews, or coming up during the time spent together. In that way, '[t]he field site transitions from a bounded space that the researcher dwells within to something that more closely tracks the social phenomenon under study. The site is constructed in terms of how such a phenomenon is perceived and acted on by participants' (Burrell 2009, 195). In the continuation of my research I thus focused on the economic field of mobile phone economies and the working conditions of young male airtime sellers in Yopougon and Koumassi. I reached out to the companies which organized airtime distribution, and also did interviews with professionals of one subcontracting firm that distributed communication credit in one district of Abidjan. This was an important part of the research process, as it showed the relevance of formal labour organization in the seemingly informal street vending market of airtime.

I started with interviews and participant observations with airtime sellers and actors in the airtime economy in Abidjan, to develop conceptual lenses with which I then looked back to Berlin. At the time of research, I was living in Berlin – formally employed there and registered as resident and as a German citizen. The choice to focus on gig workers in Berlin resulted from preliminary analyses of the material in Abidjan. Hence, the collection of empirical material and the conceptualization of the empirical realities in the two fields was an iterative process, during which I travelled between Abidjan and Berlin and was inspired by readings and conversations in the street. In Berlin, my entry to the field was marked by the beginning of riders' mobilization against their working conditions. I assisted some of their meetings and public gatherings, through which I met many riders. The dominant discourse in the media in that time was about the riders' protests, and hence a reference for many riders I spoke with too – no matter if they took part in meetings and gatherings or not. But besides meeting riders at moments of protest, I waited for them in front of the restaurants and in public squares and parks or at the riders' offices where they gathered often while waiting for new gigs.

In total, my research builds on in-depth interviews with around thirty-four airtime sellers in Abidjan and twenty-six food delivery riders in Berlin, and participant observations in both cities. Along with several times in which I spent one to two hours at a selling spot of airtime sellers in Abidjan, I spent several hours at a riders' office, at several public demonstrations of riders and at a private gathering of a couple of riders in Berlin. In Abidjan, I complemented the interviews with the young airtime sellers by four formal interviews with professionals of a subcontracting distribution firm (including one director of distribution) and did two interviews and several go-alongs with one of the employees responsible for dispatching airtime credit to the airtime sellers in the neighbourhoods. These additional interviews helped me to better understand to what extent and in what way the airtime sellers were part of the formally organized system of distribution of multinational companies like Orange or Moov, as it was less visible to me than in the case of the delivery platforms in Berlin. In Berlin, I did not approach workers in other management positions in the start-up companies who owned the platforms, as the incorporation of the riders into formally organized work as well as their strong ties to the platform were recognizable in their contractual arrangements and their algorithmic management through the platform.

The interviews were conducted in French, English and German, recorded and transcribed, and included a short standard questionnaire about demographics. In Abidjan, I interviewed the airtime sellers and professionals either at their working spot or at a bar or restaurant. In Berlin, all of the interviews took place at a coffee place or a bar. Interested in the young men's viewpoints on their everyday hustle to make a living, the conversations were focused around their everyday activities and the ways they made ends meet. Even though all of them earned money in the domain of the digital economy of their cities, I explicitly studied how these practices were connected to other domains, such as the household, the neighbourhood or the street/public space. I developed an interview guide[4] that asked first about the organization of livelihood in the everyday and then elaborated from the interviewees' stories on the social relations that mattered in these practices. I asked about role repertoires and what meaning the interviewees attributed to this social tie that they evoked during the interview, and which mattered to their organization of livelihood (i.e. as open questions: how would you describe the relation with person XY, what do you contribute to the relation, what does the relation enable you to do?) By inquiring into their understanding of the transaction, I aimed to assess the 'mixture of idioms that is available to be drawn upon by given groups' (Emirbayer and Goodwin 1999, 1439f.), in resonance with Viviana Zelizer's economic sociology on relational work.

I used these idioms to study 'what governs the conduct of this relationship' (Hannerz 1980, 321). Here, I draw on Ulf Hannerz, who problematized the link between (meaning) structure and relations by looking at role constellations and the involvement of people in situations (see also Blokland 2003). People act within these situations as they are recruited into roles (Hannerz 1980, 317), which depend also on 'where they have been before, and where they may be at some later time, because they are people with memories and plans' (Hannerz 1980, 273). To access these situations, I structured the interview around the following questions – the organization of everyday needs (such as shelter, food, mobility and communication, plus personal needs), and the evaluation of the person's own material situation, including their own explanation for the lack of resources for getting by. I added to this a question on the organization of resources in times of need or difficulties in getting by. A third block was focused on current activities, and here I discussed the organization of work, work relations and the person's own evaluation of the conditions. A fourth topic revolved around money and practices of borrowing and lending. A last block was again more biographical, and focused on future projects and imaginaries of success. During the entire interview, I deepened the information about social ties that was mentioned, and at the end I asked if any people that mattered for the interview partner to be able to get by had not been mentioned so far. A block on demographics and important steps in the life course constituted the final part of the conversation.

The interview guide allowed me to gather stories about everyday practices and how they were embedded in the life course of the person. My approach expands on existing research on social support and work conditions, two fields which are often approached independently of one another. Sociology of work then focuses on the work status and how this affects social networks (see e.g. Marquardsen 2012) and individual coping strategies (e.g. Busch *et al.* 2010; Hepp 2012; Reckinger 2010; Reiners 2010; Scherschel *et al.* 2012; Sommer 2010; Sutter 2013; Vogel 2009). Social support is most often studied as formal network analyses (e.g. Alonso 2012; Diewald 1991; Jansen 2003, 81; Taylor *et al.* 2001; Wellman and Wortley 1990). Integrative approaches, such as livelihood studies, remain narrowly focused on singular cases and risk reproducing individual-centred perspectives instead of relational explanations (cf. De Haan 2012). In general, I adapted the interview guides to the local meanings and relevance of aspects of organizing livelihood. For example, I asked in more detail about unemployment benefits and experiences with the agencies for social benefits in Berlin than in Abidjan.

I used the juxtaposition of lifeworlds of young men in their twenties and thirties making money in two distinct urban economic settings to carve out new connections, rather than exposing similarities and differences based on prior analytical frameworks. As Peck argues with Mignolo (2013), it is not about finding similarities and differences through deploying a fixed 'third' parameter against which sites are brought into relation, but it is about dialogue: a theory culture that 'enables conversations across contextually sensitized positions, while guarding against the uncritical circulation of taken-for granted assumptions borrowed from one context and applied to others' (Peck 2015, 171f.). Chris Pickvance stresses that '[o]n different occasions, different causes or causes with different weights can bring about the same value of variables of interest' (Pickvance 2001, 20). His plural causation model (2001) as well as Sayer's critical realism (1992, 2015) serve as epistemological background for the comparative analysis of the empirical material.

All interviews were transcribed and coded. The analysis focused on interview passages which indicated how social ties were built, maintained and regulated. At this moment, the inductive coding (cf. Przyborski and Wohlrab-Sahr 2009) was a rather descriptive process through which notions such as friendship, respect, reciprocity, norms of deservingness, kin (to name a few) emerged as relevant concepts to develop further. They all seemed important for understanding the social economy of getting by. I began conceptualizing economic practices in the empirical material of the Abidjan case, by 'collect[ing] examples of things we recognize as embodying what the concept refers to, and then look[ing] for what the inevitably messy and historically contingent ideas people routinely use have in common' (Becker 1998, 110f.) 'Doing kinships', 'doing markets', 'doing friendships' were categories of practices I carved out and focused on. I furthermore looked at the conditions which give rise to them and the consequences that result from them (cf. Corbin and Strauss 1990, 420, quoted in Przyborski and Wohlrab-Sahr 2009, 201). With these preliminary categories of practices in mind, I then also began coding the Berlin case. During the coding process of the material in Berlin, I began to look more carefully at the settings in which practices of doing friendships, kinships and markets occurred. Following Becker, I placed the 'term[s] that seem … to describe a trait of a person or group in the context of the system of relations [they] belong … to' (Becker 1998, 132f.). To show this, I started at the workplace itself, as a focus of activity. 'A focus of activity is defined as any social, psychological, legal or physical entity around which joint activities are organized, such as families, work places voluntary organizations, neighbourhoods' (Becker 1998, 136, quoting Feld 1981, 1016). Then I began to look for the way in which practices of friendships, kinning[5] and market transactions were relevant in other domains. This comparative analysis of 'the set of relations' of each category of practices (Becker 1998, 138) showed variation in the properties, conditions and consequences in which 'doing kinships', 'doing markets', 'doing friendships' were embedded in the system of relations and combined to organize livelihood.

On positionalities

In all my eagerness to learn, the context of discovery in this research process was deeply informed by my own positionality in the encounters with young men in Abidjan and Berlin. Independently from the location, doing research incites reflection on one's own legitimacy to seize information from one's interlocutors for the purpose of gaining reputation in the academic field. These worries can easily be washed away by referring to the rewarding effect of just listening and showing interest in the subject's life – what Jordanna Matlon (2014a, 9) calls the legitimating force of doing research. Researching as a white German woman in Abidjan introduced yet another dimension of doubts about my own legitimacy of being 'there' conducting interviews. How would I be able to convincingly practise alternative modes of conceptualization, if I myself was born, raised, educated in Germany – to what extent is it possible to turn off the 'white gaze' (Fanon 2008) as a West European sociologist? Would I be able to disrupt universalizing narratives? I do not deny the possible 'coloniality' of knowledge (Mignolo 2007) produced through my work. To make this visible at least can hopefully contribute to a better understanding about how power relations get reproduced in knowledge production.

As Cindi Katz reflects convincingly, ethnographers are to some extent 'displaced persons … one goes to the field as a kind of "stranger," and draws on that status to see difference and ask questions that under other circumstances might seem (even more) intrusive, ignorant, or inane to those to answer them' (Katz 1994, 68). My presence in the field(s) was characterized by multiple and shifting positionalities (Dery 2020; Sultana 2007). For instance, my positionality as white woman in Abidjan did invoke an *elsewhere*, a place of desire and privilege, in those with whom I spent my time and conducted research in Côte d'Ivoire (cf. Matlon 2014a). But by presenting my research as comparative, I provoked reflections about new possible connections between life in Abidjan and Berlin amongst people I encountered during my research (in university settings and in the streets alike). My presence in the field in Abidjan hence not only evoked in the actors in the field the desire to experience an *elsewhere* through collaborating with me; as someone living in Abidjan, I was also positioned in the *here and now* of an urban society in Abidjan. I was simultaneously 'insider' and 'outsider', and these positionalities were not fixed but rather fluid (see Bilgen *et al.* 2021, 524; cf. Mullings 1999; Sultana 2007; Dery 2020).

My positions in the field were shifting according to circumstances, and were part of negotiation processes in which every party gained and lost in some way (for a similar account see Matlon 2014a). These 'trades' (Becker 1998) took place in my position in the household of my Ivoirian tutor, where I lived during my research stays in Abidjan; they shaped my part in the reputation building among Abidjanese men and my role as patron and donor. These trades were part of a social infrastructure that had to be kept running through small gestures of attention and favours, and in which I was for some people one node, among many others. Also, in Berlin I had to negotiate my positionality as researcher in a highly politicized work environment. Let me explore these different trades in more detail.

I lived as invitee (guest) at the house of Dr Dembélé, which gave me a particular status as a white German woman in Abidjan: my interlocutors in the field located me as a stranger from *elsewhere*, while at the same time they perceived me as a student who lived under the guardianship of an Ivoirian big man, a professor at the university. In this way, I was not only a stranger, but also had a particular position within Ivoirian society as a student who was not yet financially autonomous, and who depended on someone else's resources and protection. My position as a white woman taught me a lot about reputation building in Abidjan; that is, all the ways in which hierarchical positions were sustained and contested – reputation was a means to obtain status. First of all, it mattered for my access to the field – I was able to conduct research in a low-income neighbourhood in Abidjan, in Yopougon, because I was recommended to a young resident there, who took me under his guardianship and opened doors for me. He, in contrast, gained reputation in the neighbourhood as a 'friend of a white woman'. Part of this relationship's value was its exclusivity. I felt this most strongly when I started to hang around with other young men in the area, as it created tensions between us.

The use of the other's status was not only a unidirectional endeavour. As Dery (2020) suggests, fieldwork is an 'intersubjective' process characterized by power sharing – both the researcher and participants are agents with "own agendas" and data collection is a deeply relational and multi-dimensional endeavour (Dery 2020, 1781). I did not only use my status or the status of someone else to gain information in the field, but also the other way around – I accompanied my research assistant and fieldwork partners to different public institutions (the prison, the court, the police, etc.) and my presence seemed to matter for them having access to these public institutions, and to the services they offer. In a way, I became part of a 'node' of a social infrastructure (Matlon 2014a), and meeting young men and the sites in the city where I could go and hang out with them in Abidjan was very much shaped by the way this social infrastructure operated. Access depended on the capacity to reciprocate in the right measure, to uphold your reputation and confirm your status, and to be able to maintain your social contacts by calling them regularly, or contacting them in an appropriate manner – for example, asking them routinely about their health and their plans, or greeting them regularly. Being 'not available' to someone who called was a means of sanctioning that person, or of making clear the difference in rank between you and them.

While in Abidjan, I was perceived as someone with (more) resources; differences in class positions were not openly addressed in my conversations with riders in Berlin. Material conditions of existence, in general, were more difficult to talk about during my research in Berlin than in Abidjan – an experience that informs my sociological analysis about the relevance of the norm of 'doing it alone' in organizing resources, as we will discuss further along in this book. That said, in Abidjan my interlocutors all stressed their need for resources, and presented themselves as deserving the support offered by me or my network, as to them I represented someone with more resources (not only as a foreigner, but also as a result of my position as a student tutored and hosted by an Ivoirian professor). In Berlin, in contrast, neediness was not often expressed. If it was, it was often as a side note, when some interviewees 'admitted' that it was hard sometimes to fully flourish according to their capabilities. As I was in a similar position to many of the interviewees – a young scholar with temporary contracts, a scholarship in which I didn't pay into pension funds nor into unemployment insurance, and in which I had to pay my health insurance myself – it was rather a moment of sharing the difficulty of transitioning into adulthood and make a living as a young scholar. Some interview partners suggested that I should become a rider too, as it presented a means of earning some extra money in a side job.

In Berlin, I did not so much engage in keeping networks going, but I tried to attend social events organized by riders, like picnics around a park bonfire at night or meetings for a beer, whenever I was invited. Also, I sometimes met two of the interview partners (one female, one male) outside of their work hours for biking, having dinner or watching movies, and befriended them. The political mobilization of some riders at the moment of my fieldwork was a crucial infrastructure I used to contact other riders. This entry point had its own challenges: I had to balance between, on the one hand, remaining open to the variety of experiences and practices of riders (by using multiple interviewees, recruiting strategies and semi-structured interview guides that did not focus on working conditions and mobilization), and on the other hand, asserting my loyalty to the riders' protest for better working conditions. I participated in demonstrations and activities that supported these labour struggles, but did not further engage in political action. In this sense, I did not embrace an action research approach. The participant observations at demonstrations served to get me access to the field, as it helped me to build trust with the riders. I could gain reputation as someone who was not an intruder from the other side (i.e. the company direction), or someone who would use the information gathered against the riders. I explicitly limited the recruiting of interviewees through these events, in order to avoid biasing the sample. All in all, there is clearly an imbalance in the intensity with which I immersed myself in the lifeworlds of urban youth in Abidjan in comparison to Berlin. In the latter, I very much remained a researcher who occupied a more distant role conducting semi-structured interviews; and I focused on riders and constructed a narrower field site than in Abidjan.

In both settings, however, gendered and racialized status differences between me and my interlocutors shaped the power relations in my fieldwork (cf. Sultana 2007; England 1994). Power influences knowledge construction and production at all stages of the research, but the interview setting and the points of asking and listening are crucial moments in which research relationships are negotiated (Doucet and Mauthner 2008, 337). Power relations are dynamic: on the one hand, as interviewer I was supposed to orient the conversation through my questions, and as such gained authority to frame the problem, and decide which topic should be discussed in more depth, by asking follow-up questions etc. This role as interviewer, even though I was supposed to conduct open-ended interviews, led in some situations to mismatches between my perspective on the problem and the perspective of my interview partner. The participants in interviews in Abidjan most of the time tried to answer the question anyway (except in one situation), and when expressing doubts, they referred the mismatch between my questions and their everyday to my foreignness, or to a misunderstanding in language. It recalls the observation by S. H. Chen (2011), who argues that non-native interviewers can defer to the native interviewee's language authority to elicit more information. Indeed, as non-native French speaker, I could ask about the meaning of friendship, or ask for more details to explain a situation of their everyday. In Berlin, in contrast, interviewees formulated their doubts about questions I posed. For example, interviewees denied the relevance of my inquiries and dismantled my role as interviewer who guides the conversation by interrupting me, or asking me about my own experience of family support. I interpret these dynamics as an indication of gender roles that inform the relation between interviewer and interviewee. Power relations based on gender and race positions can produce conversational situations that evoke moments of symbolic violence (Bourdieu 2003; Moebius and Wetterer 2011) in which the authority to speak is unequally distributed. In the aforementioned case, being a young white female researcher interviewing young white male adults can invoke situations in which my authority to ask questions can be put into question by my interlocutor, who instead sees himself as authorized to teach me 'a better way' of interviewing. This shows, how we, as researchers, 'do not conduct fieldwork on the unmediated world of the research, but on the world *between* ourselves and the research' (England 1994, 251). It requires an autoethnographic sensibility to recognize 'our research subjects' struggle to create themselves for themselves while also creating themselves for us' (Butz and Besio 2004, 358).

The context of discovery of the field was shaped by my own positionalities and the process of gaining access to the lifeworlds of the young airtime sellers and food delivery riders. At the same time, the experiences of the young men's everyday are embedded in the economic and social histories of each city. This is to what we will turn now: I introduce the context and set up of both areas of work, the airtime economy in Abidjan and the platform economy of food delivery in Berlin. In both cases, mobile devices are crucial digital tools to work with, and we will explore now in more depth how digital economies take shape in and shape the two cities.

Abidjan: mobile phones as provider for urban social infrastructures

When I lived in Abidjan in 2015 and 2016, for most of urban residents, a life without mobile phones was barely imaginable/thinkable, so normal had the technical device and communication tool become in their daily routines. Especially for the younger population and the young men I spent most time with, my own technical abilities and habits often seemed out of date: for a long time, I had no smartphone and no mobile Internet connection, and asked my contacts in the field where to buy a simple *bescla*,[6] which they commented on with a raised eyebrow and doubting laughter, asking me if I was serious and didn't want a 'real' phone?

Mobile phones arrived in Côte d'Ivoire in the 1990s, and since then their use has grown tremendously, particularly in the urban areas like Abidjan. Between 2010 and 2018, the number of new mobile phone subscriptions increased by an average of 2.4 million per year (ARTCI 2015).[7] 'The phone has become a vital cog in the navigation of everyday life' (Archambault 2013, 91) as lubricants of redistribution networks and as devices to build and maintain social infrastructures in the city. Promotional videos, like the one by Orange Côte d'Ivoire,[8] portray the new communication technologies as tools to maintain social connections even at a distance, to 'get closer to the essential' – meaningful and important social relationships. This way, the main providers of mobile communication in Abidjan – Orange, Moov and MTN – fuelled a narrative as facilitators for building social relationships. In my urban everyday in Abidjan, the mobile phone became a crucial device to negotiate distance and intimacy as well as hierarchies and relations of power within webs of social relations. Often, I received messages wishing me a good day, asking me if everything was fine, from urban dwellers I had met once or twice, at a bus stop, or at a marketplace, and these small messages were ways to keep oneself in play, showing attention – a gift that was carefully weighted in the politics of reputation. This shows that information and communication technologies redefine the 'ways in which individuals everywhere imagine, experience, as well as navigate material and social spaces' (Archambault 2013, 98) – through multiple scales, as mobile devices enable reaching out to sites and people that seemed out of sight before. Mobile devices give actors new possibilities to play with appearances and to become visible (i.e. through messages and phone calls) and invisible (i.e. by not picking up phone calls, keeping your phone number unknown), which Julie Archambault has convincingly circumscribed as 'cruising through uncertainty' (Archambault 2013, 2017). The telecommunication companies used these dynamics to offer specific packages of subscription to their users, with free calls to a set of numbers of 'family members' for example (Akindès and Kouamé 2019, V), or by offering messaging packages at low cost for the younger generation, particularly invested in messaging (e.g. Moov's subscription package 'Fun' at the time of research in 2017). Airtime sellers were part of my basic infrastructure, and I was not the only one. Spread out in the city at almost every corner, on pavements or at boutiques, recognizable through their umbrellas, desks or signposts, they attracted passers-by who needed to top up their phones, to make a phone call or to simply have a chat, ask for directions or leave messages.

Phone boxes, or the selling of airtime, emerged as a practice in the course of the 2000s, when the mobile phone was not yet as widespread as today and people used the airtime selling spots to make phone calls – calls via mobile phone were cheaper than via the landline. For those offering the call-by-mobile-phone service, it was a welcome opportunity to make some money. For many of them, this was money badly needed, as shortly after the interventions by the International Monetary Fund (IMF) and their changes in development policies, Côte d'Ivoire was drawn into a decade of political and economic crisis. Indeed, the structural adjustment programmes of the 1980s were a turning point for Côte d'Ivoire and its post-independence development model and political compromise around capital, labour and the state. Twenty years before, in 1960, Côte d'Ivoire became formally independent from France, its colonizer since 1893. Félix Houphouët-Boigny 'ushered Côte d'Ivoire into its independence and became president for life' (McGovern 2011, 151), until his death in 1993. Under Houphouët-Boigny's single-party rule, Côte d'Ivoire experienced a period of political and economic stability – a time that has been memorialized as the 'Ivoirian miracle'. However, the country's success relied heavily on a neocolonial relationship with France (McGovern 2011, 142) and old and new systems of 'political and economic control and patronage that have been part of the cocoa sector since the colonial period, but took on their current form during the Houphouët-Boigny years' (McGovern 2011, 138). The so called 'cacao-coffee-motor' was in large part the continuation of a colonial and extractivist cash crop economy – still today, Côte d'Ivoire exports 40 per cent of the world's cacao.

With the fall of cocoa prices in the 1980s, the system grew untenable. Côte d'Ivoire's debts rose, from 25 to 60 per cent (Cooper 2002, 215), and unemployment rose (Bamba *et al.* 1992). In 1990, Côte d'Ivoire counted among the most indebted countries in the world. The amount of the budget deficit was estimated at 11.2 billion dollars in 1990. Adjustment programmes were implemented by the IMF, which put an end to an idea of development that prioritized stabilizing the livelihood of the majority population. Instead, the IMF privileged the logic of the market, pushing for cuts in public spending (Cooper 2002, 221). Adjustment programmes included the privatization of the fixed telephony firm (Laffont and N'Guessan 2002, 6f.), and legal as well as technical reforms enabled the entry of mobile phone operators into the market.[9] These opened up the market for mobile phone subscriptions. At the same time, they turned into crucial agents to expand the telecommunications infrastructure, which, historically, 'emerged in the context of the French conquest, organization and control of the country ... The telecommunication infrastructure was closely tied to the economic exploitation of the country' and was an exclusive project – back then, 'the telephone remained largely inaccessible to the local population' (Koné 1999, 145).

The parameters not only changed economically and in regard to international dependencies, but also politically. The Ivoirian political system allowed for a multi-party system and president Houphouët-Boigny died in 1993. Consequently, the legitimacy of political leadership became contested, and escalated into militarized conflict (McGovern 2011; Akindès 2004; see also Akindès 2003, 2008). The young men with whom I spent much time in Abidjan were born shortly before these troubled decades. For the majority of them, growing up in families who had lived the city's image as the

Ivoirian project of modernity, they experienced how these promises of a golden era became out of reach. Abidjan was once famous in the subregion as the '*perle de la lagune*'. In its postcolonial condition, it was imagined as the city of 'modernity' where the 'civil service was the formal economy's major employer and provided educated Ivoirians the ultimate modern employment and the central path to middle-class status' in administration and civil service (Matlon 2016, 8). These imaginaries of success that focus on wage labour in the public sector have roots in the colonial project of France in Cote d'Ivoire. Since the French colonization, the administration has been considered the principal employer and regulator of the labour market. The *Code du Travail*, introduced after the Second World War, remained in force after Côte d'Ivoire's independence. This legal document reinforced a distinction between the formal and informal sectors, by omitting all other forms of work than wage labour as outside of the *Code du Travail* and as 'informal' (Bazin and Gnabéli 1997, 692). This official recognition of particular types of work promoted a social division of labour that was gendered and ethnicized (Banégas 2007; Dembélé 2009).

Throughout the 2000s, in the face of the increasingly shrinking work opportunities in the so-called formal sector, Abidjanese youth began to reinvent themselves in the '*bizness*' and new cultural universes around music, dance and linguistic creativity, known as the world of *Nouchi* (cf. Gawa 2014; Kohlhagen 2005; Konaté 2002; König 2014; Newell 2012). In addition, parts of the urban youth in Abidjan mobilized as important actors in the conflict, for example in street debates of the so-called '*parlements de la rue*' (cf. Cutolo and Banégas 2012), and as militias in the *Galaxie Patriotique* pro-Gagbo FANCI (pro ex-president Laurent Gagbo) forces or the pro-RDR groups (the party of the current president Alassane Ouattara) (Arnaut 2012; Banégas 2007, 2011, 2012; Cutolo 2015; Koné 2015). When I arrived there in 2014, Abidjan continued to transpire some of its glamour and economic thriving. For the airtime sellers I met, the hustle of the world of *Nouchi* was part of their everyday. They moved between circuits of money, phones and drugs, and a moral economy around work, education and expectations of the proper job and a role as provider (cf. Newell 2012). Hence the phone box was an activity in transition, done in a situation of permanent temporariness, labour in time.

The *cabines* or 'call boxes', as the Abidjanese residents called them, were important nodes in this infrastructure of communication. As nodal points of infrastructures, they were elements of 'built networks that facilitate the flow of goods, people, or ideas, and allow for their exchange over space' (Larkin 2013, 328). As prepaid subscription packages were widespread in 2017, one needed to get communication credit and top up the phone very regularly. At the corner of every street, you could find someone who was able to top up your phone with fresh airtime. To call them 'cabines', call boxes, was a reference to the physical boxes used for landline calls in earlier times. Often, a cabine did not consist of any fixed materiality. Some call boxes were nothing more than a removable desk on the roadside, which disappeared from the pavement if there was heavy rainfall, or at times when the person selling airtime was busy with other activities – attending university, travelling or working in industry as a daily labourer, for example. Only visible if one looked twice were the range of mobile phones at service for the sale: bigger call boxes had one phone for each provider. The call box owners sometimes differentiated between devices reserved for calls and devices to top up communication credit. Most of the time, however, the technical devices were stored in pockets, bags or in spaces under the desk – to avoid attracting attention and inciting potential thefts. Common spots for cabines were crossroads or pavements on streets with lots of traffic – the more people passed by, the better the turnover for airtime sellers. As the call box didn't consume a lot of physical space and didn't need a heavy material set-up, I often met airtime sellers in front of their residence – sometimes literally at the doorsteps. Others combined the sale of communication credit with other businesses – frequently the offer of mobile phones and other accessories. In any case, airtime was available almost everywhere in the city – as an everyday commodity, its market expanded from the administrative centre of the city to the urban fringes, from the parking lot in front of the supermarket in an upper-class neighbourhood in Cocody (a district in Abidjan) to the kiosk at a street corner that provided residents living in provisional housing, under the radar of the state, with their daily needs.

The disposability of underemployed youth was an important element on which telecommunication companies could draw in order to expand their markets to urban areas in which formalized market structures were not the mode of provision for the majority of residents. To this end, an easy entry to the business of airtime distribution was beneficial. Indeed, it didn't seem to require much to sell airtime in Abidjan. All the airtime sellers I met described their entry into the business as easy and quick. At the moment of the research in 2016, one needed only an ID and a mobile phone, and a locality with which a person could be identified by the franchise of a telecommunications operator on the basis of their SIM card and a unique telephone number. 'Everyone can do this activity, no, there is no selection. If you want to do the activity, you do it without constraints [*librement*]' (Interview with dispatcher Daniel, Yopougon, 13 October 2017).

Call box workers[10] got a percentage of their sales, which meant that their profits depended on the amount of airtime they sold – for call box workers in Abidjan there was competition for clients (with high purchasing power), and for credit in airtime. The working arrangements of those young adults I met were diverse. Some of the young men were self-entrepreneurs. They borrowed starting capital from relatives or donors in their social networks, and then started to sell airtime. Others were contractors, who got paid for their service work biweekly or monthly. Depending on their work status, they had either a fixed salary, or were remunerated on the basis of their sales, from which they were getting a percentage of each sale, from 4 to 6 per cent, from the telecommunication operator. For most of the interviewees, their earnings did not exceed the Ivoirian minimum wage, 60,000 FCFA[11] (€100), which, given the living costs in Abidjan, would not allow them to start their own household and live by themselves. In Abidjan, airtime sellers had to register with a company and worked under arrangements that were concluded orally and were not legally coded. Airtime sellers didn't pay taxes to the city government; they sold either in front of their family residence or arranged deals with shop owners or other residents to install their phone boxes in semi-public or public spaces.

What began as an incremental economy among residents, became more and more standardized over the years. The telecommunications firms each had different strategies to make use of the airtime sellers to distribute their products and enhance their market. One model was based on the creation of subcontracting firms, in French *franchisé*. These held the exclusive rights of distribution in a concise urban area. Instead of relying on private individual contractors as middlemen between the telecommunications companies and the local distributors, the airtime sellers, this enabled the franchises to have control over the number of sellers and the transactions in a particular area. With the help of a platform, it was possible to track all transactions, from the local airtime seller to the franchise (see Touré 2010, 412f.). 'RESUS'[12] was the central platform with which the telecommunications firm I focused on was able to connect the subcontracting firm of distribution (*franchisé*) and the micro-entrepreneurs who sold airtime as call box workers on the street level (Interview with the responsible manager of this platform, 8 April 2016). The tracking of the transactions through the platform was also a means to get hold over the airtime sellers. As I learned in an interview with the director of one such franchise, the airtime sellers were seen as a labour force that needed to be evaluated, classified in competition to each other, in order to advance and improve the service (Interview with franchise CEO, 11 October 2017). Airtime sellers with the best 'numbers' got recompensated, according to the CEO, with tools to work (umbrellas for the sale's spot against the sun; tables and advertising tools). The classification served the company to identify 'the value of a worker, what (s)he is worth', as it expressed degrees of commitment, perseverance at the working spot, and business (Interview with CEO, 11 October 2017).

Even though these telecommunications firms are not configured as 'lean platforms' (like Uber, Airbnb; cf. Srnicek 2016), their network infrastructure displays the characteristics of a platform: it has the potential to bring 'together different … service providers and clients, and provides them with a core functionality they can use to transact' (Kendall *et al.* 2012, 49). Platforms like RESUS have turned into providers of a 'network infrastructure for storing and moving money that facilitates the exchange of cash and electronic value between various actors, including clients, businesses, the government, and financial service providers' (Kendall *et al.* 2012, 49). The platform character of telecommunications comes through even more if we contextualize their role in urban development policies in the last decade. The distribution of communication credit, and the roll-out of communication networks in the urban areas also prepared the distribution of financial products (Carroll 2014, 538). One of the paradigmatic sectors for the digital transformation in Africa is the banking sector, most visible with the introduction of mobile and digital banking by telecoms operators such as Vodafone in Kenya via its M-Pesa system (Akindès and Kouamé 2019, VIII). The telecommunications operators provide the infrastructure for financial products such as mobile money and banking. In this sense, the sale of airtime can be seen as a start; in 2017, the telecommunications operators had already shifted their attention to mobile money and banking. At the same time, more broadly, the communications infrastructure that airtime sellers uphold through their services gives way to new social practices, new forms of selling and buying, and new potentialities for artistic creation via the social media platforms YouTube and alike. Moreover, we can observe the introduction of platform-mediated work, for instance in the transport industry (Akindès and Kouamé 2019).

The airtime economy is an example of new forms of economic incorporation through entrepreneurial activity and gig work that is done temporarily, as part of a portfolio of multiple activities, and in which informalization does not constitute a fraud, but a welcome status for companies to outsource any potential risks to the shoulders of those who labour for them. These shoulders carry a heavy load: inequalities have risen and economic hardships expanded in a country that experienced a decade of civil war, and whose leaders invest in huge infrastructure projects to incite economic growth, but have less concrete plans for how to resolve social fragmentation. Hence, the proliferation of economic opportunities as informalized, entrepreneurial activities sits within the current post-conflict governance of economic liberalism under the presidency of Alassane Ouattara (Akindès 2017). A rhetoric of 'emergence' 'seemingly takes precedence over every other aspect of national life. It therefore defines the new [post-war] period, whose ambitions somewhat incoherently combine the desire for rupture, for a "new Ivoirian" and a new constitution' (Miran-Guyon 2017, 10). The imaginary of the new Ivoirian breaks with the old ideal of the 'civil servant', itself deeply embedded in the colonial legacy of Côte d'Ivoire (Banégas 2007, 28; Bazin and Gnabéli 1997), and instead favours a spirit of entrepreneurialism and inventiveness (Schilling and Dembélé 2019). Political programmes to combat youth unemployment proclaim support to help jobseekers into entrepreneurship and the expansion of micro-financing systems (see Ministère d'Etat *et al.*

2012). Aside from its focus on entrepreneurship, the government invests in huge infrastructure projects, with the promise of 'trickle down effects' that would redistribute among the Ivoirian population. A vain promise so far, as it had so far not been proven to work. '[T]he fruits of growth are not well distributed. The poverty level fell from fifty-one per cent in 2011 to forty-six per cent in 2015, but remains higher than in the late 1980s. Income inequality, regional inequality, and gender inequality are all provoking increasing social unease' (Miran-Guyon 2017, 10). Airtime sellers that we will get to know more extensively in the next chapters make their living against this background of increasing inequalities under state liberalism, characterized by development policies that foster entrepreneurship and that keep believing in economic growth as a redistribution machine.

Berlin: mobile phones as devices of convenience to navigate the city

The delivery of food by bicycle in Berlin attracted the young men I spoke with as a temporary means to make money, similar to the perspectives gathered from airtime sellers in Abidjan. Food delivery platforms had recently established their services in the city, and needed a flexible and temporary workforce to get the meals from restaurants to the clients. Young urbanites didn't need much to start the gig: a bicycle and smartphone was enough, so that they can receive orders through the platform. The platforms were flagships in the growing start-up scene in Berlin: start-ups comprise small or medium-sized enterprises (SMEs) mostly funded through venture capital or angel investment[13] and characterized by fast growth potential and highly adaptive organizational structure.[14] The annual Startup Monitor places Berlin as one of the leaders in terms of spatial concentration of start-up companies reported to the monitor (Kollmann *et al.* 2020). Already in 2013, McKinsey assigned Berlin the status of the leading start-up hub of Europe (McKinsey 2013).

Mobile phones can be called devices of convenience to navigate the city of Berlin. Companies advertise their app-based platforms by promising efficiency and quick access to services. Their ubiquitous presence in all areas of urban life – from ordering food, renting out living space, to cleaning the house – causes Lyster to argue that the city turns into an 'integrated platform of services' (Lyster 2016, 13; quoted in Altenried *et al.* 2021, 75). When the Berlin Senate decided to shut down the city in March 2020, due to the rising numbers of people infected with Covid-19, for many people, their daily income to make ends meet was disrupted: actors couldn't play any more, taxi drivers didn't find any clients to bring from A to B, as airports were shut down, bartenders were jobless, etc. But in the midst of all this loss of economic opportunities, there was one field of activity that certainly thrived economically: the delivery of food, ordered via online platforms.

The digital economy builds on the thirty years of tertiarization of Berlin's economy. After the fall of the Berlin Wall, in the early 1990s, Berlin turned into a destination and platform for innovation. In a sort of 'gold rush mentality', the local government promised in 1992 'that Berlin would soon play in the same league as London, Paris or even New York, and rise to a global city status' (Bernt *et al.* 2013, 23). Berlin gained a reputation as a city where 'anything goes' (Haid 2017, 174), as the city 'became the projection surface' (Cupers and Miessen 2002, 78, quoted in Colomb 2012a, 135) for new ideas and cultural practices, such as techno clubs. The availability of vacant land provided space for this, mostly for temporary uses (see Colomb 2012a, 135). In reunified Berlin, the earlier expectation of the city becoming a 'slick new business hub yielded after 2000 to a new emphasis on diversity, youth, and creative cultures, an image succinctly captured by Mayor Klaus Wowereit's characterization of the city as "poor but sexy"' (Ladd 2012, 478, reviewing Colomb 2012b).

The successful implementation of the gig economy in the Berlin context can be discussed against the background of broader transformations in Germany's labour market and social welfare politics, often subsumed under labels such as flexibilization, precarization and informalization of work. The gig economy is paradigmatic for the emergence of new 'grey spaces' of work. Two trends predominate here: first, the distinction between employees and employers blurs, with the increase of contractual arrangements such as micro-entrepreneurship, bogus self-employment, freelancing and contracts for services. Second, being involved in multiple labour relationships, mixing part-time employment with self-employment or a second dependent employment relationship, becomes more and more a common situation in

Germany. 'Employment hybridisation', as Jansen pins down, 'has gained significantly in importance since the beginning of the 2000s' (Jansen 2020, 9). The pluralization of sources of income, including the growth of platform work, can be seen as part of larger trends – such as the 'drop in value of real earnings in Europe in the aftermath of the financial crisis of 2007–8 and, in some countries, the impact of accompanying austerity policies including reductions in benefits and cutbacks in public services … and the general growth of non-standard forms of employment' (Huws *et al.* 2019, 19).

For Germany, the national reforms of the German social security system in 2005 (known as the Hartz IV reforms) certainly pushed this trend forward, as they marked a turn towards an 'activating' and punitive welfare state (cf. Butterwegge 2007). So-called atypical employment arrangements, midi- and mini-jobs,[15] were implemented and made side jobs more attractive, while at the same time dismantling the institution of the normal employment relationship, which remains a strong basis for access to rights to social security in Germany (Jansen 2020, 12). Eventually, 'access to paid employment […] was no longer a guarantee of being protected from poverty or social exclusion' (Laruffa and Schilling 2016, 7). Precarization was the term that enabled sociologists in France and Germany (Castel 1995; Castel and Dörre 2009; Freudenschuss 2013; Motakef 2015; Paugam 2000; for an overview see Laruffa and Schilling 2016; Schilling *et al.* 2019) to highlight the new processes of marginalization in this context of 'the weakening of the link between work and social rights' (Laruffa and Schilling 2016, 7).

In view of this debate, the narrative around food delivery as precarious work conditions is not astonishing, as the contractual forms of the riders I got acquainted with in Berlin reflect the 'atypical' arrangements discussed under precarization in this peculiar national context: the companies hired workers as freelancers, midi-jobbers or as '*Werkstudenten*' – student jobs. Some companies even contracted full-time employees. The freelance contract most prototypically stands for the 'piecework' character of the job: it is concluded between a rider (as contractor) and the platform (the client). Workers work on their own and are remunerated for a job done independently.

Whether or not the delivery riders were 'independent' workers was hotly debated in Germany. According to the German Federal Labour Court, the guiding principle of personal dependence in work relations is the question of whether the worker is subject to directives and if the worker is integrated to the organization (i.e. the person depends on the personnel and work equipment of the client in a particular way) (see Dietrich and Patzina 2018, 1[16]). In the course of the legal dispute over this, Deliveroo backed out of the business, as the company mainly employed freelancers and was sued by the court for bogus self-employment. Foodora, instead, adapted its strategy to this local context and renounced freelance contracts. The young men who worked for this platform were contracted as mini- or midi-jobbers – two marginal part-time work forms. While the mini-job paid up to a threshold of €450 per month, the midi-job is defined by a maximum threshold of €850 per month.[17] Access to statutory welfare contributions is only guaranteed to midi-jobbers. Mini-jobbers need to get their health insurance elsewhere, as health insurance has become compulsory for anyone resident in Germany since 2009.

This detailed description gives an idea about the entitlements mini- and midi-jobbers have to social protection due to their labour position. Given the low income and only partial coverage for social security benefits, most of the time platform work is pursued as a 'side activity' next to other sources of income, and part of a 'piecing together [of] a livelihood from multiple sources of income, not all of which involve the sale of their labor' (Huws *et al.* 2019, 19). 'Platform workers' cannot be used to designate a 'particular group of workers'; they demarcate not a 'distinct group' in the labour market – rather, we need to acknowledge their compositional heterogeneity (Cansoy *et al.* 2021; Huws *et al.* 2019, 19).

In Berlin, several companies compete for the biggest market share – the key actors change over time, quickly, which is typical for platforms' business model: organized as start-ups, their value is centrally defined by their potential for innovation (cf. Kollmann *et al.* 2018, 18), often independent from the concrete success in the operational business and their profitability. Foodora and Deliveroo, for instance, both recorded losses in 2016 (Schreyer and Schrape 2018, 9). Nevertheless, Foodora and Deliveroo were the most prominent food delivery platforms in Berlin back in 2016/17. Even though both providers have since then left the Berlin market, cyclists in their uniforms and square box on their backs still populate the streets and the pavements in front of restaurants in the city centre of Berlin. Only the colour changes from time to time – from pink to orange to light blue. Each company forges its own brand identity, although the financial entanglements might be more tense than the colourways suggest. The investment fund 'Delivery Hero' who owned Foodora Germany, for example, also ran another delivery platform at the same time, to capture different food segments – until it sold its brands to its rival Takeaway in 2018.[18]

No matter which brand they were working for, delivery riders' principal task consisted of transporting food from restaurants to clients who had ordered meals online via an app. Most riders did so by bicycle. As is characteristic for gig workers in general, their services were engaged via platforms, but performed offline – with bicycles, cars or motorbikes. In their work arrangements, they had 'flexibility in terms of work schedules and autonomy', but at the same time they 'must not only assume responsibility for operating costs and risks and forego protections enjoyed by employees but also conform to the temporal rhythms of customer demand, which can reduce their autonomy substantially' (Vallas and Schor 2020, 275, quoting Ravenelle 2019; Rosenblat 2018; Schor 2020). Their autonomy was particularly limited by the fact that the orders were dispatched via their smartphone, using algorithmic matching as technology. The platforms themselves earn from each transaction: as intermediaries, they coordinate and match suppliers – the restaurants, who present their offers on the digital marketplace of the platform – and demanders – the consuming customers who command their desired food on the platform. Both the restaurant (for example, at that time they paid Foodora 30 per cent of the price announced at the digital marketplace) and the consuming customers (in the form of a delivery fee of €2.50 to Foodora at that time) pay a commission if the matching is successful (Schreyer and Schrape 2018, 14). As intermediaries, the platform-operating companies are also remunerated more implicitly through the user data they extract (Schreyer and Schrape 2018, 8; see further van Doorn and Badger 2020). Data on transactions feeds the matching-algorithm and is combined with data received from constant evaluations and instant feedback on the 'delivery experience' – all meant to create trust for the consuming customers and control over the delivery process. Ordering food online was – and still is – supposed to be smooth, easy and quick.

Not only customers were teased into the app-based command of food through a rhetoric of convenience. Also the workforce, the food delivery riders, were attracted by the relative ease with which they could start the gig work: one didn't need to hand in a CV or a motivation letter. Instead, an applicant filled in an online questionnaire to check if he or she fulfilled the basic conditions: these were, first of all, the availability of a smartphone new enough to run the application that coordinated the distribution of food, and which had sufficient data volume 'to stay connected to our community at all times' (see Foodora 2017).[19] Besides this, the future rider needed a bike (even though other means of transport were possible too) and a work permit for Germany. The applicant, at least 18 years of age, needed to have the 'flexibility to work on weekends', and to be 'responsible and reliable' (see Foodora 2017). Another company, Deliveroo, advertised the job as giving one the possibility to decide when to work. 'You decide when you work. With Deliveroo, you obtain high flexibility that enables you to organize your day according to your rules' (Deliveroo 2017).[20]

This rhetoric around flexibility and autonomy was referenced widely among the young men I encountered during my research. They unanimously described access to the job as easy and quick, and shared the feeling of having flexibility in choosing when to start their food delivery shifts. Riders had to select at the beginning of each week on a digital schedule the time slots on which they committed to work. The way in which shifts were assigned changed frequently. At some point during the research, interviewees reported that they were allocated shifts on the basis of their preceding work schedules. The platform also calculated the need for labour power flexibly depending on the demand (season, weather, day and time of the week). As gig workers, food delivery riders were a contingent labour force, a characteristic feature of labour platforms' business model:

> Companies no longer need to buy employees' compliance by assuming market risks for them, as they do for permanent staff members … Those who offer their labour and are not associated with an institution face contingency in two respects: they depend systematically on the congruence of demand (tasks, assignments) and supply (availability of their labour at the conditions offered) but lack effective influence on the price of their own labour, which depends chiefly on the size and composition of the digital reserve army. (Staab and Nachtwey 2016, 469)

In 2017, when I got to know some of the food delivery riders and learned about their making a living in the city, the imaginary of Berlin as a city where you can invent yourself was still vivid amongst my interlocutors. Victor – born in Romania, and grew up in Spain before he came to Germany at the moment when the financial crash reverberated in Europe – held up Berlin as the city that gave him 'insurance that [he] will find something'. 'Sooner or later, you will find something to do, to keep going.' Berlin's imaginary as a city in which it was possible to keep going, without much money, was still alive, helping to sustain a thriving low-paid sector and unstable work arrangements. The start-up culture and the digital entrepreneurs seize on this image of Berlin as 'creative city'. As 'entrepreneurs of the self',[21] urban dwellers are for themselves their own capital, their own producer and their source of earnings (Rossi and Di Bella 2017, 1001). The young men who began to deliver meals, by logging their phones into a platform that organized the delivery of the meals from restaurants to customers, while calculating the most efficient placement of orders to their flexible workforce the riders, expressed in our conversations these struggles to make ends meet in a context where they are supposed to be entrepreneurs themselves. The self-reflexivity and self-monitoring 'is premised upon the availability of, and access to, discourse and cultural resources, and the techniques and practices necessary for producing, but also knowing, a self' (Skeggs 2004, 20). These expectations and silenced preconditions turn the instability of work into a locus where inequalities in youth transitions unfold in contemporary Berlin.

Taken together, the new forms of work emerging in the course of digitalization in cities like Abidjan and Berlin are fruitful cases to depart from the coevalness of these spaces.

> What are opposed ... are not societies at different stages of development but different societies facing each other at the same Time. [This is not to state] a romanticised/exoticised radical difference or a blandly relativistic denial that there is any such a thing as ‚progress', say, or ‚development', at all ... Coevalness concerns a stance of recognition and respect in situations of mutual implications. (Massey 2005, 69)

In both cities, Abidjan and Berlin, the technological transformation is discussed as contemporary development invested by the state. The processes of informalization and precarization that these transformations bring about are then not a relict from the past, and Abidjan does not need to catch up with Berlin, but can be theorized upon equally to produce knowledge about the urban present. Both groups of youth work flexibly, temporarily and with low remuneration and few formal entitlements to social protection from their work status. The platform-operating companies in Berlin are different to the telecommunications operators in Abidjan in their organization of the labour process, but we can bring both work settings into relation: they challenge, in both their contextual specificities, clear-cut distinctions of employee and employers, as grey spaces of labour that transfer to the workers a lot of independency and responsibility in organizing the workplace and the working tools. Telecommunications as well as platform companies are carriers of innovation and represent economic sectors that attract capital and build their reputation on technological development as a solution for societal challenges, be they inclusion, efficiency or comfort (see further Nachtwey and Seidl 2020). At the same time, they rely on human labour, invisibilized forms of labour that make their technological infrastructure and markets run on a daily basis: those bodies that stand at the crossroads, day and night, in the rain and in the sun, to be at disposal to sell airtime to customers – and equally, those bodies that cycle around the city from restaurant to restaurant, or waiting in parks or public squares to be ready to deliver food to customers waiting in their homes.

Notes

1 'Urbanizing Faith' led by AbdouMaliq Simone and Talja Blokland, University of South Australia / Humboldt Universität zu Berlin (2014–15).
2 SICOGI stands for Société Ivoirienne de Construction et de Gestion Immobilière, which was founded in 1962 by the Ivoirian state. It is a company with a capital of about 4.5 billion FCFA. The State of Côte d'Ivoire owns 80 per cent of the company, and the remaining part is owned by various private companies. See their homepage (SICOGI 2020).
3 SOGEFIHA stands for Société de gestion financière de l'habitat, which is a state real estate company, founded in 1963 (see Antoine *et al.* 1987, 86).
4 I expanded on the interview guide developed by Blokland with project members in the project 'Urbanizing Faith', which was centred around 'narratives of how youngsters created resources, ties, skills, expectations,

aspirations and plans to realize livelihoods (beyond work for wages) in the contexts of home, neighbourhoods and places of faith' (Schilling *et al.* 2019).

5 By 'kinning', I mean the practices of doing kinship – that is, the mutualization of resources (see Chapter 5).

6 *Bescla* is *Nouchi* for a simple mobile phone without any Internet capacities or extra accessories.

7 Nguessan 2019: Panorama des Télécommunications/TIC, Autorité de regulation des telecommunications/TIC de Côte d'Ivoire.

8 Orange Côte d'Ivoire 2020 (26 May 2020).

9 At the beginnings of this drive towards liberalization, three mobile phone operators conquered the market, under very favourable conditions: IVOIRIS, TELECEL and COMSTAR. Seventy per cent of IVOIRIS was owned by France Telecom, which was rebranded as Orange in 2002. At the time of my fieldwork, this picture had changed: Orange, MTN, Moov, Green and Comium were the five companies offering mobile phone services to the population of Côte d'Ivoire, with Orange holding a market share of almost 50 per cent in terms of sales figures (see ARTCI 2015, 22).

10 This is another term for airtime sellers.

11 This is the Ivoirian currency: 1 FCFA is equivalent to about €0.0015. Antoine earned the equivalent of €45 a month as an airtime seller, which was half of the official minimum wage (60,000 FCFA or €91) in Côte d'Ivoire. As waged employees, in 2013 people earned on average 105,731 FCFA (AGEPE 2014, 37).

12 Anonymized.

13 The UK Business Angels Association presents angel investment the following way: 'Angel investing is equity finance. An angel investor is a high net worth individual who makes use of their personal disposable finance and makes their own decision about making the investment.' See online: UKBAA 2022.

14 See the definition given in Businessinsider Lexikon 2019.

15 Midi- and mini-jobs are two marginal part-time work forms: a mini-job describes a job paid up to a threshold of €450 per month, and the midi-job is defined by a maximum threshold of €850 a month. As a mini-jobber, you 'do not have to make **any** contributions to health, long-term care and unemployment insurance. In the pension insurance there is also Mini-jobber compulsory insurance, but you can apply for an exemption from this' (Federal Government Commissioner 2022). Midi-jobbers, in contrast, are obliged to pay into social security funds (see Arbeitsvertrag 2022).

16 OECD data – see online: OECD 2019.

17 See Eurofound 2019 for 'Individual employment relations'.

18 See Handelsblatt 2018.

19 See Foodora (2017), 'Du entscheidest, wann du arbeitest. Mit Deliveroo erhältst du eine hohe Flexibilität, die dir ermöglicht, deinen Tag nach deinen Regeln zu gestalten', https://deliveroo.de/en/apply [accessed 8 November 2017]

20 See Foodora (2017), on the website of Deliveroo (2017), 'Du entscheidest, wann du arbeitest. Mit Deliveroo erhältst du eine hohe Flexibilität, die dir ermöglicht, deinen Tag nach deinen Regeln zu gestalten', 'Apply as partner courier with Foodora', https://kurier.foodora.de/en/?utm_medium=ats&utm_source=greenhouse&utm_campaign=foodora.contents [accessed 8 November 2017]

21 'Entrepreneurs of the self' is the English translation of the concept '*Unternehmerisches Selbst*', a term coined by Ulrich Bröckling (2007) which describes a form of subjectivity, a 'set of interpretative schemes with which people today are supposed to understand themselves and their lives' (Bröckling 2015, xi).

2

Conceptual devices: inequality at work in comparative perspective

If we broaden our perspective and study the role of work for the organization of livelihood, we also need conceptual tools that allow us to capture livelihood as a more nuanced set of practices, one that exceeds the dichotomy of informal work vs. formal employment. This chapter discusses possible conceptual devices to study the reproduction of inequalities in variegated processes of commodification in the context of digital urban economies. We will explore possibilities to carve out similar mechanisms in the making of livelihood in diverse economies, in the light of globalized precarities. This perspective starts from the everyday and refutes a view 'from above' that maps urban life using a conceptual mode of governing (Smith 1990) with a focus on state policies and official labour markets. How unequal access to resources is legitimized and how it comes about remain the overarching questions. The analytical lenses derived from the conceptual framework I present in this chapter structure the three subsequent chapters of this book. The conceptual devices themselves are already the product of comparative analysis of my observations and conversations in the fields. Most importantly, they are a result of probing to what extent important mechanisms in Abidjan matter for the context of Berlin.

Work as economic practice in processes of commodification

In order to grasp subtle and ordinary ways of making ends meet, without using terminology that above all defines them through all that they are *not*, I situate work in a broader range of possible economic practices: with Polanyi, I understand the term economic as describing 'the interchange with [our] natural and social environment, in so far as this results in supplying [us] with the means of material want satisfaction' (Polanyi 1957, 244). People try to make ends meet not only in market transactions, but also for instance by means of bestowing, sharing or redistributing goods. The making of livelihood consists of a variety of economic practices (Bourdieu 2000, 23; Smith and Stenning 2006). Practices are 'routinized ways in which bodies are moved, objects are handled, subjects are treated, things are described and the world is understood' (Reckwitz 2002, 249f.). *Economic* practices, then, are all practices that organize the 'satisfaction of human needs in a specific context' (Hann 2018, 2). They are the organization of livelihood, 'the means and mechanisms' through which people try to make ends meet (Lont and Hospes 2004, 6). Making a living includes resources generated through market exchange and commodified labour, as well as resources accessed as rights to a share. This wider perspective enables us to show *how* work plays a role in the organization of livelihood, and how it is articulated with other means and mechanisms to make a living. The focus on 'economic practices' allows us to see how the boundary drawing between economic and non-economic or work and non-work itself plays an important role in blocking or facilitating circulations and flows of resources. Means to make a living are not distributed equally. Inequalities in organizing livelihood are then, first, not only explained by the actors' inclusion or exclusion from a market or their sale of their efforts as labour, but can be shaped by other forms of economic integration. Second, economic practice is not only a matter of individuals' striving to accumulate resources as capitals (a starting point of much research using the livelihood approach (see De Haan 2012, 348)), but economic practice includes transactions and gaining value as a person in varying interdependencies, as it is 'socially, culturally and historically embedded' (De Haan 2012, 348).

Here, Pierre Bourdieu's understanding of economic calculation expands the ideal of the *homo economicus*. Bourdieu suggests to

> extend economic calculation to ALL the goods, material and symbolic, without distinction, that present themselves as RARE and worthy of being sought after in a particular social formation – which may be 'fair words' or smiles, handshakes or shrugs, compliments or attention, challenge or insults, honour or honours, powers or pleasures, gossip

> or scientific information, distinction or distinctions, etc. (Bourdieu 1977, 178)

According to Bourdieu, an economy of symbolic goods, as for example the good-faith economy, consists of the 'fiction of a disinterested exchange' (Bourdieu 1977, 171) – 'the emphasis on the symbolic aspect of the activities and relations of production, to prevent the economy from being grasped as an economy, i.e. as a system governed by the laws of interested calculation, competition, or exploitation' (Bourdieu 1977, 172). Symbolic investments, like spending time with others, and gifting, are practices to build symbolic capital (i.e. prestige, reputation), which is 'credit, in the widest sense of the word, i.e. a sort of advance which the group alone can grant to those who give it the best material and symbolic guarantees' (Bourdieu 1977, 181).[1] These practices can turn into valuable forms of accumulation of resources and forms of economic calculation. Drawing on this broader understanding of economic calculation, I pay attention to how material and symbolic goods become important in mechanisms of organizing livelihood.

The entry point to this comparative crafting of connections between young gig workers in Abidjan and Berlin is thus a study of their organization of livelihood as a set of economic practices. Very prominently, Simone (2004) and others, e.g. Thieme (2018) and Monteith *et al.* (2021), have shown the mundane and diverse ways in which urban residents collaborate through an intersection of socialities so that 'expanded spaces of economic and cultural operation become available to residents of limited means' (Simone 2004a, 407). Against this background, grammars of the market or the distinction between formal and informal economies are difficult to maintain; instead, we could describe these practices as 'an amalgam of efforts on the part of the urban majority to constantly re-open the question of value – what is to be valued, by whom, and how?' (Simone 2019, 618). To open this question of value also informs the analytical lenses to study commodifications – and precarity as their product. We need to carefully look at the way things and people are turned into commodities, and appropriated by capital. 'Commodification entails a relationship between labour market dynamics … and processes of marketisation of common social goods, land [… or] social security benefits' (Barchiesi 2006, 94). Precarity is not necessarily based on the commodification of labour, and the recommodification of welfare states (Burawoy 2015; Paret 2016), but can also be a product of ex-commodification and non-commodification (Burawoy 2015). Paret (2016, 120) distinguishes 'precarity rooted in the commodification of labour, the classic case of exploitation, [in contrast to precarity] rooted in the commodification of labour-power, based on exclusion from various sources of social income'.

To keep spaces and populations outside of the market is an integral part of global capitalism, and this gains particular relevance in the current era of digital capitalism: extracting rents from consumption and unpaid labour, by framing the labour as gift and sharing, is one constitutive feature of platform capitalism and the gig economy (Fourcade and Kluttz 2020; Sadowski 2020; Srnicek 2016). This underpins a critique of commodification as an encompassing process in which capital rationality as a dominant form of living and thinking is implemented (Münnich and Sachweh 2017, 12; Tsing 2009; 2013). As Williams and Zelizer (2005) have argued, it is not useful to think of commodification as an either/or question. Commodification can possibly be fed by very different cultural repertoires, also those which are not close to the 'liberal credo'. An analytical perspective on commodification gains from considering the interaction between market-critical and market-friendly cultural forms (Münnich and Sachweh 2017, 13). This implies we should also take into account the moments and configurations in which transactions and relations are kept out of the market to further propel capitalist accumulation.

Economic practices as social relations

Work as economic practice can be classified not only according to the kind of economy in which it is taking place (market exchange, reciprocity), but as a socially embedded practice. In the following, I will lay out in more depth what this means, and what follows from this for an analytical framework to explain the reproduction of inequalities in precarious work conditions.

Prominently, new economic sociology has laid the groundwork for bringing back social networks into the analysis of economic organization. Most importantly, Mark Granovetter (1985), Harrison White (1981) and Richard Swedberg (1990) rediscovered at the beginning of the 1980s the potential of economic sociology and its social and theoretical relevance (see Maurer 2017, 12f.). Social capital, 'the ability to gain access to resources by virtue of membership in networks or larger structures' (Portes 2010, 27), has become a crucial factor to consider in economic organization. New economic sociologists have not only focused on the importance of social capital in terms of closed networks, but have also looked at the role of 'weak ties' in social mobility, such as in Granovetter's book, *Getting a Job: A Study of Contacts and Careers* (1974), and his seminal study on the role of weak ties for accessing employment (Granovetter 1973). Despite all the valuable results that studies on the role of social capital for social mobility and access to work have produced, I see some shortcomings. First, the economy is still perceived to be an autonomous field, in which social relations, external to the economy, are influential. 'Skeptics complain that the concept typically assumes a social container within which economic processes, not fully conceived as socially constituted, operate' (Zelizer 2012, 148). The market remains intact as a unit outside of the social. Second, economic practice is not only embedded socially, but also politically and culturally (Smelser and Swedberg 2005, 15).

To bring the latter back in, let us turn to new institutionalist approaches to discuss the role of institutions in shaping economic practices. Neo-institutionalist[2] scholars criticize Granovetter's sole 'emphasis on the nature of interpersonal ties and the structure of networks' (Nee 2005, 53). In contrast, they pay attention to the structures of meaning that actors draw on in their economic practice, and follow here a Weberian tradition of the analysis of social action. The question remains as to what institutions are. In the discussion of the elements that orient actors in their practices, a division into formal rules and informal elements is quite prominent (North 1991). This division is problematic, however, as informal institutions are transformed into a deviant form of economic regulation. In various analyses, the lack of formal institutions is described as a source of insecurity: for Elmar Altvater and Birgit Mahnkopf (2001, 25ff.), informality is then 'the loss of security' that has been guaranteed by formal institutions – informalization increases insecurity, as institutions that were supposed to limit uncertainties were destroyed in the name of deregulation and flexibilization. They deduce from this an increasing uncertainty about the results of actions and about the endurance of their consequences, on the individual and the collective level (Altvater and Mahnkopf 2001, 25ff., my translation).

Even scholars who try to overcome the idea of a lack of regulation in the informal economy use the distinction between informal and formal institutions to establish a shared reference (e.g. Ayimpam 2014; Hillenkamp *et al.* 2013; Lourenço-Lindell, 2002; Neves and du Toit 2012). For instance, Kate Meagher (2005, 2007, 2010) prominently promotes an institutionalist approach to social network analysis in order to understand the role of informal institutions organizing economic fields in African societies and beyond. However, the definition of informal institutions as 'alternative forms of regulation operating outside the framework of the state' (Meagher 2005, 217) remains vague. I argue that we need to open this black box of the informal, for instance through Portes's differentiation between values, norms, roles and institutions. This allows us to analyse economic practices as culturally embedded in structures of meaning, or the symbolic realm. Values are 'general moral principles', whereas norms are 'concrete directives for action' (Portes 2006, 237). Norms, according to Portes, 'come together in organizational bundles known as roles[, ...] generally defined as the set of behaviors prescribed for occupants in particular social positions' (Portes 2006, 238). Roles, norms and values are part of institutions, but they are not equivalent to them (Portes 2006, 238). '[I]nstitutions represent the symbolic blueprint for organizations' and guide the relationships between roles. However, it is not the case that 'once institutional rules are established, role occupants blindly follow. Instead, they constantly modify the rules, transform them, and bypass them in the course of their daily interaction' (Portes 2006, 241f.).

Portes's working definitions of institutions, roles, norms and values allow for a consideration of economic practices as practices in which these institutions are actualized, realized and modified. The question of what actors do, and how they make use of institutional rules – which may be legally codified or not – and how this produces social structures, then becomes more important to examine than the distinction between informal or formal institutions. Rules do not exist as reified culture – there is no 'clear logic dictated by shared values and behavior' (Benton 1994, 238). But actors actualize rules in practice, and shared values derive from a shared experience, as a 'negotiated agreement from participants to act as if they had such shared experience and values' (Benton 1994, 239).

With cultural sociologist Viviana Zelizer's (2012) approach to economic practice, we can grasp the realization of rules, values and norms in interactions as repertoires of meaning that inform relational work. According to Zelizer, economic practices are 'relational work', a 'process of differentiating meaningful relations' (Zelizer 2012, 146). For each category of social relation, people erect boundaries, mark these boundaries through practices and designations, and establish a set of meanings that carry these relations. In other words, they define what kind of economic transactions fit to each relationship, and also define the means by which these transactions should be carried out (money, phone calls, etc.) (see Zelizer 2012). Relational work consists in the creation of 'relational packages', that are 'viable matches among those meaningful relations, transactions and media', in which people use the relational category that defines their relations and the respective meanings and forms of transactions that match to this relational category (i.e. friends, lovers, etc.) (Zelizer 2012, 151). The meaning that actors attribute to their transactions stands at the centre and as a starting point for understanding economic lives. With these questions, the focus shifts away from analyses of how social networks affect economic actions and market positions, to the analysis of how social relations constitute the economy (Zelizer 2012, 147–9). To understand making do beyond wage employment, I suggest we look at the meaning people attach to their efforts and relationships in which resources circulate. This meaning-making is a relational process – who is accepting which efforts as 'work', what does the remuneration of efforts enable people to do, and what is the remuneration worth in negotiating access to care, shelter or food?

Still, there are important limits to Zelizer's approach. First, although she traced social transformation through an examination of the monetization of the economy in the US as a case study to elaborate on the meaning of money (Zelizer 1994), she does not provide analytical tools to explain 'cultural, historical and institutional variation in the assembling of relational packages', a limitation that she herself recognizes as important for future research (Zelizer 2012, 164). So far, the separation between intimate ties and impersonal market exchange defines how relational packages are assembled in Zelizer's work. Her analytical framework in her article 'Payments and social ties' (1996) attaches the meaning of money to a specific quality of social relations, and she states, 'entitlements and gifts imply a more durable social relation between them than does compensation' (Zelizer 1996, 482). In other words, when monetary transactions are seen as gifts, actors conceive their relations as intimate and strong ties – but how can we explain situations in which actors who do not know each other personally nor durably transact money as gift *and* define their relationship as business partners? What is considered a legitimate relational package can differ between contexts.

Ulf Hannerz's (1980) work provides an analytical lens to account for variation in the assembly of relational packages. He focuses on relational categories and not so much on the meaning of the medium of exchange (as Zelizer does), and understands the relational categories as 'roles' on which people draw in interactions. Importantly, these roles depend on context. For Hannerz, 'social order' consists of role constellations, which are more or less recurrent, institutionalized solutions to problems (see Hannerz 1980, 174). Social life consists, perhaps most concretely, of situations. People involve themselves in these through relatively standardized modes of purposive behaviour (and also with parts of their consciousness and material resources) which we call roles. The total array of such modes of behaviour known within some major social unit, such as an urban community, may be described as its role inventory. The particular series of modes of behaviour in which one individual is involved is a role repertoire. '[Both these kinds of role collections are] divided into domains (household, kinship, provisioning, recreation, neighboring, traffic), containing greater or smaller numbers of roles' (Hannerz 1980, 317). What kinds of roles actors do or do not take on, depends on role-discriminatory attributes (i.e. sex, age, ethnicity), and the way role repertoires of one domain influence what kind of role repertoire an actor can take in another domain (the governing of role relationships, as Portes (2006) would call it) (see Hannerz 1980, 318). To expand on Zelizer's relational work, I look at role constellations as elaborated upon by Hannerz, as these shape the assembling of relational packages in economic practices. Second, for Zelizer, the trouble comes when categories of payment get 'chaotic' – different kinds of organizations concentrate on one category of payment, compensation entitlement or gift, and people get into trouble if there are discrepancies (see Zelizer 1996, 483). 'My own research shows how at each step in money's advance, people have reshaped their commercial transactions, introduced new distinctions, invented their own special forms of currency, earmarked money in ways that baffle market theorists and incorporated money into personalized webs of friendship, family relations, interactions with authorities and forays through shops and businesses' (Zelizer 1996, 484).

In contrast, I challenge Zelizer's assumptions that matching processes tend towards consistent relational packages. Social roles are not 'coherent sets of normative expectations', but 'ambivalence, conflicting norms and counter-norms associated with particular social positions' (Merton 1976; Merton and Barber 1963, both quoted in Hillcoat-Nallétamby and Phillips 2011, 203) can produce social order, too. Relational packages can consist of relational categories, forms of transactions, and media that are in tension with each other, as contradicting normative expectations, but this can become a tension that actors want to maintain in order to uphold positions of power or access to resources more generally.

Third, Zelizer does not account enough for the existence of power dynamics, and for ways in which inequality is reproduced in relational work, a limitation she recognizes herself (see Zelizer 2012, 164). In relation to this matter, I will discuss next how economic practice and inequalities can be articulated, and how these inequalities can be studied across contexts. As the last step of the theoretical framework for this study, I will lay out below the three entry points into the empirical analysis. Each entry point enables us to see inequalities in the making of livelihoods.

Economic practices and inequalities: three lenses

Precarization describes processes of marginalization, which are deeply embedded in power relations and social inequalities (Lorey 2017; Munck 2013). Marginalization is a process, subtle and explicit, 'through which specific sections of an urban population are pushed out of resourceful settings, not because of anyone's intentions, but because the mechanisms in place and the capital in various forms that is needed to make them work for oneself are effectively keeping them out and, in some cases, [pushing them to the edges of urban life]' (Blokland *et al.* 2016, 8). Comparing these mechanisms can then be a way to bring into relation different contexts, acknowledging their differences, but at the same time exploring new ways to relate them to each other. Three mechanisms are central to showing how inequalities get reproduced in precarious work settings: social closure, domination and exploitation. By starting in Abidjan, I show that mechanisms visible there are also operating in Berlin –different in content, but similar in form. In both contexts we can ask when do particular resources, and work, turn into capital; and how is value attached to things and people in social relations. These questions help to see how resources circulate and how (dis)advantages are reproduced at and through work.

Social closure or the symbolic value of work

Work, on the one hand, constitutes a means by which people can satisfy their material needs through the compensation they receive for deploying their labour power. On the other hand, work also has a symbolic value. The kind of work one does matters not only in terms of income or material gains, but also in terms of the status associated with it. What is considered to be valuable work varies. The status of work can be institutionalized, for example, through *professions*, defined by the acquisition of a 'specific set of competencies and skills' through training, 'which guarantee material survival on a long-term basis' (see Weber 1972, 80, author's translation). The status of work entails processes of social closure (Weber 1972, 201–7). Under conditions of competition for scarce resources, actors try to monopolize access to these (Weber 1972). Consequently, work opportunities are not equally accessible, but monopolized (see Weber 1972, 202). The monopoly is created through opportunity hoarding, a relational mechanism that Tilly (2001, 366) defines as the limitation of use 'of a value-producing resource to members of an ingroup'. It often involves boundary work. Hence, it is not enough to probe in what way symbolic capital becomes attached to occupational positions; it is equally important to analyse how this serves the monopolization of resources through processes of closure.

Moreover, these processes of closure matter in transitions from youth to adulthood. In the sociology on youth transition and coming of age, work status is discussed as an important indicator for adulthood (for an overview see Furlong 2009), particularly in Côte d'Ivoire (see Bazin and Gnabéli 1997; Matlon 2016), but also in Germany (see Kohli 2002). That said, we can say that the value we give work is structured by time – not every kind of work has a similar value at every moment of our lives. The temporality of work is closely tied to ideas about the life course and politics which institutionalize certain norms about the way we structure our lifetimes. Life course politics constitute all those (state) regulations relevant to the temporal order of life (Kohli 2002, 538). In seeking explanations for the marginalization of young adults, then, we must look at their position in regard to life course ideals and the possibilities available to them to find activities which are in accordance with them. As Mains writes in relation to urban youth in Ethiopia, 'stress is generated for young men not because of a lack of productivity but because their social relations are not changing in accordance with an abstract notion of time' (Mains 2012, 85).

Pelizzari and Krämer both acknowledge time as a factor when discussing precarity. They consider precarious working conditions in relation to the professional trajectories of actors, and explore how transitory precarity becomes enduring for some but not for others (Krämer 2014, 444), as a result of different work habitus (Pelizzari 2008, 207ff.). However, by focusing on actors' work habitus, Pelizzari approaches the practices of actors as though they move within a field of the labour market that, while transforming, remains intact as an autonomous field with the same 'rules of the game' and logics of exchange. The cases of airtime sellers in Abidjan and food delivery riders in Berlin challenge such notions of 'foundational stability implied in the idea of field' (Vigh 2010, paragraph 47). The actors here negotiate the meaning of their practice as work or non-work. The shifting boundaries of labour markets themselves are at stake, and I argue that it is important to study these and how they are redrawn in practice. These cases reveal the limits of an understanding of social mobility that looks 'synchronically at the way in which agents move within solid social coordinates or structures. [Such a perspective] implicitly or explicitly consider[s] the surfaces, be they fields, frames, maps, structures or stages, in which agents act as imbued with a stable and solid quality' (Vigh 2010, paragraph 47). With Henrik Vigh, I ask: what if actors begin to worry about the movement of the field itself and how this movement in turn moves them (Vigh 2010, paragraph 47)?

I pluralize concepts of status and the making of personhood, pointing to the importance of wealth in people and other forms of storing and converting value that all together go beyond the self-accruing individual. As a first lens, I focus on the symbolic value of work, by analysing how status is built in processes of closure. I turn to the meaning the young men pursuing this activity attach to the airtime selling and food delivery jobs. Yet, this analytical lens does not focus on the subjective meaning only, but rather on how dominant perspectives on the symbolic value of work organize processes of closure among youth and risks for precarity in the longer term. I expand on the work by Pelizzari and Krämer on precarity as a *floating situation*, which stresses fissures, splits and hierarchies within groups of workers that from the outset share similar conditions of work. Precarity as floating situation has open ends, leading upwards or downwards (Krämer 2014; Pelizzari 2008). Drawing on feminist and postcolonial sociology on work, the hustle and youth transitions (Guyer 2004; Skeggs 2011; Thieme 2018; Vigh 2010), this first analytical lens challenges the Bourdieusian foundations of fields as stable and autonomous. I understand value as being created relationally and situationally, but not so fixed throughout time as the notions of field and of capital may imply (Schilling *et al.* 2019; Skeggs 2004, 2011).

Domination or regulatory practices at work

When it comes to domination in the area of work, sociological theory discusses above all the appropriation of labour power. At the focus is often mainly the working contract, and with it, the legal arrangements that tie workers to work. This is problematic, as it universalizes the empirical particularity of industrialized societies to theoretical concepts applied elsewhere. This is why it is important to broaden the perspective to other forms of domination than those in which labour power is appropriated as wage labour. Bourdieu (1976, 1977) stresses the significant differences in modes of domination, that is, how privileges in a social space are maintained by the dominant class. He is interested in the historically grown structures of power and power struggles that constitute the field of the economic

(Bourdieu 1997, 2005). By using the metaphor of a field, Bourdieu acknowledges that the social space behaves 'as a field of struggle within which agents confront each other, with means and ends differentiated according to their position in the structure of the force field, thus contributing to preserving or transforming its structure' (Bourdieu 1994, 55, my translation) Bourdieu understands the economy as a field with specific rules ('doxa') and actors with different possibilities to use these rules to their advantage. The rules create opportunities and constraints for actors at the same time. However, different to a game, rules in social fields are constituted as legitimate through social struggles – and are not created by a single person (see Costey 2005, 14). These struggles are often not explicit. Actors in the field are 'caught in the game, in the *illusio* understood as fundamental belief in the interest of the game and the value of the stakes which are inherent in that membership' (Bourdieu 2003, 25, my emphasis and translation). That said, the rules might appear natural to those who have a 'sense of the game' (Bourdieu 1994, 155). They exist without 'anti-thesis', but prescribe what is sayable and thinkable, and in that they are like 'the principles of visions and divisions' (Costey 2005, 14). Once actors accept the constituting perspective of a field, it is no longer possible to take an outside perspective (Bourdieu 2003, 140). Actors accept the rules of the game, even if they might oppose them or circumvent them, because their ways of perceiving the world are structured by their social position. As such, the agents' thinking is not determined, but has a limited and conditioned spontaneity (Münnich 2017, 115, quoting Bourdieu 2005, 86). Bourdieu acknowledges actors' space for manoeuvre, in that he does not assume that 'institutions generate meaning for people' and as such, determine their action (Hanappi 2014, 165; Münnich 2017).

Different economic systems require different modes of domination (Bourdieu 1976, 1977). Legal regulations are then only one mode of domination. Law 'does no more than symbolically consecrate – by recording it in a form which renders it both eternal and universal – the structure of the power relation between groups and classes which is produced and guaranteed practically by the functioning of these mechanisms' (i.e. the distinction between the position and the person, the power and its holder, together with the relationship obtaining at a particular moment between qualifications and jobs)

(Bourdieu 1977, 188). In what Bourdieu calls 'elementary forms of domination', in contrast, a person is directly dominated by another person (see Bourdieu 1976). To appropriate labour, services, goods, homage and the respect of others, the dominant class has to 'win' them personally – they have to create a bond between persons (Bourdieu 1977, 190). The differences in modes of domination then lie in the 'degree of objectification of accumulated social capital' (Bourdieu 1976, 122). On the one hand, we find relations of domination that are constantly made, un-made and re-made in and through the interaction between agents. On the other hand, there are social formations in which objective and institutionalized mechanisms guarantee the distribution of titles (monetary, scholarly etc.), and these mechanisms are so opaque and permanent that they are beyond individual consciousness and power (Bourdieu 1976, 122).

Bourdieu's theory on the economy of faith and its forms of domination, and his genesis of the capitalist economy as an economic field with its own *illusio*, shows that economic practices and the relational work they entail reproduce relations of domination. This extends Zelizer's theory on economic practice, where she herself recognizes the missing attention to power relations. Zelizer looks at the tensions that arise when actors translate the 'continually negotiated categories of social life' into legal conceptions, and shows that people differentiate 'forms of monetary transfers in correspondence with their definitions of the sort of relationship that obtains between the parties. They adopt symbols, rituals, practices, and physically distinguishable forms of money to mark distinct social relations' (Zelizer 2000, 819). In her work, Zelizer doesn't focus on the ways in which social practices' tensions with legal categories are powerful. She argues that matching goes in both directions: forms of payment are used to define relationships, and relationships define meaning and forms of payment.

With Bourdieu, however, we could argue that it is important to consider how these matching pairs come about. For what purpose does matching happen? By asking these questions, we could understand the power of the symbolic, and would pay attention to the fact that intimate relations and the corresponding payments can constitute important relational work for maintaining a form of domination. To expand on Zelizer's concept of relational work with reference to Bourdieu's focus on inequality, I look at the ways in which relational work is embedded in an *illusio*, in which relations of domination at work are understood as legitimate, and hence actors reproduce their unequal positions in the field. I use Bourdieu's elaboration on the economy of symbolic goods (Bourdieu 1977, 1998)[3] in comparative perspective. Symbolic economies might exist in both contexts, Abidjan and Berlin, but with other functions in the reproduction of positions.

This is why, as a second analytical entry point, I examine the power of the symbolic and discuss asymmetries and power relations emerging in fragmented work contexts. This entry point addresses in more depth the particular organization of work in platformized companies of the digital economy. New technical devices such as applications that track movements and locations, and software for instantaneous feedback on transactions, are used to organize the work necessary for the service to deliver, while at the same time attachments to companies are informalized. Drawing on theoretical innovations in the debate on (in)formality (Benton 1994; Hilbrandt 2017; Ledeneva *et al.* 2018), I discuss regulatory practices in these emerging work relations, and analyse how labour is appropriated there. Most importantly, I stress the importance of personalized attachments between workers and managers as sources of authority, in contrast to objectified power relations represented for example through legal regulations. This helps to see how ambiguity in rules and ambiguous roles can become powerful in establishing authority and forms of attachment, despite the increased use of technological devices that standardize rules and work relations. I study how official legal rules are applied and rendered effective in the relational work of agents. Authority can be established in personalized *and* impersonalized relations. This can be explained by variation in which interviewees reproduced an *idea of the state* and the functionality of official rules for establishing relations of domination.

Exploitation or the articulation of work and care

Broadly speaking, '[e]xploitation occurs when persons who control a resource a) enlist the effort of others in production of value by means of that resource, but b) exclude the others from the full value added by their effort' (Tilly 2001, 366). As I refute a narrow understanding of work as labour and the economy as autonomous area of market transactions, I want to understand how relations of exploitation cross capitalist and non-capitalist economies and mobilize the boundary of labour and work, of unpaid and paid labour. This requires us to overcome wage labour centrism, as in the classical Marxist conceptualization of labour commodification and surplus generation. Marcel van der Linden's concept of the subaltern worker is useful here, as it acknowledges forms of labour that are in between wage labour and self-employment, or slavery and wage labour. The term 'subaltern workers' aims to broaden a Marxist conceptualization of the working class. These 'make up a variegated group, including chattel slaves, share-croppers, small artisans and wage earners' (van der Linden 2008, 32). The multitude is characterized by the common condition, that they must sell or hire their labour power to another person under economic or non-economic compulsion, and this regardless of 'whether the carrier of labor power is him- or herself selling or hiring it out, and regardless of whether the carrier him- or herself owns means of production' (van der Linden 2008, 32). Workers who take their own tools to the workshop are examples of such intermediate forms between wage labour and self-employment (see van der Linden 2008, 25). Here, we can see connections to the gig workers, the riders and airtime sellers in this book, who represent such intermediate forms of work.

Moreover, the articulation of production and reproduction must feature prominently in studying mechanisms of exploitation. Capitalist accumulation uses and also depends on spheres of care (see feminist critique, e.g. Federici 2012; Fraser 2016), and public and social spaces of consumption (see e.g. Lefebvre's [1991 [1974]] theory on the production of urban space). Marx did not consider the effort of making consumer items suitable for consumption, a process that Marxist anthropologists and feminists discussed extensively in the 1960s and 1970s (cf. Thelen 2015, 501; van der Linden 2008, 28). More precisely, feminist Marxists focused in the following decades on the practices of 'social reproduction', defined by Cindi Katz as all the practices that allow the reproduction, on a daily and long-term basis, of the means of production and the labour power to make them work (Katz 2001, 711). Consequently, I argue that relations of exploitation are not only based on the principle of equivalent exchange, but generated through the entanglement of different economies. The Marxist anthropologist Meillassoux (1972, 1979), for example, explains the dialectical relation between capitalist and non-capitalist modes of production: maintaining a domestic, 'non-capitalist' mode of production reduces costs of reproduction and, as such, is beneficial to capitalist exploitation. This resonates with Klaus Dörre's concept of 'secondary exploitation' (Dörre 2012; Dörre and Haubner 2018). Characteristics of forms of secondary exploitation are that the rationality of equivalent exchange does not apply, or only to a limited extent.

> We can thus speak of secondary exploitation whenever symbolic forms of pressure and pressure applied politically by the state are utilized in order to preserve differences between 'inside' and 'outside' with the aim of pushing the labour force of certain social groups below its actual value or of excluding these groups from the actual capitalist relationship of exploitation. (Dörre 2011, 77f.)

As Dörre puts it: dominant capitalist actors draw on different forms of exploitation to overcome limits of accumulation, and to conquer new social territories to produce surplus value (see Dörre 2012, 111). Politics of commodification can maintain spheres of non-capitalist modes of re/production for enabling the accumulation of capital, or (re-)commodify these spheres of re/production and introduce logics of market exchange there.

As a third entry point to studying inequalities in the making of livelihood, then, I study the entanglements of market-work and care through the concept of distributive labour (Ferguson 2015). I look at the contradictory relationship between capitalist production and care, and show that selling airtime and delivering food was work entangled with care practices. This addresses precarity in its existential dimension: the precariousness of life itself and the human need for care (cf. Butler 2009). Drawing on feminist and postcolonial economic sociology (Ferguson 2015; Fraser 2016; Seekings 2008; Vuarin 2000), I conceptualize care relations and their entanglement with market-work as distributive labour, where the radius of responsibilities is negotiated based on norms of deservingness. Asking how honour and reputation demarcated when and how support by others is legitimate helps to see variations between the cases. The organization of care relations, and with it the negotiation of deservingness and entitlements to support, turns into a crucial element where urban precarities crystallize. This becomes particularly visible by looking at the contradictory relationship between capitalist production and care and its current articulation (Fraser 2016; Meillassoux 1972, 1979).

In conclusion, the previous sections lay the groundwork for my own perspective on economic practices and an analysis of the reproduction of inequalities in work settings characterized by instability. While Zelizer helps us to grasp the entanglement of social relations and economic practices beyond the embeddedness paradigm in new economic sociology, Bourdieu's early economic sociology directs attention towards power relations in the relational work. Moreover, Hannerz and Portes highlight the institutional embeddedness of relational work and allow us to employ a comparative lens on economic practices. In sum, economic practices of making livelihood comprise work, understood as all 'efforts adding use value to goods and services' (Tilly and Tilly 1998, 22), and other practices that allow the satisfaction of human needs. Economic practices are hence more than exchange relations in the market, and they are constituted by relational work. Economic processes are instituted, and as I focus on practices, I look at the role constellations and norms that actors reproduce in their practices and in the relational packages of their relational work. Moreover, economic practices are shaped by values that define which transactions are possible at what moment in time and place, as *illusio* of the field, and perspectives that privilege certain things and persons to become valuable.

That said, rather than comparing the platform economy of food delivery and the airtime distribution economy in the way they organize labour processes, the focus lies on the economic practices of those selling airtime and delivery food. Most importantly, we will learn how these practices are connected to other domains, such as the household, the neighbourhood or the street/public space. Given the temporary and unstable character of these economic activities, we further ask: how are advantages maintained when institutionalized forms of capital are not the only ways to ensure social position, and no longer even provide a means for doing so? How do the deinstitutionalization of professional roles and the instability of rules operating at work make 'ambivalence' productive in power relations? What sociability do actors need to invest in and how do they build symbolic capital (i.e. reputation, prestige) to secure distributive outcomes, when access to employment positions and to the associated rights to welfare is difficult? With these questions in mind, we craft connections while comparing the practices of young airtime sellers and food delivery riders. We first of all assess how actors negotiate their occupational positions in accordance to the symbolic meaning of work, which has to be seen in its temporality, or situated in life course politics. Second, we analyse the different modes of domination in economic fields, be it more systemic or personalized – which in consequence also defines what kind of resources are valued, and are significant for the reproduction of inequalities. Third, we address how different economies intersect – the economy of reproduction and production, for instance (Meillassoux 1979). In the following chapters, we will explore the making do of airtime sellers and delivery riders through these three entry points.

Notes

1 Bourdieu stresses the relational production of symbolic capital. Ordinary properties of agents (e.g., physical strength, wealth etc.) turn into symbolic capital of recognition and become symbolically efficient, because it is recognized as such. Symbolic capital appears 'in the social relations between properties possessed by an agent and other agents endowed with adequate categories of perception' (Bourdieu 1998, 104). It is a specific form of capital produced and accumulated in an economy of symbolic goods (cf. Bourdieu 1998, 104).

2 I use neo-institutionalism and new institutionalism interchangeably.

3 An example of an 'economy of symbolic goods', is 'the economy of good faith'. Bourdieu uses both terms to elaborate on his theory of the importance of the symbolic – so do I in the following.

3

Hustling: the symbolic value of in-between work

'Why we are doing this?', Antoine intuitively began to explain, when I presented my research interest in call box workers to him. 'It is to not stay here *bras croisés*.[1] Otherwise we wouldn't choose to *be* phone box guys. If we had something else somewhere else, we would stop it' (Interview with Antoine, Koumassi, 10 March 2016, my emphasis). Antoine was studying sociology at the main university of Abidjan, but also sold airtime for a neighbour. The neighbour paid him a monthly return of 30,000 FCFA, which remained the same amount, no matter how much profit he made through sales. For Antoine, this allowed him to have some pocket money for his own needs, as his parents were not able to take care of everything. In Antoine's reaction to my research interest, we can grasp a little bit how the sale of airtime is perceived by young men in Abidjan: it is a temporary economic activity for them, a way of getting by and preparing for the future. The flexibility and ease with which you could start the activity was beneficial here.

Also for the young men we encountered in Berlin, the delivery jobs for platform companies like Foodora and Deliveroo were income-generating activities to keep going but not to enter a fixed professional career. Most interviewees acknowledged that the job was not for a lifetime, but stressed the temporary character of the job. Dennis, a full-time rider, put this in a nutshell:

> It's not real work. It is a job, for students or for young people, you know. For young people in particular, you know, because you cannot ride your bike your entire life and deliver stuff. It's a job for a limited amount of time in your life, it's not a job with a future. (Interview with Dennis, Prenzlauer Berg, 24 February 2017)

The easiness with which one could start the gig work helped to make the delivery job an attractive temporary activity. In Berlin, most jobs required a lot of paperwork and official documents to prove one's capacities and identity. Not so the gig economy. There was no need to hand in a CV or a motivation letter. Instead, an applicant filled in an online questionnaire to check if he or she fulfilled the basic conditions (availability of a smartphone new enough to run the application that coordinated the distribution of food; sufficient data volume; a bike (even though other means of transport were possible too) and a work permit for Germany). As a second step, applicants were invited for a test ride. Job applicants followed an experienced rider[2] along their daily routes: waiting for an order, receiving the message on the smartphone that indicated a new order, getting the address and the name of the restaurant, riding to the restaurant, picking up the order (e.g. the food ordered by a customer of the Foodora delivery service app), receiving the delivery address by app/phone message, riding to the delivery address, delivering the food ordered to the customer, waiting for the next order, and so on. There was no transparent goal to achieve at this test ride, to my knowledge.[3] The test ride was framed as an opportunity to learn about the routines of the work, and to speak peer-to-peer about the job. But the test ride was also about getting a sense of the candidate's capacity to do the work. Another rider I met, Salomon, explained the procedure in this way: what made him 'get in' to the delivery job in the end was his speed and efficiency, which he proved during the test ride. That said, access to these delivery jobs had low barriers in terms of formal requirements and institutionalized cultural capital – such as a diploma or a professional CV (cf. Bourdieu 1983) – but required skills, most obviously knowing how to ride a bike.

Both selling airtime and delivering food were income-generating activities, and hence could be considered as work. For the majority of the young men I encountered in both cities, however, it didn't constitute a profession, defined by the acquisition of a specific set of competencies and skills through training, which guarantee material survival on a long-term basis (Weber 1972, 80). The young men in Abidjan didn't invest in the accumulation of specific cultural and symbolic capital attached to the sale of airtime. Instead, they used the activity to maintain their status as people who were trying to get somewhere, people who were not standing still, stuck in permanent temporariness, but would move on to become something else, professors or businessmen for example. In the following, we will show how, in such contexts of apparent convenience and freedom, risks of enduring precarity result from processes of closure among workers. To this end, we look more closely at the symbolic economy at work and how work serves to construct status in both settings.

'In-between work'

What is considered to be valuable work varies. The value of certain activities is a historical product and closely linked to moral economies of work (Dawson and Fouksman 2020; Fouksman 2020; Newell 2006), in which norms about deservingness or aspirations and expectations about the relationship between work, wealth and reward are articulated (Fouksman 2020, 288f.). Holding a particular job can give someone status and prestige, and in this sense, work matters for young men to construct status and become a person of value in their environments. If we start asking how does work play a role in achieving status, self-esteem and social recognition as young men, and when we decentre the construction of person value from a focus on institutionalized work status, then we can include a broader range of practices of personhood, and multiple ways in which people can be put into value.

Actors move within time in a constant shaping and reshaping of actions. Value, i.e. as a person, is created relationally and situationally, but is not so fixed throughout time as the notions of field and of capital may imply (Schilling *et al.* 2019; Skeggs 2004, 2011). With Skeggs, we understand value as contingent and situational, based on practices, and ask how value can be lived and materialized, carried, inscribed and recognized on bodies, on persons and in practices. Like Jane Guyer, who confronts us with the idea that 'value is contingent, hermeneutic, negotiable, and non-natural', and that 'if people inhabit choppy waters, perhaps they do not anchor at some fixed point at all. In fact, the literal condition of seasickness is much better corrected by focusing one's eyes on the horizon than by attaching the boat to the ocean' (Guyer 2004, 13). We pay attention to possible shifts in the rules of the game, and a 'focus on the relationship between what is happening with and *within* structures' (Beck *et al.* 2003, 3, quoted in Vigh 2010, paragraph 48).

Building status through work is then more than the accruing of value as individuals. Status is acquired as symbolic capital in webs of social relations, rather than being a state attached to an 'autonomous' individual, accruing credits and entitlements as individual assets. This view is prevalent in a sociology of professions by Weber and other modernist sociologies. Weber focuses on the status of work as institutionalized in *professions* (see Weber 1972, 80). But achieving status, self-esteem and social recognition is not only the result of the accumulation of resources as capitals for themselves. The imaginary of personhood as singular self and possessive individual is a bourgeois model – other forms of value practices need to be included in the picture. 'Not everybody can extend their opportunities for exploitation by loading themselves with value that is convertible into capitals for themselves and Capital more generally' (Skeggs 2011, 508). People can be put into value in different ways and not only as labour power (Guyer 1993, 1995; Skeggs 2011). In other words, value is attached to different conceptualizations and practices of personhood. Personhood describes 'the legal, social and moral states generated through encounters with others' (Skeggs 2011, 498). Material conditions of living different relations to capital produce different orientations to others (cf. Skeggs 2011, 507). 'Different circuits and exchange mechanisms exist, some enable capital/s accumulation; others exist alongside and others are autonomist, based on reciprocity, care, shared understandings of injustice, insecurity, precarity. All these values circulate through the person as they face capitalism in very different directions' (Skeggs 2011, 509). Skeggs proposes three different spatiotemporal configurations of value: '[A] model of extraction from (surplus value extraction from labour power – time and energy), a model of accruing to (time and energy on self-development), whilst the other is based on relationality (time and energy with and for others)' (Skeggs 2011, 509). Investing time and energy with and for others is particularly relevant in Africanist scholarship on person value. The self is formed by relationships. Persons do not 'have relations, they are relations' (Piot 1999, 18, quoted in Mains 2013, 336). Exchange of resources as gifts is hence not a 'transfer of resources from one individual to another ... Rather, the exchange of gifts and affection modifies relationships and selves' (Mains 2013, 336). Transactions as gifts and commodities are not mutually exclusive, or part of entirely contrastive systems, but instead can become both relevant and converged.

> Only certain kinds of activity that we would include under the rubric of 'work', however, were considered to create value, or in Melanesian terms, conferred authorship ... The Western concept of 'labour' merges the two in ways that mask the interplay of quality and quantity in the cultural and historical dynamic. The kinds of work that created personal 'reality' were culturally delineated; they excluded but also included activities that a Western concept of labour does not. (Guyer 1993, 255)[4]

That said, Guyer, Mains and Skeggs show that value practices are 'made not (just) through self-value accrual but through the gift of attention to others over time and space, through relational extension' (Skeggs 2011, 509).

In the following, we illustrate the marginalizing effects of respective 'dominant symbolic model[s] for proper personhood, legitimated through law and the social contract, extended through commodification and morally legitimated' (Skeggs 2011, 501), without portraying the other practices as a lack of value. More concretely, the apparent accessibility and flexibility advertised by the delivery companies, and which many of the interviewees presented as an advantage, represents a discourse and *perspective* on the work setting that overlooks the unwritten rules of the game there. This discourse conceals the unequally distributed opportunities to gain shifts and thus money as a rider. Floating in and out of work required habits, skills and cultural resources. What constitutes 'making the most' of a situation is a question of analysis, and does not only circumscribe the accruing of resources to a singular self. Hustling points to a different understanding of the production of value, not as fixed capital through time but as situational. In a situation of floating (Krämer 2014), showing attentiveness and the ability to act in relation to the movement of one's own surroundings is important. In the following, I analyse how cultural resources were differently valued in the work setting, and how these legitimized processes of social closure among those selling airtime and delivering food as rider.

'Super riders' and 'bike monsters': the symbolic value of delivering food

At the beginning of this book we met Tobias, a young rider who was attracted to Berlin as he saw in it a place where everything was possible. Riding a bike and enjoying the race was a cultural practice that became to him a valuable card to play, an expression of distinction, in the particular socio-spatial setting of Berlin in which it took place. The image of Berlin as fresh, fun, cool is not only evident in the discourse of my interviewees, such as Tobias, as well as that of their acquaintances, but is also part of the official place-making of Berlin. It is staged as a youthful, culturally diverse metropole (cf. Colomb 2012b; Lanz 2007). Since the early 2000s

> internationally, Berlin was also increasingly perceived as an exciting metropolis characterized by a dynamic cultural scene, social liberality, and the availability of spaces that had not yet been commercially exploited. Once again, the label of Berlin's youth came to the foreground of the city's official marketing … Berlin was conceived of as a city of the future, as the cultural capital of the twenty-first century with the attributes of cosmopolitanism, urbanity and diversity. (Lanz 2013, 216; see Colomb 2012b; Lanz 2007)

This perspective on Berlin (see Skeggs 2004 on perspective) makes certain areas and certain diversities more valuable than others. Kreuzberg, Friedrichshain, Southern Neukölln, Prenzlauer Berg were districts in which the delivery platforms made most of their revenues, as the density of restaurants and customers was highest. Outer districts in the former East Berlin turned into the 'Other' of the cosmopolitan Berlin that Stephan Lanz describes (see Lewek 2016). In this particular urban setting, Tobias's praise of the cyclocross bikes and of the joy he experienced when riding worked as practices of distinction.

Similarly, Carl, 27, who was intrigued by the rider's job because it enabled him to discover Berlin, consumed the 'cool' atmosphere of Neukölln and Kreuzberg by taking photographs, getting to know restaurants and districts in which he was eager to cycle more often. Carl studied electrical engineering for his bachelor's degree. After having completed professional training as an electrician at a renowned company, and living in a student residency in Lichtenberg, an outer district of East Berlin, he wanted to apply for residencies in the 'best locations' [*coolste Lage*] (he did not specify but referred vaguely to Neukölln, Kreuzberg and Prenzlauer Berg as districts). But as places were scarce, he followed advice to apply for a residency that was located more 'outside' of the city (even though administratively it still belonged to Berlin, and also in terms of physical distance it was not necessarily further away from the geographical centre of Berlin than Prenzlauer Berg or Neukölln, for example) (Interview with Carl, Prenzlauer Berg, 5 March 2017). He had grown up in Saxony. His parents had both attended university and were employed in technical professions. When asked about young people's everyday lives, he began describing his recent experiences at a bicycle fair. He had just spent his weekend at one in order to look for new bike models. He already owned two different bikes, a racing bike and a mountain bike, and he was now looking for something that he could use everywhere – but which was nevertheless not standard, mass-produced but 'individual'. 'I don't want to have a bike which is serial. A bike that could [belong] to everyone, and could stand around everywhere … I want to be a bit individual' (Interview with Carl, Prenzlauer Berg, 5 March 2017).

He also observed the messenger riders on the street and copied some of their ways of equipping themselves, and their way of behaving in the street. When asked for examples, he explained that 'he would avoid routes where he would be stopped and slowed down by red lights, or by cobblestone', and that 'real messengers, they don't have uniform clothing but a uniform *look* [he says this in English, H.S.], cycling trousers, often shorts in Army style … and a belt pouch'. He adopted these accessories and made a special torch construction for his helmet, as his bike's handlebar lamp was stolen while he was working. Carl cultivated a messenger cultural identity, as revealed in his explanation about how he tried to professionalize his riding style and equipment, copying the practices and dress code of the messengers.

Displays of being 'individual' and 'well equipped' for speed and sportiness counted among the riders. Their individual accounts on the styling of the rider's activity were also reproduced in interaction with other riders. These cultural practices became valuable and enabled practices of distinction. Prestige was attributed to those riders who embodied these styles most successfully. Rumours that the young riders shared with me with admiration about specific workers who were 'monster[s] on their bike[s]', or 'super riders', illustrated this.

Next to the cultivation of style, risk-taking and fighting spirit were important habits expressed among the riders I encountered. In conversations, they affirmed the 'game character' of the job. This included the calculation of speed records and records in the length of shifts one could make, as well as stories about how to subvert the regulations of red lights and the street. One night, after a shared evening around a bonfire in one of the Berlin parks, three riders and I cycled down the hill, and as I rode in front of them, I passed a red light. I got caught by one of the riders, who said: 'Ah, now you are one of us, Hannah!' (fieldnotes 21 June 2017). Wolfgang, a rider from Poland, who even before starting delivery work was attracted by urban cycle races organized all over the world (so called 'bad trails'), showed me an application on his phone through which he calculated the records he was doing on his daily rounds of delivery. He could follow riders and see at what speed others rode through a given street segment/route in Berlin (Interview with Wolfgang, Friedrichshain, 1 July 2017). By distributing 'likes' to each other on the basis of their rides, they inculcated a particular working culture.

Research on messenger work shows interesting parallels to delivery work. Messengers are discussed as a group of workers 'for whom the binary distinction between work and life, work and leisure and not work are relatively meaningless' (Fincham 2008, 619). Messengering is different from other service work because of the 'incorporation of play into the workday, and play is the starting point for unravelling the puzzle of the messenger subculture, understood as "un-instrumental human activity" produced for its own sake' (Kidder 2011, 11). The delivery job is similarly a job in which lifestyle, subculture and identity-making intersect with the process of selling labour power. It is not so clear if people invest in an occupational identity, or use the occupation for constructing an identity. 'In the case of bicycle messengers, the identification with a particular way of being as a messenger was strong for many of the men and women … [t]he maintenance of a particular image, makes tolerable the poor conditions and pay of the work' (Fincham 2008, 621).

Coolness is part of this particular image, as well as fashion, or style, according to Fincham. 'You can see the freedom … like surfers or skateboarders', interviewees in Fincham's (2008, 622) research explain. It not only produces a self-image and reputation, but also matters for building a sense of commonality among workers (Fincham 2008, 622). Berlin, as an urban context staged as youthful and not mainstream, offers a particular scene in which cycling became coded as valuable as style and practice of distinction.

Food delivery platforms picked up on the 'playful character' of delivery work. Game systems – competition, rewards, quantifying player/user behaviour – were applied to the domain of work (see Woodcock and Johnson 2018 on 'gamification'). The companies, with the help of app-based technology, tracked the speed of each worker and classified workers according to their weekly 'efforts'. They also introduced incentives to encourage quicker delivery – when riders hit a certain level of orders per week, they got an extra pay bonus. In this way, the companies were able to control the riders' efficacy as labourers. The statistics on speed, amounts of orders/week, etc. had consequences for the workers: when riders failed to achieve the average riding speed, they could be dismissed.

The practices of personhood valued by 'biker culture' converged with practical regulation of the working process and the possibilities available for a rider to earn money. In that sense, the work setting emphasized self-agency, and labour value was generated through the production of a particular sort of person. Here, '[t]he ability to capitalize or not upon culture and use it as a mobile resource is fundamental' (Skeggs 2004, 76). Not only on the organizational level, but also in the relationships among workers, the valuing of a certain *perspective* on the job created a sense of commonality – but organized processes of social closure, too. This was also used to monopolize resources and prestige, with the effect that others could be excluded from access to scarce resources, which is what defines social closure (Mackert 2004, 11; Weber 1972, 199–211).

Indeed, not all the riders expressed an attitude of play towards the delivery job. Practices of personhood differed in classed and gendered ways. In conversations with riders, speed and sportiness were valorized and admired, however not everybody was similarly enabled to perform this ideal. Gabi, for example, a woman in her twenties, didn't sign up for the 'challenges' (extra payments if one hit a goal of x deliveries per hour) set up by the platform, as she felt 'stressed'. 'She was just not as fast as a rider', Gabi explained in an informal conversation (fieldnotes, 14 June 2017). This self-perception and self-rationalization is inscribed in the interplay with how agents are seen by others: in other meetings in a park around a self-made bonfire, one of the male riders called Gabi 'mother' [*Mutti*], for bringing lots of food and for taking care of the physical well-being of everyone. When we rode back home at night together, she told us how happy she was that we had come, so that she was not the only woman there (fieldnotes, 21 June 2017). This shows 'how difficult it is for many woman workers to achieve identities beyond that of women worker because their labour of identity is naturalized as part of their selves and cannot be used and exchanged as a mobile resource' (Skeggs 2004, 74).

Also, those who saw the delivery job primarily as a means to make money were marginalized in a dominant *perspective* on the delivery work as fun and play. This became most evident in my encounter with Dennis, a Spanish man in his late twenties. After college, he had completed professional training to install air conditioners. He had lived in Austria for several years before coming to Berlin some time ago. He was one of the few full-time riders I met. He cycled 160 hours a month and earned between €1,000 and €1,300, which was enough to pay for rent and food, and some leisure expenses – but he 'couldn't really afford much' (Interview with Dennis, 24 February 2017). Dennis also acknowledged the job's flexibility, but in his everyday life, flexibility meant being able above all to be flexible in accepting overtime hours. He had fixed scheduled shifts, and normally he would not cancel any shift, because he needed a full-time position to be able to 'take something decent [*Vernünftiges*] home at the end of the month'. When describing the good atmosphere, he stressed how one worked on one's own, independently, and portrayed a work setting characterized by impersonal contacts. Dennis was sometimes 'tired to death', because he needed to be fast so as to deliver orders in time. A chronometer in the app indicated how much time he had to ride between restaurant and client.

As riding a bike every day for eight hours was exhausting, especially under these conditions, he bought an electric bike so that he could be quicker while conserving his energy. When he had to set up his new electric bike, he called us and not one of his colleagues – even though we barely knew each other and had just met for a one-hour interview – to help him to repair/set up his bike, as he needed help with the German instructions. We went to the riders' hub, and started to set up the electric bike. In one corner of the hub, a carpet was laid out on the floor, on which some tools were scattered. It was a repair space for riders, back then installed as a self-help space. Riders often had to fix flat tyres, and could do so on their own, bringing their own tyres and materials for repairs. One of the riders, Frieder, was a trained bike repairman, and he was paid more per hour and had some shifts dedicated to helping repair riders' bikes. Frieder invested in cultural practices and lifestyles that were valued in the work setting – the way he was dressed and spoke about his speed when we met him at public meetings in the park indicated this. When we went to the office to set up Dennis's bike, Frieder was hanging around in the office. Instead of helping him with the bike set-up, he only greeted me briefly, and let Dennis figure things out on his own. Dennis, in contrast to Frieder, didn't approach work as a means to produce personhood as an 'enterprising self' (Skeggs, 2004) (i.e. loving to cycle and seeing in it a moment of self-realization) – he worked full time, to be able to get enough pay to make ends meet. As such, Frieder and Dennis did not connect and their membership in the company as workers did not turn into resourceful ties, and so Dennis didn't receive help setting up his new bike.

We see different abilities to capitalize on cultural resources in a work context that formally and in its discursive framing was open to everyone. The organizational culture valued countercultural habits such as rule-breaking and individual style, as well as risk-taking and flexible selves. In view of a habitus 'in and for action' (Schilling *et al.* 2019; Wacquant 2016), we see how this perspective on work enabled ties between workers who 'made group', for the majority who were studying alongside the work and didn't depend entirely on the job to make ends meet in the city. It also fed into performances of masculinity, and as such reproduced gendered divisions at work.

It also reproduced class: the interviewees who were actively pursuing qualifications in higher education were likely to take the gig work as play and a challenge in which monetary compensation was important and critically evaluated, but not an everyday issue to worry about. Those who were making ends meet with lower qualifications (high school) had a different perspective on the gig work, as it was their main source of income – investing in voluntary meetings as riders to fight against the unbearable working conditions was difficult. These voluntary meetings, however, were useful sites for encounters and mutual support. What began with occasional bike demonstrations became institutionalized in regular sessions at the office of the trade union, to which only riders and members of the trade union were invited. Gina was one of the riders who attended those sessions regularly. She was a bachelor's student of political science, and when I met her was also undertaking an internship in the editorial office of a professional journal for political affairs in Germany. She was given the opportunity to write an article about the problems riders were facing, and turned into a spokesperson dealing with media journalists interested in the riders' mobilization. Because of the internship, she did not have much time to take shifts as a rider, and feared that the company might end her contract as a result. In this situation, the relationships she had built with colleagues were helpful as they enabled her to keep the contract at a time when she was busy with her internship, and this allowed her to use the job flexibly according to her needs.

The previous year, she had become familiar with other colleagues, as she and some other riders had begun to meet regularly to discuss whether to do something, given all the things that were going wrong at the workplace. One of these riders was Ludwig. He was a 'head of riders', and through his position had relationships to other staff at the platform company. He inquired at the company about what would happen if someone, hypothetically, didn't take any shifts over a period of two months. In this way Gina learned that a rider would be fired if they didn't take any shifts in a four-week period. Gina said, 'So I just watch out that I take a shift two or three times during the two months [of the internship]. In order to be able to keep the contract' (Interview with Gina, 19 May 2017). Shifts were difficult to get, particularly when one had not taken many shifts for a while – the shift plan was programmed in a way that every week, shifts were assigned to the riders on the basis of the distribution of the shifts of the week before. In this way, one could easily get kicked out of the system.[5] The meetings at the union's office were also an opportunity to share these experiences with others, and to find ways to handle these difficulties. Gina managed to maintain and control her time, and could work as a rider *and* pursue her professional career as a political scientist for a professional journal. This was not, however, because she had asked for help explicitly, and Ludwig did not offer Gina shifts because he favoured her specifically as a person. Rather, their complaining about working conditions created a sense of commonality, leading to regular meetings and a familiarity among colleagues, through which resources were shared. Other riders were also very unhappy with the working conditions, but did not invest in these meeting times – because they had to work as riders or in several jobs simultaneously and had no time, as they told me in informal conversations. Or they did not share cultural resources which turned into the legitimate cultural capital at work. Such misfits of investments fed into processes of social closure, as complaining about the job turned into a valuable cultural practice, generating social capital, at least from my standpoint in the field.

The promise of options to become who you wanna be

For Tobias as well as for all the other riders I met in Berlin, the delivery job was not supposed to become a job for a lifetime. They all stressed the temporary character of the job, which fitted their expectations of flexibility. Many riders appreciated the possibility to decide when to work, to be able to work as much as they wanted, in principle, so that they could make the work fit to their life rather than vice versa. Sam explained that he started delivering food as he wanted to do something he could 'enjoy' and do 'alongside studies'. 'What was appealing to me about the [delivery job] was that I could be outside, that I could cycle with my bike and that I could divide my working time quite freely', he added (Interview with Sam, Wedding, 15 February 2017). Understanding the job as temporary and flexible was a *perspective* shared by all interviewees and reflects the way the company advertised the job. Most of the interviewees did not want to work conventionally, that is, having a job from nine to five in an office. More important for riders like Victor, was to be able to 'do everything that [he] really want[ed]' (Interview with Victor, Friedrichshain, 3 April 2017). More than the pursuit of a concrete plan, Victor valued the act of autonomous decisions in which the 'individuality' was enacted and realized anew, until 'one feels complete'. This reflects the ideal of becoming a successful self-manager – 'feeling complete with yourself' once one has realized oneself as an individual actor. Being able as an individual to maximize options and to manage oneself accordingly is part of status constitution, or one's constitution as a person.

Victor did not have a clear professional career path in mind, but continuing his studies was important to him. His parents were born in Romania, but he had lived with them in Spain for most of his life. Victor had come to Berlin two years earlier through the mobility programme 'Mobipro', financed by the German state to allow young residents in European countries to come to Germany to find an in-house vocational training position, and to bring them together with project providers and companies in Germany.[6] In his attempts to begin professional training, he realized that he had to go step by step, and learning German was a prerequisite for studying (Interview with Victor, Friedrichshain, 3 April 2017). Participating in a German language class to obtain the required language certificate, however, was incompatible with his full-time job at the delivery platform – hence, accruing value was difficult for him. After one year of full-time work at the food delivery platform, he had to quit because of health problems. He was again back in the low-income sector in Berlin, with no further qualifications to enter other domains, or higher education institutions. For Victor, the floating situation did not turn into an opportunity for accumulating resources.

Gabi, as a woman in her mid-twenties, had taken a loan to enrol as a student in a private distance learning university. Besides her job as rider, which she was doing as *Werkstudent*, she was pursuing another freelance job as a tutor on an online platform. A couple of months after our first interview, she told me that she worried about how to make ends meet and project a future: she was no longer needed as a tutor and had lost the freelance job. At the same time, Gabi began to feel exhausted by riding the bike throughout the year in rain and heat alike. In her studies, she didn't advance as planned. Her boyfriend, after having dropped out of his studies, worked in the call centre of a start-up company in Berlin, and their income situation worked well only because they managed to live in a one-room apartment at a very low rent. The possibility of planning a family, and organizing space and material securities accordingly, was very difficult for Gabi (informal conversation, July 2018).

Young residents like Victor and Gabi who took up the job as a means of earning money while preparing to enter or to find alternative entries into the German education system, were stuck in a delivery job that required energy and time, especially as they needed to work full time in order to get by in the city. As delivery riders, they were not gaining recognized qualifications for building careers in professional areas other than the low-paid sector in Germany.

Most interviewees did not consider this long-term outlook, pushed instead by immediate needs (to earn money) and an atmosphere at work in which the joy of the ride and the gameful character of the job is much more at the forefront for the majority. For German, male, student riders, the floating situation at work was even beneficial: they could realize an 'asset acquiring self, obsessed with increasing the volume of its cultural capital … They start from a position of advantage and optimize from this' (Skeggs 2004, 75).

They perceived their studies to be their main activity, and a temporary job was nothing serious. The physical activity was not exhausting to these riders, as they worked only a couple of hours a week, and they had a safety net of parents and kin that had enough resources to share in case of financial problems. Those who lived the job as a temporary side activity, while being able to invest in institutional cultural capital (i.e. formal qualifications), were also strengthening the dominant *perspective* through which particular skills and habits were valued more than others in the work setting.

Flexibility is the ideal and at the same time a norm, as 'only some people can accumulate the required cultural capital to become a self, only some people can acquire the right dispositions to become the selves that can be reflexive, and only some selves are seen as capable of acquiring the knowledge for self-monitoring and self-responsibility' (Skeggs 2004, 20). The self-reflexivity and self-monitoring 'is premised upon the availability of, and access to, discourse and cultural resources, and the techniques and practices necessary for producing, but also knowing, a self' (Skeggs 2004, 20). Dörre confirms this thesis:

> The way in which individuals deal with insecurity depends, according to the thesis defended here, inevitably on the availability of specific material and cultural resources. Uncertainty can only be deciphered as a productive biographical challenge if a certain level of income and employment stability is ensured. (Dörre 2010, 140, my translation)

If the resources required for being able to 'plan' are lost, actors might experience dreadful situations (Dörre 2010, 140f.). These resources for becoming an effective 'self-manager' are distributed unequally, and this inequality is obscured by a discourse that praises flexibility. Seizing opportunities, maximizing one's options as a young adult also depends on acquiring legitimate cultural capital in the form of qualifications obtained at official educational institutions. The emphasis that interviewees (and companies alike) place on the ease with which one can access the delivery job (as no formal qualifications are required) elides the fact that, at the same time, formal qualifications are important for getting ahead in the German labour market. Despite the rise of atypical employment, the normal employment relation is still an empirical standard in Germany – it is the most prevalent form of work in the country (in 2012, 41 per cent of the working-age population were in long-term, full-time employment [Eichhorst 2015, 5]). Those who have lower or average qualifications are most likely to be in atypical work. Put differently: the likelihood of being unemployed increases if you have no professional qualifications, and this is more likely today than it was thirty years ago (the unemployment rate has been increasing since the 1970s). Also, in terms of income, those with university degrees earn more than employees without formal professional qualifications, assuming that one's qualifications correspond to one's occupation. This produced lock-in effects for young riders who had difficulties accessing formal qualifications.

The focus on convenience and temporariness is complicit with the companies' advertisements about the freedom workers gain by making money on the side. In this discourse, risks are framed as freedom to work by yourself and in an easy way, by using your own bike and phone and working the hours you like. This rhetoric silences discussions around requirements and preconditions that make this freedom possible. These requirements include language skills, but also the social capital and the physical energy that the job demands. In portraying the riders' activity as convenient because of its flexibility, riders and the company overlook the question: flexible for whom, and with which preconditions and in which temporal perspective? Flexibility is liveable in the long term only from a particular starting point and position. Resources that make the flexibility liveable long term are distributed unequally. As a young, male, white student, it is most likely possible to convert and reuse cultural capital throughout the life course and reproduce one's own privileges in that way. The analysis has shown that gender, ethnicity and class do structure the ways in which the job can be used as a prop to navigate transitions into adulthood, but also risks entrapping young residents in permanent temporariness.

It's all about credit – airtime selling in Abidjan as investment in social relations

At the crossroads of a residential area in the West of Yopougon, in front of a shop that sold rice and so on, we met Raphael. When we arrived he was not at his spot, but the neighbouring businessmen indicated that he didn't go far and would be back soon. Raphael seemed to be known as an integral part of the marketplace that flourished at the crossroads.

Raphael's success in the market depended very much on his ability to build social relationships that enabled him to get things done. To secure a spot to sell in the first place, he needed to negotiate with the owner of the store just behind the pavement where he wanted to set himself up. Raphael agreed with the shop owner that he would pay 5,000 FCFA every month for the spot. Ultimately, he ended up paying only 2,000 FCFA, contending that he did not have more at his disposal, and compensating for the lack of monetary payment with services instead. For example, he would help the shop owner cover his electricity bills, which had to be paid electronically through the money transfer service of one of the telecommunications companies. Raphael was familiar with the use of 'mobile money' services, not least because he was selling airtime and needed to use these services regularly. Hence, he knew people working in the domain and could help the shop owner to transfer the money electronically. Then, besides a selling spot, he needed a place to store his box and table. Raphael became friends with another young man who worked in the market repairing mobile phones. As they worked in similar domains, they started to 'tittle-tattle' and developed business ideas together (Raphael didn't specify what exactly they discussed). Raphael described his friend as a guy who smiled a lot – like him.

> I am a guy who loves to put others in a good mood, I like to motivate them, I like to play comedy. You know, so [inaudible] he really appreciates my style. And I love to tease him, that's all. [...] He told me that I am a *chercheur* [literally: a seeker; or: someone who has goals and doesn't stop trying]. I am not a fake guy. He said to me, no matter what day I want to store my table/box, no problem. (Interview with Raphael, Yopougon, 19 March 2016)

The friend offered him a storage place for his table and things, and Raphael didn't pay anything for this. But from time to time, to please his friend, he invited him to a restaurant. Furthermore, he had built a good reputation at the market crossroads at which his store was situated, as he proved his trustworthiness in storing other people's money.

> I am a guy, I store the money of others. They give me 50,000 FCFA and I take it for one month. And work with it [investing with it]. And while I am working with it, I know what the money means to the others, as they, too, they count on it. So they have trust in me, here at the crossroads. Really. (Interview with Raphael, Yopougon, 19 March 2016)

Selling airtime was part of a series of transactions through which Raphael created and maintained social capital, or '*entregent*'.

> *[E]ntregent* (disposing of people) means having a capital of relations as friends, family or neighbours, professional or political relations, which are important and solid [relations], that is to say that [*entregent*] implies esteem and trust. Thus, social capital. It is somewhat the personification of the *credit* we have. (Vuarin 1994, 255, my translation)

Raphael gained prestige and status not because he was an airtime seller as a profession: he could not accumulate competencies (e.g. making the deals to top up the phone) more efficiently to capitalize on them and create institutionalized cultural capital to transfer into a professional status which guarantees economic income. Instead, the sales were meaningful in his construction of a status as a businessman, in which being sociable, cheerful and honest constituted the social prestige that opened up social relationships that allowed him to get things done. Teasing was a way of growing familiar with others as a means of building credit with people (*entregent*).

The *maquis*, open-air bars where people gathered to drink beer and other beverages, were important places to meet and chit chat. Being sociable was a way to find and seize opportunities. One of the airtime sellers, Timo, explained this well. He stressed that the primary purpose of these meetings was to pass time.

> We can talk about life. How it is going … if something has happened. About everything. For example, if someone has discovered a good business. He can talk about it, and if everyone is interested in it, everyone gets into it. At the end, the question is if it is profitable, if you can earn something good. And if the people are interested, we set ourselves in motion. And if no one is interested, he talks about it, and well, we listen. And we talk about it to others, if they are interested. And in case, we put them in touch with the person who has started talking about the matter, and we move forward. (Interview with Timo, Yopougon, 10 October 2015)

The time spent at the open-air bars and restaurants is not only an important focus of interaction to re-actualize existing social relations, but it can generate resourceful exchanges with people who don't know each other personally, too. Raphael told me how he got to know someone who could deliver to him very popular mobile phone SIM cards that were difficult to get hold of. He went alone to the restaurant he regularly ate lunch in.

> Yeah, you can go alone, and you notice that there is one seat empty, but another person sits at the same table. But the restaurant is full! [And I approach him] 'Ah, brother, excuse me, could I?' – 'Sit down!' And that way, you start to exchange a bit. 'But I know you, you have the phone box over there?' – 'Yeah, it's me, [Raphael]!' – 'I am a delivery agent for a telecommunications company, you know!' – Ah, everyone wants to work with me.
>
> [Raphael said to me, the interviewer, and explained to the agent:]
>
> 'Ah brother, to be honest, I would be interested in buying these SIM cards, but I already have someone who delivers to me. And as he needs the business and we already have a long-term collaboration, you cannot let someone down like this. That's not easy. So what you

> will do, give me your number, and if I am in need of anything, I will call you'. [This is how I would talk to the agent.] (Interview with Raphael, Yopougon, 19 March 2016)

Time spent together, chit chatting, without defining the interaction in terms of interest in each other's resources, but rather just for the pleasure of being together, was a resourceful practice for organizing livelihood. Actors inhabited a personhood through these practices that was not self-accruing, but rather they invested in relationality in order to move along (cf. Skeggs 2011, 509; see also Newell 2006, 2012).

Privileging the maintenance of social relationships over the importance of profit was situationally normal (Blokland 2017; Misztal 2001) in the context of airtime sellers. This *situational normalcy* also created marginal positions for those who did not primarily invest in relationality through the sale of airtime.

Adou sold airtime at a call box in the North of Yopougon to provide a livelihood for himself. He established the call box in 2012, after the crisis in Côte d'Ivoire, with 20,000 FCFA as starting capital. At the time of our encounter, which was later during my fieldwork in 2017, he was buying airtime credit for 100,000 FCFA daily from the telecommunications company's wholesaler, which he then resold to his customers. This brought him about 60,000 FCFA (a minimum wage) per month of income. He was able to pay the rent for his own apartment and could get by on his own. In approaching the sale of airtime as a commercial activity on which he could base his livelihood, Adou deviated from the established view of airtime selling as a practice through which one could build person value through social relationships and reputation. In principle, he didn't care about the image that others had of him as an airtime seller:

> [T]here are people who have a bad image of me, and there are those who have a good image of me. This is not what preoccupies me. I am here, I manage my call box. If you want, you come and top up your phone, if you don't want to – that is your problem. I am here, God sends me my customers, and I am managing my call box. I succeeded to pay my rent, I succeeded to clothe myself, and to buy food. (Interview with Adou, Yopougon, 3 November 2017)

Adou qualified 'being strict' as an important skill for succeeding in the sale of airtime. If one wanted to build one's livelihood on this activity, one needed to be strict, in the sense of not participating in an economy of debt by selling airtime on credit.

> So you need to be strict, avoid [sales on] credit. It's true, they will make problems for you, they will criticize you, but you mustn't care about it. You only manage your phone box. (Interview with Adou, Yopougon, 3 November 2017)

The refusal to sell on credit represented a break with the *normalcy* of investing in relationships rather than material profit. His customers' anger and the bad image the neighbourhood had of him expressed disapproval of this rule-breaking. He explained how he was caught between these two economic logics, one based on market exchange and one based on reputation building and *entregent*:

> Here, the people, if you give money, that means you are good. If you give them money, they don't see your suffering. If you share the things, you are nice … If you say, it's not possible to buy or give credit, they say he doesn't give credit, he is bad … So in that way, I am doomed here in the neighbourhood. They speak bad about me, if they sit together, they speak bad about me. No, he is mean, he is like this and that … The phone box, you cannot get anything. If you are not strict, you will not make it. There is nothing to get through a phone box. If you give credit, at the end of the month, you have not enough money to pay your house – the landlord, what will he say if you tell him to wait, as you cannot pay because you gave a lot of credit to others? He wants his money! (Interview with Adou, 3 November 2017)

On the one hand, Adou was sanctioned by his customers, the residents of the neighbourhood to whom he was selling airtime, for not participating in an economy of reciprocal exchange, in which giving and receiving happened within a flexible temporal gap, and in which the maintenance of relationships was more important than the object exchanged. On the other hand, he relied on income from the call box to pay his rent – he depended on market relations to secure his livelihood.

This tension became even more acute when he realized that his activity would be rendered superfluous in a restructure of the distribution of airtime in Côte d'Ivoire. The telecommunications companies were changing their business strategy and replacing the work of call box workers by virtual phone top-ups, through the customer's mobile money bank account. Adou feared losing the basis for his livelihood and was very keen to speak to me.[7] To protect himself against the forthcoming restructuring of the service, he believed his best bet would be to reorient himself towards the business of mobile money. Mobile money was a service offered by the telecommunications companies and consisted of a banking system that operated with mobile phones. One could send money from one's mobile bank account to others, and to this end, one needed an intermediary, a mobile money store, which could execute the transaction.

Adou wanted to open such a store, but it was tricky: it required a lot of daily expenses such as the rental of a store space, electricity bills, and investments such as painting the store in the colours required by the telecommunications company. Also, even though he had applied for a mobile money SIM card some time ago, he had not yet received a response from the telecommunications company. To Adou, it seemed like the company was slowing down the process so that he couldn't open the store, even though he had already begun to rent store space and paid rent and taxes on it. From the point of view of the company, it was not possible to reintegrate all the call box workers as mobile money store keepers, as not so many were needed. With the restructuring of the phone credit distribution, job cuts were an evident side effect. My observations and conversations at the franchise office of one of the companies showed that labour power was used in flexible ways, and was not incorporated into the business itself. The consumption of airtime, on which the profit of the companies depended, did not need labour, only incentives to communicate, navigate more, and hot spots through which the service could be dispersed. This could be achieved through a peer-to-peer economy, and later as automatized e-recharge.

Also, attempts on the part of call box workers to professionalize as workers were in vain. In a conversation (not recorded) with a member of the 'association of call box workers', which had organized to improve work conditions for airtime sellers,[8] the airtime sellers revealed that they were not only making demands for more income, as portrayed in the media, but were also trying to regulate the airtime business by imposing a uniform, the provision of stable selling points and registration of the localities in which the call box workers were selling. These instances show the difficulties for young residents to change the *perspective* on the job as an airtime seller, and realize person value as a labourer.

> Individual citizens, a lot of them marooned by a rudderless ship of state, try to clamber aboard the good ship Enterprise. But in so doing, they find themselves battling the eccentric currents of the 'new' world order, which short-circuit received ways and means. Caught up in these currents, many of them come face to face with the most fundamental metamorphoses wrought by the neoliberal turn: the labile role of labour in the elusive algorithm connecting production to consumption, the pro to the con of capitalism. (Comaroff and Comaroff 2000, 299)

Adou attempted to climb the 'good ship Enterprise' to make a living through business as commodity exchange, and experienced the risks of an economy in which labour was used in highly contingent ways: what Comaroff and Comaroff call the 'labile role of labour'. In this context, selling airtime could only be a way to make money on the side, and a means to invest in other economies than that based on the sale of labour power. Otherwise, the risk of redundancy was real.

However, investing in relationality to get things done did not simply consist in the accumulation of any kind of personal relations. Guyer stresses this too, in her critique of the concept of wealth in people. Wealth in people comprises 'a regime of quality as well as quantity' (Guyer 1993, 246). Wealth acquisition as a system was 'compositional as well as accumulative' (Guyer 1995) and becoming a valuable person depended as much on quantity as on quality of social relations.[9] Moreover, status was not an institutionalized position, but 'more a function of one's reputation and social connections' (Newell 2006, 195).

While not all the interviewees, and more generally certainly not all call box workers, stressed that they were going to school or university (see Raphael's account, for instance), formal education mattered in the production of personhood. Those interviewees who had obtained A-levels or had continued in secondary education were particularly cautious to maintain their status as educated youth. Marian provided an example of how certain habits became valuable, too:

> I am at my call box, I am someone who is calm, and the people are observing me/look at me I am always with a smile on my face. [A

> client…], a 'grand-personne' … [told me:] 'petit' that is good, you have to continue like that. You have which level? I tell him that I am a student, I have my A-levels and finished the second year of my bachelor's. My parents are alive, and I live with them. (Interview with Marian, Yopougon, 4 March 2016)

To keep this image, he emulates[10] these classification schemes as symbolic boundaries in building friendships with other young residents: 'If you want to evolve', Marian explained, you need to follow the advice of 'grandes personnes'. This advice included, besides behaving with respect, 'to never drink to be drunk, and never to steal another person's valuables'. He also avoided consumption practices involving cigarettes and drugs, following the advice of the 'grandes personnes'. This is why most of the friends with whom he went walking [*marcher avec quelqu'un*] were not smoking. Also, they would often sit and think about how to realize working together in the future, and how to achieve their projects (Interview with Marian, Yopougon, 4 March 2016).

Marian didn't want to be seen as a potential criminal by other adults who lived in the same neighbourhood – and was careful not to hang around with the wrong people, who might damage his image. One of the practices of distinction in which Marian participated was playing scrabble, a game he loved to play during his free time, because 'it cultivates and elevates the mind' (Interview with Marian, Yopougon, 4 March 2016). Scrabble requires players to compose randomly given letters into words. In Côte d'Ivoire, playing the game is a way to show your versatility in the French language. Through this game, Marian met and befriended Christian. Their meeting occurred in 2008 or 2009, when Christian approached the scrabble players and began keeping track of who was winning the games in a sketchbook. The two began to chat – they were both going to school, but as Christian wanted to become famous in show business, he also realized that in order to get somewhere he needed money and connections, as Marian explained. Christian had decided it would be better to go to school. 'While waiting', he intended to hustle, in his case not by sitting at a call box, but by selling clothes. Christian then became an important person in Marian's everyday life. He managed the clothes store next to the call box. There, Marian could ask for new shoes, and pay later.

These conversations at the scrabble games show that these young residents attending high school (Marian was in the last years of high school at that time) were aware of the importance of 'money and relationships' to 'evolving', and were not necessarily interested in seeking employment in the public sector (i.e. Christian wanted to go into show business). Nonetheless, having a cultivated grasp of the French language mattered – and was best acquired through school.

Another call box worker, Boris, told me that he couldn't work with someone who did not go to school. He wanted to improve his French – and having a co-worker to sell airtime who was currently going to university helped.

> Myself, in school, I was not going far. It's only now that I am in the evening classes – [my colleague] has gone far, and I cannot allow myself to walk with someone who is not going to school currently.

When I asked him why, he responded:

> Because ... if I walk with someone who is illiterate, what will I earn in return? ... [The person I am working with right now] he is here in Cocody, and I walk with him because that way, I will be able to express myself easily, although I didn't go far in school ... [O]ften when people approach me they will say, ah, but you have been to school, no? I say yes, a bit, because when I am with him, [I learn] to speak French and to express myself well, he corrects me and I think that is good. (Interview with Boris, Yopougon, 8 March 2016)

His customers made remarks about how well he expressed himself, thanks to his co-worker who, attending university, was able to teach him proper French.

In Boris's and Marian's accounts we see reputation building through symbolic boundary work (Lamont and Molnar 2002). Both interviewees distanced themselves from those with different consumption practices (drugs and alcohol) and from people who were not oriented towards education in school or university. Formal education was not cultural capital on which actors focused as self-accruing individuals, but cultural resources – literacy in French, for example – were important in constructing person value in the social relationships among youth in their collaborations as hustlers. This shows how relations mattered for person value, not only in terms of quantity, but also in terms of quality. Interviewees could hoard opportunities through symbolic boundary work.

Permanent temporariness in the long term

In this symbolic boundary work, the young men used symbolic references that are embedded in the country's history of labour. Some activities were undesirable not because workers received low payment for the work, but because of 'the fear of what others might think or say about one or one's family if one were seen performing this type of work' (Mains 2007, 661). Historically, salaried employment became a crucial denominator of social status in Côte d'Ivoire in the 1930s (Le Pape 1997). Back then, salaried employment was introduced by the colonial administration and instituted as a kind of work opposed to '*la débrouillardise*' which designated everything else: the work done by the (colonized) Other (cf. Bazin and Gnabéli 1997).

Even in national legislation after independence in 1960, only salaried work was taken into account and regulated. Family allowances, pensions and other welfare programmes were only attributed to those receiving a salary (cf. Bazin and Gnabéli 1997; MacLean 2010). The state administration was considered to be the main employer. Only a select minority of the population pursued salaried work (cf. Bazin and Gnabéli 1997; Le Pape 1997). However, or perhaps precisely because of their rarity, wage earners constituted part of a privileged minority with particular relations to the state. In fact, the salary did not simply remunerate workers' productivity. As a state employee, one did not sell one's labour power to the state as a commodity. Instead, civil servants claimed for a salary, and in return were indebted to the state, a debt they repaid through obedience. The salary helped to establish 'a particular type of civility: authoritarian civility' (Mbembe and Roitman 1995, 348f.).

> This type of citizenship was not, above all, founded on the principle of political equality and representations thereof. It was based on 'claims' [i.e. salary …], from which the state created social debts. The construction of the political relationship was thus enacted in redistribution and not on the basis of representations of equivalence between human beings endowed with their own natural and civil rights, and thus able to have an effect on political decisions. By transforming the

> salary into a claim and a formality, the state granted subsistence to its subjects. But these means did not sanction a conversion of energy into wealth; they resulted in a specific figure of obedience and domination. This is, moreover, why, in public discourse, these claims are sometimes represented as favours, or at least, privileges. (Mbembe and Roitman 1995, 349)

Thus, the salary constituted an 'indispensable cog in the dynamics of the relationship between state and society' (Mbembe and Roitman 1995, 349). But it also defined a relation of domination in the worker's web of relations. It was

> a relationship that could be described as 'paternalistic', i.e. one that is played, explicitly or not, on the model of an elder–junior relationship – in this case, it is a tie of personalized subordination that implies for the higher party a moral obligation of assistance. (Bazin and Gnabéli 1997, 698, my own translation)

Part of the construction of a status as wage earner depended on the use and display of symbolic references to a white, European modernity. As product of the institution of colonial state power, wage labour was the 'work of whites'. It was important to show 'the signs of an anchoring in modernity, such as diplomas and salaried employment' (Bazin and Gnabéli 1997, 698, my own translation). Salaried workers had the right to speak and express their opinions regarding important family matters, in associations, parties, etc., but their status came with financial obligations of redistribution (Bazin and Gnabéli 1997, 700). That said, the salary was an important regulation of social life in Côte d'Ivoire.

> The regularity of salary payments allowed for the regulation not only of the lives of those who earned them, but also those who depended on them for their survival, according to the principles of redistribution, allocations, transfers and reciprocity. The cycle of debts, contracts and obligations was stimulated in this way. (Mbembe and Roitman 1995, 348, referring to Mahieu 1989 writing on Côte d'Ivoire)

Salaried employment was a category organizing the economy of social debts and the popular economies of redistribution, and was set in opposition to *la débrouillardise*. As Newell put it, labour is an index of cultural hierarchy. This includes that sometimes it is better not to work in order to control resources (see Newell 2006, 184f.). It is better to say that one isn't employed but is searching for employment, rather than admit to a low-status activity such as airtime selling. The image that one projects through one's activity is important, as it determines how one can contribute to redistributive economies.

Against this background, it is not surprising that the majority of the young men presented themselves to me as hustlers, and contrasted the situation that they occupied to being employed. This, first of all, also regulated their credit relations. Boris saw himself as someone who was not currently working, and therefore did not like to borrow money from others.

> Why should I go take credit from someone? I don't like that, because … maybe one day, I have taken credit, and things don't go well, it's falling – and how will I reimburse? I don't work currently, we are not working, we are hustling, and so if I take credit, and we are about to speak about the terms of our deal, and the other asks, well and you, where are you working? And I tell him, well I don't work – and the other: but you are not working, and you take credit – How am I supposed to get along then? (Interview with Boris, Yopougon, 8 March 2016)

These perspectives revealed that to be able to participate in the economy of debt and credit, it was not enough to have money. More important was having an employment status which served as an insurance by which people could calculate when, and if, you would be able to repay your debts. Hence the importance of the regularity of a salary, which, as already discussed, has served historically not as remuneration for labour, but rather, designated a status, organized the claims one could make towards others.

Others pointed to this when they stated how they would be able take on responsibilities once they obtained employment and a stable income. In their view, the main difference between selling airtime and working was the regularity of income, not necessarily the amount, but the fact that one could earn a salary which was consistent and regularly paid, independent of one's actual effort. Aimé mentioned a change in his work situation as a crucial precondition to having enough resources to make a living.

> Aimé: As always, it's the work that makes a man. This here [selling airtime] are small activities. To have some liquidity, that's all.

Interviewer: Well, then work, what would that be – can you describe a bit what would be real work?

Aimé: Yes, work in the administration, something like that, so that you are remunerated every end of the month, that's all ... Then, at least, you know that every end of the month you have money somewhere. But this here [selling airtime] doesn't work. It doesn't work. (Interview with Aimé, Yopougon, 26 March 2016)

In the words of the interviewees, having stable work would also change their status as young men. They would become able to carry/assume responsibilities, they would be able to distribute to those who had been supportive of them, and they would be able to have children and a wife, and their own residence. This indicates a different realization of oneself through work to that dependent on the sale of one's labour power to increase economic capital as a possessive individual. Rather, specific work, or stable employment as a civil servant, is of important symbolic value in constructing social prestige, and achieving a change of status within the web of social relations.

To confront the risk of loss of status, Ivoirian high-skilled young men like some of my interviewees represented themselves as 'busy', and portrayed their activity as temporary, a simple way to make some money while pursuing educational training (cf. Baumann 2003, 237f.).

> The graduate pursues both short- and long-term objectives. On the one hand, he has urgent material needs and satisfies, even if only very superficially, his need to send back to his entourage an image of activity. On the other hand, he invests in social relationships that may provide benefits of all kinds in the more or less near future. (Baumann 2003, 263, my translation)

Many of the interviewees, like David, invest in public competitions to enter the civil service. However, in 2009, the ratio of admissions to enter the state function was 13.2 per cent (see Ministère de la Fonction Publique 2019), and these numbers are unlikely to have improved ten years later.[11]

Selling airtime to earn money and building social relationships to increase the chances of entering the civil service constitute a response to the devaluation of formal qualifications as well as the increased competitiveness in the acquisition of positions in the public sector. Laurence Proteau has described this devaluation more generally, as a 'crisis of belief' in formal educational institutions as a means of social reproduction of privileges in Côte d'Ivoire (Proteau 2002).

Gérard, 28, sold airtime in Koumassi, alongside his contract as a day labourer at a factory in the industrial zone in Koumassi. According to him, nothing would change until he secured employment. He, too, stressed the value of getting work in the public sector, as this would ensure a regular income. He had started training to obtain a BTS (*Brevet de technicien supérieur*, a national diploma of higher education), but hadn't finished. He described the competition in the labour market in the following way:

> When there are these kind of job interviews, your friends call you: 'Ah, someone looks for a technical assistant' … Often we are more than one thousand, although they [only] need three or four workers … This is why you need to have … a contact, a relation behind so that it works … So that makes it difficult … [If] [y]ou don't have chance, you don't have God behind you, they will reject you … The truth is, if you have degrees here, they represent nothing. It's about relations or money. If you have money everything is possible here. (Interview with Gérard, Koumassi, 11 February 2016)

Such discourse is supported by economists' analysis which shows that employment opportunities are positively affected by social capital. The network of acquaintances is more important than competence. This reinforces inequalities: it is becoming increasingly important to belong to a well-connected family and thus have good networks of acquaintances rather than having a high level of education. Meritocracy is becoming increasingly irrelevant in the labour market (Kouakou 2011, 11). But the advantage of a higher qualification to attain stable employment (see Kouakou 2011, 34) cannot only be explained by the increased probability that higher qualifications can be better converted into work positions, as these qualifications are better recognized in the labour market (e.g. Kouakou 2011). My analysis showed a more complicated picture. Educational qualifications were not easily transferable as institutionalized cultural capital into positions in the labour market and the respective economic and symbolic capital attached to professional status. Cultural resources acquired through being at school (e.g. language skills, being perceived as someone who is on the right track, having good manners) became valuable resources in building social relationships. They were used in practices through which the interviewees realized themselves as persons, investing in relationality (time and energy for others, for instance, through providing credit, humour, disinterested chatting, or services). Cultural resources turned into prestige and symbolic capital.

This also adds to Baumann's analysis linking the advantage of high educational qualifications to social capital. Her research on university graduates in Senegal shows that the more educated one is, the more likely it is that one can build social networks outside of family (Baumann 2003, 234). Baumann points to the importance of universities as 'foci of interaction' (Feld 1981) where social relationships are built (see Baumann 2003, 247). We can expand her argument by pointing to the process by which cultural resources derived from formal education – such as French language skills and literacy, and an educational degree – even though devalued when it came to entry into the labour market, became valuable as symbolic resources in the building of social capital.

Practising the sale of airtime as a side activity of hustling, while keeping a status as a student was valuable in a context of changing rules of the game, where former objectified mechanisms through which positions had been reproduced (education, degrees, the schools as institutions) didn't work any more. But wage labour was still a valuable social status for some interviewees and their social environment, and holding on to this ideal of transitioning into adulthood was of value for generating social capital. This reproduces advantages for those interviewees who have capacities to invest in their status as students.

The role of culture in reproducing advantages through social closure

This chapter has focused on the cultural resources that became valuable skills in the hustle practices in Abidjan and Berlin. Hustle practices are 'situated cultural economic practices' (Thieme 2018, 530) within which inequalities are reproduced. Young people organized resources by riding their bikes to deliver food, and by selling airtime.

They hustled, making money on the side. They conceived these activities as temporary, carried out on the side and while waiting. Formal qualifications and institutionalized cultural capital were not prerequisites required to undertake the activity. One could be hired by a platform company or could register as an airtime seller at a store of a telecommunications company with relative ease. Yet *culture* mattered for the symbolic economy at work and how the activity was used for status construction by young men. Cultural resources were differently valued, and this served the monopolization of resources for those who were able to take advantage of this symbolic economy.

I identified processes of social closure through which transitory floating positions become an enduring situation for some, but also a resourceful position for constructing status as a person to others. To explain this process, I looked at the ways riders and airtime sellers talked about their work, built social relationships with other workers and symbolic capital through work. I showed that value is attached to different conceptualizations and practices of personhood, and refer these differences back to politics of the life course. Seen that way, marginalization occurred when hustling turned into the main occupational status, and no longer served as a bridge, or parallel activity. As such, hustling as a way of life could be celebrated and used as a norm to the detriment of those who risk getting stuck in a permanent temporariness. This worked as social closure: actors monopolize resources, privileges, power and prestige to the detriment of others (Mackert 2004, 11). By identifying processes of social closure, we saw 'the making of class', or more generally status, not only in the exchange of labour power, 'but also [through …] the accrual of cultural resources to oneself, be they commodity objects or cultural practices' (Skeggs 2004, 15).

The analysis of practices of young airtime sellers in Abidjan and delivery riders in Berlin show different ways in which the economy is premised on the symbolic and how economic activity is constituted through social relations. Relational work consisted in the attempt to maintain a status of in-between work and non-work, giving oneself hope for social mobility in the future. Those selling airtime and delivering food understood their practices not as labour; instead, they framed these activities as side jobs or as a way to avoid staying at home, 'doing nothing'. They *detached* (Schilling *et al.* 2019) from their work, calling it 'fun', 'temporary', 'not an activity'. Interviewees emphasized the flexibility of the work and the autonomy the job promised them. In their view, the job enabled them to become financially more powerful and to be 'their own boss' by allowing them to decide the way they set up their sales, and the way they rode their bike. This indicates practices of personhood aimed at achieving self and social esteem, that is, status, in which the sale of labour power was not the primary value. The interviewees' perspective on their activity was a perfect match to the companies' hiring practices: they had very few formal requirements for job applicants to become accepted. Accordingly, everyone seemed to be able to participate formally, and to undertake the job as a rider or an airtime seller. Yet I identified processes of closure. Gaining access to resources at the job required the young men to be able to follow a certain way of doing things. The work setting was one of 'open relations' (Weber 1947, 139). Open relations are those relations in which participation in a social practice is not prohibited to anyone, to the extent that they are able to practise the same way:

> A social relationship, regardless of whether it is communal or associative in character, will be spoken of as 'open' to outsiders if and in so far as participation in the mutually oriented social action relevant to its subjective meaning is, according to its system of order, not denied to anyone who wishes to participate and who is actually in a position to do so. (Weber 1947, 139)

The formal openness came along with closure in practice, in both cases. Keeping the status of the activity blurry – that is, as temporary, transitory or floating – is in itself an approach that organizes opportunity hoarding for some, to the detriment of others.

In Berlin, cultural resources like style, attitude towards cycling, the relationship to your body and work on your body and language skills enabled relationships and resourceful transactions among riders. The accessibility to these resources, and the value of these resources was contextualized and embedded in the actors' life course. Those who could understand the work as a game, as they were materially less dependent on it and had bodies that could keep up with the game (which was not the case for some female riders), gained symbolic capital. Embracing the game character of the job meant, too, not caring too much about rules, the future or money. Being bilingual and knowing what kind of accessories mattered, and having those, enabled access to social capital. These cultural resources were exchangeable and valuable as symbolic capital. Being less dependent on the job, because of parents who paid one's rent, for instance, or as a student who had the possibility to render knowledge of the delivery job valuable as a cultural resource at an internship to advance one's professional career, was an advantage. These interviewees integrated the job in the advancing and accumulation of resources as accruing self. Flexibility of work served the individual actor to accrue value through the seizure of opportunities, and the disciplining of oneself. Making money on the side worked in a context in which the legitimacy of diplomas and the value of cultural capital in the market economy persist. Commodification processes restructured the labour market, while being strongly regulated by the state, which maintained a monopoly over symbolic capital. Institutional cultural capital worked as capital to enter the labour market. Those who were advantaged in cultural capital could even increase their advantages. This worked also as closure: those who approached the job as a means for making money on the side adopted a *perspective* that enabled particular relationships. This access to social capital helped to make the flexible work environment work for one according to one's needs, as demonstrated in the example of Gina.

In Abidjan, selling airtime was a means to develop relationships, and the possibilities that come with them: organizing a workplace, a store and clients to sell mobile phones, as the story of Raphael showed. Investing in relationality, in time and energy for others, was key, and the skills, styles and habits that were required to do so became most valuable. It was important to project an image of uninterested relational work. The signification of sitting together at bars or in public spaces was to pass time together – as revealed by Timo in the interview. Furthermore, being in a 'good mood', and having the ability to create a good atmosphere, constituted very important relational work. Interviewees stressed this when explaining how building resourceful relationships had worked out for them. So, hustling was a *cultural* economic practice, and as such part of a symbolic economy in which uninterested sociability enabled resourceful transactions.

Investing in market transactions was less beneficial here. When selling airtime was not used as a way to offer services to others – neighbours and strangers alike – it got difficult. The companies that monopolized the airtime economy did not offer stable working contexts that could provide the continuous revenues that one would require in order to make a living through investing in market transactions, only based on commodified transactions. The example of Adou indicated this problem. In other words, those who were not investing in relationality, in being and spending time with others, were more exposed to the risk of being marginalized. This way of constructing personhood was a *normalcy* – and it worked in institutional settings too. For example, relationships and money were *situationally normal* prerequisites for getting good grades to pass the exam to enter the civil service. Having relationships required spending time with others, making oneself familiar with them, offering them services, so that in times of need, they could work things out for one. One invested in relationality as a way to earn status.

Status frustration was not so much linked to the impossibility of having a career. The young adults I interviewed in Abidjan wanted to assume responsibility, which was closely attached to consistent income that allowed for redistribution. Wage labour had for a long time functioned to offer this, but was becoming less and less accessible to young men. The hustle happened in the context of the devaluation of formal qualifications and the destabilization of educational institutions. The rules of the game were changing. Those who experienced the devaluation of this cultural capital in the institutional setting reproduced classificatory schemes that designated value to work as a form of opportunity hoarding on the 'street', a sphere of commerce and forms of work which had historically stood in opposition to the sphere of the administration and the attached privileged social status.

In conclusion, this chapter has focused on the cultural resources that become skills to hustle in the respective work settings. The symbolic value of work mattered in personal relations; cultural resources deployed in the work turned into symbolic capital organizing processes of closure. As variation between the two cases, I showed that in Berlin, objectified and institutionalized mechanisms of social reproduction (Bourdieu 1976)[12] were structuring the symbolic value of work in the long-term perspective: school titles and institutionalized cultural capital turned into labour positions. In Abidjan, interviewees invested their cultural resources and the symbolic value of work into building social capital, as a way to ensure social reproduction in the context of devaluation of institutionalized cultural capital.

Notes

1 Similar to the English expression: better than sitting around and twiddling your thumbs.
2 In both companies, some of the riders were assigned particular tasks, including testing the riding skills of new candidates for the job (see Chapter 4).
3 Ludwig was one of the riders who led the test rides and had to assess whether new candidates were suitable for the job. As a side note to a conversation we had about the importance of getting engaged with the matters of your job, in spite of – or just because of – the difficulty involved in changing conditions you didn't like, Ludwig showed me a picture on his smartphone. It showed a to-do list. The company he was working for had sent the picture to him to inform those leading the test rides about the company's 'hiring rules'. Even though he would not be held accountable for hiring decisions, Ludwig could give recommendations. Some 'no-gos' stated in the list he showed me were: 'expresses criticism to the employer', 'presses ahead and is arrogant', 'doesn't have a bike/smartphone and doesn't want to provide him/herself one', 'is too late', 'indicates that he already knows that he would not respect the minimal working time and does not plan to work for the company for long', 'lives in another city, needs longer than one hour with public transport to get to a log-in point', 'is too slow, doesn't keep up', 'does not speak good enough English or German' (Interview notes attached to interview with Ludwig, Köpenick, 17 August 2017).
4 When Guyer speaks of 'conferring authorship' and 'creating personal reality', she describes how actors gain person value or build status.
5 The shift plan and the procedures for distributing shifts to the riders were constantly changing during my fieldwork and afterwards. The rules described here might not apply consistently throughout the interviewed riders' working experiences.
6 The pilot programme has existed since 2013. The eligibility criteria are residency in another EU or EEA country, state-recognized school qualification (and no completed vocational in-company education and training or master's degree), and being between the ages of 18 and 27 years old (see TheJobOfMyLife 2019)
7 Probably he saw it as opportunity to improve his situation, as I might have connections to one of the telecommunications companies, which he

had an application pending with for a new business. I was introduced to him by the company's dispatcher, and was a white woman interested in the conditions of airtime sellers.

8 Similar to workers' unions, a group of airtime sellers founded an association to organize for better work conditions. See Abidjan.net 2016.

9 Guyer expands further: '[The] Western concept of "labour" merges the two in ways that mask the interplay of quality and quantity in the cultural and historical dynamic. The kinds of work that created personal "reality" were culturally delineated; they excluded but also included activities that a Western concept of labour does not. Only certain kinds of activity that we would include under the rubric of "work", however, were considered to create value' (Guyer 1993, 225).

10 On emulation see Tilly (2001, 366): he defines emulation as the 'transfer of existing organizational forms, representations, and practices from one setting to another'.

11 Author's note: I did not find more current statistics. The '*concours*' designates the public service entrance examinations.

12 Bourdieu designates by that: 'les univers sociaux où les relations de domination se font, se défont et se refont dans et par l'interaction entre les personnes, et les formations sociales médiatisées par des mécanismes objectifs et institutionalisés, tels que ceux qui produisent et garantissent la distribution des titres, nobiliaires, monétaires ou scolaires, elles ont l'opacité et la permanence des choses et échappent aux prises de la conscience et du pouvoir individuels. L'objectivation garantit la permanence et la cumulativité des acquis, tant matériels que symboliques, qui peuvent ainsi subsister dans les institutions sans que les agents aient à les recréer continument et intégralement par une action expresse, mais, du fait que les profits de ces institutions sont l'objet d'une appropriation différentielle, elle assure aussi, inséparablement, la reproduction de la structure de la distribution du capital, qui, sous ses différentes espèces, est la condition de cette appropriation et du meme coup, la reproduction de la structure des rapports de domination et de dépendance' (Bourdieu 1976, 122).

4

Trust and rule: tying workers to work

Wolfgang was a musician from Poland, and he started to deliver food in Berlin as a freelancer to make some extra money to get by. As with the other riders, his pay was calculated on the basis of the app's tracking of his rides. In this sense, it was highly standardized. At the same time, the way these technicalities worked produced uncertainties and required extra-work. Wolfgang checked every invoice he received from the company, to be sure that every order he delivered was remunerated, and that the bonus was calculated correctly. This constituted work time he did not get paid for.

> [S]ometimes some orders are missing, and they say it is because there is some problem with the application. It is quite complicated this computer system, because there are different applications for booking shifts, different applications for work. And the, like, the way those applications work with each other, sometimes, something is fucked up and some orders are missing. So you have to check if everything is ok, add missing orders if there are any. Ah, then count, [whether] you have a rain bonus for some day [or] a summer bonus. Like right now we have the summer bonus. And you have to put it on your invoice, it's like, they will not tell you you got the bonus. You have to figure it out by yourself. (Interview with Wolfgang, Friedrichshain, 1 July 2017)

Recently, Wolfgang added seven deliveries to the number of orders he took according to the invoice he got from his company – which also made him eligible for one of the current bonuses. 'So their invoice was like, 570 euros, or 560, and after my recounting it was almost 700 euros!' Wolfgang recalled. Riders like Wolfgang were remunerated formally, with the application counting their deliveries and calculating their pay. However, Wolfgang described how he had to revise these bills and check for consistency, as some of the remuneration rules officially declared (in emails), such as the bonus system, didn't figure in the bill. By using labour force in a freelance capacity, it was easy for the company to outsource responsibility for financial control that concerned workers' benefits to the workers themselves. This shows formality as 'piecemeal' (Neves and du Toit 2012, 144): technological tools documented the riders' activity, but workers like Wolfgang needed to undertake a hand-sorted listing of their activity too, and calculate their entitlement for pay by hand, just to formulate their claims through the medium of an official document, the bill.

In Abidjan, the distribution of airtime was also increasingly standardized, with the help of platform technology. Airtime sellers were ranked according to their sales, and eventual inactivity could be detected instantaneously. However, within these standardized technical arrangements, airtime sellers challenged the idea of them being 'individual entrepreneurs'. Boris, for example, established a phone box along with a neighbour his age, in his mid-twenties. They had been neighbours for about eight years, and became friends. They decided to start a company together, after they saw that selling merchandise individually didn't bring the expected turnover. At the time of our interview, they were running several phone boxes in the larger surrounding area, and were looking for more staff to manage these. They placed a job announcement in front of the phone box desk they took care of together. Their collaboration worked, according to Boris, because they respected each other, and neither of them thought he was superior to the other. When necessary, they took over the other's shift: 'There are no discussions about who is the boss, everyone is at the same level, and when I have been managing the call box this morning, he has to organize himself to be able to do the same in the evening', Boris explained to me. They had agreed to communicate about their respective availabilities and could rely on each other's commitment. It was most important to be in constant communication and to talk about problems together, and to not be disturbed by rumours about each other, which might cause problems for collaboration:

Interviewer: What could interfere with the agreement? What could break it?

Boris: ... I think it's this gossip [you can hear,] like your guy is not at the phone box, and not managing it well ... [W]e are used to hearing that here but we trivialize it and then we move on! ... Even if someone has come to tell me something about my friend, I can't take that into consideration, because he and I know what we're doing here ... And if I considered it, I wouldn't trust him anymore ... or he will no longer trust me. (Interview with Boris, Yopougon, 8 March 2016)

Boris stressed he didn't listen to bad gossip about his friend, as a way of demonstrating that even bad talking would not affect the trust between them. Boris's collaboration with his friend illustrates the regulation of work relations based on a 'code of honour' (Bourdieu 1977). The bond between the two was guaranteed by loyalty, and not by an abstract discipline and rigorous contracts or specific sanctions (cf. Bourdieu 1977, 190). They regulated their working time by disclosing availability and negotiating how to share the working time. What made these rules binding was mutual reliability and the desire to maintain a good reputation, so as not to hear someone speak bad about you. This is also reflected in the relationship category that Boris used to characterize his relation towards his collaborator. He considered him his friend, even his brother, and what bound them together was mutual respect; what made the collaboration work was the reliability of his commitment to stick to his word, and to be there when he said he would be there. Calling his co-worker a friend created an 'enchanted relationship' of disinterested exchange which Bourdieu sees as characteristic of an economy of good faith, in which domination works through symbolic violence, the shared recognition of the importance of personal loyalty and obligation to commit to work.

Both airtime sellers and delivery riders worked in informalized work settings. Extra-legal sources became important here to organize the labour process. At the same time, official rules remained meaningful, although actors in Abidjan and Berlin used them in different ways to organize labour relations. In both settings, a moment of ambivalence in roles and rules appears in the young men's accounts. In the following, we will explore regulatory practices in the gig economy and airtime distribution in more detail.

Ambivalence in regulatory practices

Starting from the airtime sellers in Abidjan, it becomes pressing to ask how we can understand the making of labour relations beyond the formal working contract. With this question in mind, we can also approach hybrid employment systems elsewhere. Here, I argue, the use of legal regulations is also combined with other principles and practices, that together reproduce unequal positions in the work setting. In other words, we can study here the variety of sources of authority that legitimize the appropriation of labour by others. It is their ambivalent entanglement that attaches the workers to the organization and explains unequal distribution of resources at work. Both airtime sellers and delivery riders are attached in a flexible manner to the organization they produce value for through their efforts. They have temporary and flexible contracts or are registered with the company as micro-entrepreneurs. In this way, their positionality evokes digital contingent labour, which Phillip Staab and Oliver Nachtwey characterize in the following way:

> [Contingent labour is] both 'free' from social integration into the corporate universe and integrated tightly into a company's system of control. Increasingly automated direct control has returned, albeit without the benefits that membership in an organization offers employees in classic job forms. All of this is embedded in a context of highly asymmetric constellations of power and access to information. (Staab and Nachtwey 2016, 471)

Their situation is an example of informalized working relations. Analyses of power asymmetries in digital economies have focused on the automatization of control (e.g. Huws 2016; Klauser *et al.* 2014; Sewell and Wilkinson 1992; Staab and Nachtwey 2016; Wood *et al.* 2019) with the help of the technical infrastructure of platforms and algorithms. By taking Abidjan as a starting point, I argue for the importance of looking at the social work that *does* infrastructure (Tonkiss 2015, 389), and the different economies in which the organization of work in settings of informalized labour is embedded. This is true not only for automatized regulation techniques, but also for the legal frameworks of work relations. Legal precarity needs to be embedded in the larger political institutional context, and the functionality of law in reproducing social order. To overcome totalizing views on the importance of algorithmic regulation in platform labour and the gig economy more widely, we will give a more nuanced picture of how rules are enacted, negotiated by actors in the field, by exploring regulatory practices.

The regulation of work relations comprises the organization of work: i.e. the regulation of membership in an organization such as a company. The working contract is one of the ways in which workers are attached to the organization that uses their labour power (Wilz 2005, 216). When informalized and precarious work are discussed together, the specific constellation of legal regulation in these work relations is an important denominator: both precarious and informalized work are characterized by an 'extra burden of extra-legal regulation (such as personal ties and dependencies) on top of legal regulation (employment contract, labour law, social security)' (Mayer-Ahuja 2012, 292, quoted in Burchardt *et al.* 2013, 15, my translation). To overcome analytical divides between on the one hand regulation through official labour law, and on the other hand cultural repertoires that regulate work relations in the work setting, we contest 'that state regulation has a particular boundary … [Instead,] contracts about employment, its terms and conditions, could be placed on either side of this boundary [dividing into informal/formal sectors] with an acceptable level of confidence in ANY setting' (Benton 1994, 233, emphasis in the original).

This shifts the focus to the question of how official legal rules become applied and rendered effective in the relational work of agents. Formal regulation in itself needs to be enacted and renewed through social relations (Hilbrandt 2017; McFarlane 2012). What is sought to be formally regulated is also often 'piecemeal' (Neves and du Toit 2012, 144), and formal regulation itself is often bricolage (Cleaver 2002, quoted in McFarlane 2012). State laws and procedures are only one element of regulatory structures for economic action (Benton 1994, 226; see also Meagher 2005, 2007; Viti 2013). Following Benton's (1994) intervention in the debate on legal pluralism, we can think across airtime selling and food delivery by asking more broadly about the young men's sources of authority, the ways legitimate authority is established and upheld, and the rules made and played with at work. Sources of authority are not so much seen as a tool with which actors can establish authority over one another, but rather sources of authority refer to the *illusio*, the shared rules of the game, according to which agents compete for resources in the field of the economic and create work relations that can be various. It is the 'probability of orientation to the subjective belief in the validity of an order which constitutes the valid order itself' (Weber 1972, 31, my translation).

We can learn here from Africanist perspectives on regulation: they dismantle the idea of the clearly demarcated public sphere and public authority of a modern nation-state. When the state is something else than a unified actor holding the monopoly on the rightful use of symbolic and physical violence (Bourdieu 1993a), individual and collective actors compete for investing in the state or take over functions previously performed by public authorities (Chauveau *et al.* 2001, 152). Structural adjustment programmes and the economic and political crises that accompanied these in the 1990s in many countries in sub-Saharan Africa, and also in Côte d'Ivoire (Bamba *et al.* 1992; Contamin and Memel-Fote 1997), produced a crisis context (Mbembe and Roitman 1995) in which long-standing conceptions of causality and responsibility in regard to the state apparatus, its bureaucratic procedures and legal authority, were corroded. Formal rules and conventional procedures were not absent, but respecting them did not imply that 'the prescribed results will be attained'. On the contrary, someone who followed rules too scrupulously would be likely to have contrary outcomes (Mbembe and Roitman 1995, 342). This produced a 'discrepancy between publicly announced reality and the constantly changing, unstable and uncertain, quasi-elliptic realm of the concrete bargain' (Mbembe and Roitman 1995, 342). The improvisation of efficacious action became the normal way of acting:

> [E]very law enacted is submerged by an ensemble of techniques of avoidance, circumvention and envelopment which, in the end, neutralize and invert the legislation … [A]cting efficaciously requires that one carefully cultivates an extraordinary capacity to be simultaneously inside and outside, for and against, and to constantly introduce changes in the reading and usage of things, playing, in this way, with the structures and apparatuses, capturing them where possible and eluding them where necessary, and in any event, amputating them and almost always emptying them of their formal and designated functions so one can better restore them with those that correspond best to desired goals and expected gains. (Mbembe and Roitman 1995, 340)

This created a *situational normalcy* of 'being at the same time inside and outside', and of negotiating order in intermediary zones of regulation, where different norm systems converge (Chauveau *et al.* 2001).

I will start from this *normalcy* (Misztal 2001) to look at ways in which intermediary zones of regulation are emerging in informalized work relations in Berlin and Abidjan. How can a situation of ambivalence become resourceful, and for whom?[1] How does ambivalence shape power relations in work relations? As Merton argues, ambivalence can constitute an order that works. To him, 'sociological ambivalence refers to incompatible normative expectations incorporated in a *single* role of a *single* social status' (Merton 1976, 6, emphasis in original). It is the 'product of conflicting norms and counter-norms associated with particular social positions' (Hillcoat-Nallétamby and Phillips 2011, 203).

This also affects how we think of social roles: these are not 'coherent sets of normative expectations, but ... clusters of norms and counter norms that alternatively govern role-behaviour' (Levine 2006, 236). Acting in relational roles other than those which are prescribed by an official professional status can become a valorized conduct (Levine 2006, 236) in work relations, and hence needs to be integrated into the analysis of the ways in which labour is appropriated (cf. Bourdieu 1976 on forms of domination). Ambivalence can also be produced through a particular temporality of rules. Rules 'prescribe the "*do's*" and "*don't's*" of individual everyday conduct' (Portes 2006, 237), as there is a shared belief in their validity in the future – the rules of a game, that is. This is the temporal dimension of legitimacy: the trust that in the future this rule will be valid, and the individual conduct will be sanctioned accordingly.

Law is one way to provide actors with structures for anticipating an unknown future. Legal institutions serve as stabilizers or destabilizers of expectations, thereby influencing perceptions of certainty, uncertainty and risk. But such structures of anticipation can also consist of personalized trust in specific persons (cf. Benda-Beckmann 2014). We analyse how the temporality of rules is used by actors to constitute work relations, stabilizing expectations which are based on trust in persons or in law. In the following, the regulatory practices that unfold in the organization of food delivery and airtime distribution show their plurality and ambivalence. In contrast to the comparison of formal and informal institutions, which in itself is part of an 'academic' doxa about how regulation should be ordered in analyses (cf. Benton 1994), I draw on Bourdieu's theory of domination and symbolic power. This overcomes common ways of theorizing the law's role in the economy, which is, as Benton pointed out, dominated by viewing state law as the centre around which all other legal spheres cluster (Benton 1994, 224). Even if legal anthropology acknowledges the existence of plural legal orders, it still 'stacks the formal and informal sectors one atop the other and … views them as instrumental in supporting a parallel system of economic relations that is also divided into dominant and subordinate sectors' (Benton 1994, 225). Instead, the comparative lens opens the perspective to an appropriation of workers through creating personal bonds. Such a 'good-faith economy' (Bourdieu 1977) shows that the absence of legal regulations is not always a lack and deviance from a standard, a lack that produces precarity. In addition, we will see that the temporality of rules – like frequent changes and disruption of the causality and responsibilities that they promise – is an important source of power. The notion of ambivalence captures this. Ambivalence can produce order, and also reproduce inequalities, as it asks for time and knowledge to learn about changing rules, and to organize resources at the intersection of various sources of authority.

Building and maintaining work relations/authority-upholding through trust and law

Coming back to Wolfgang and Boris, the delivery rider and airtime seller we introduced at the beginning of this chapter, we have seen that both airtime seller and delivery rider needed to build and maintain their work relations in practice. By juxtaposing both work practices, we will now explore in more depth how extra-legal regulations guided resource distribution prominently in Abidjan, and worked there but were also relevant in Berlin. We show that legal regulations, quantification through technical devices and extra-legal regulations were entangled in different ways in the two cases. We will do so by exploring authority-upholding (Benton 1994, 238) as established in social relations and emerging in contexts, rather than as strategies that individuals pursue in their own interest. The ambiguity of the roles that the work setting provides to dispatcher and monitors is used in a different manner to build authority.

Don't stop trying to keep your foot in the door

Wolfgang was not the only rider who raised concerns about the fastidious extra-work necessary to obtain a rightful compensation or the necessary information to get things done at work. Not only was the official pay check 'piecemeal' and as such, despite its standardized form, workers could not rely on its correctness, but instead needed to invest in additional calculations and control, but also the other forms of compensation and monetary regulations brought about uncertainties.

For example, it was impossible to predict when and how much you could make in tips as a rider. Yet it was a recurrent topic of conversation among riders (e.g. at meetings around the bonfire), in which they complained about the lack of tips or related their success stories about tips. As the basic payment for riders was at the level of the minimum wage, tipping complemented the regular pay check, and for some was a matter of being able to pay for daily expenses, notably the rent, or not. The rider Salomon, for example, got ill for a while, and during this time relied on his mother's support in order to be able to get by, as he did receive the regular wage, but not the tips (Interview with Salomon, Friedrichshain, 22 August 2017). Every interviewee had a slightly different story about how to make sense of the tipping behaviour of their customers. I asked the riders about their strategies for increasing tips, as I did with Jack. He was a highly educated man in his thirties from Poland, who had come to Berlin in order to secure a better livelihood than he could in Poland. He worked two jobs, in addition to studying at university, and one of his jobs was delivering food as a midi-jobber:

> I think it's a little bit random if you get tips or not. You need to be lucky because there's no approach. I tried approaching people with a smile, without a smile, being nice, being just normal, it doesn't change anything. I think people already decide before they pick up the orders if they're going to tip or not. So of course, the area where you work matters a lot because if you work here you probably won't

> get tips that much and if you work in Wilmersdorf you'll get tipped much more, a huge difference actually. (Interview with Jack, Neukölln, 10 March 2017)

Others said that the weather and the working time might matter for the tipping behaviour of their customers. Some interviewees mentioned that rainy shifts or shifts during the weekend worked better for tipping, as people had more pity then for those who biked over to bring their food. Contrary to other services, such as gastronomy for instance, the interaction between customer and service person was very limited. Hence, extra pay is difficult to attach to a personal quality of the worker himself; rather it relies more on general principles such as the weather, work time and the place (like Jack's assumption about neighbourhoods where demographics reveal more affluent residents).

Joseph, in addition, was above all frustrated by the difficulties he faced in grasping which legal rules were effective in the organization of his work. He was a man in his late twenties who grew up in a small town in northern Germany, and who moved to Berlin in his mid-twenties. He began delivering meals to residences in the Berlin neighbourhoods of Neukölln and Friedrichshain at a time when he urgently needed to earn money to pay his rent. From that time on, he regularly got onto his green mountain bike in the evenings after his mini-job in the retail sector. The bike had seen better days – some stickers with leftist slogans decorated the scratched bicycle frame. Joseph could choose his working times, as he had a contract as a freelancer with the company. When, for how long and for what pay he would do his delivery shifts was difficult to pin down for Joseph, as this varied. Per 'drop' – one delivery from restaurant to customer – he got €5 as basic pay (Interview with Joseph, Neukölln, 25 May 2017). Thus, his pay depended on the amount of deliveries, but also on the tips and on the ability to be eligible for bonus payments.

In his work contract, the company stated that he was not obliged to fill in his shifts in the mobile phone shift-plan application, but then they[2] told him to enrol himself nonetheless. 'These are the things that make it so ambiguous [*zwiespältig*]', Joseph explained, 'because it's all the time like that, that I just don't know how it really is … It's typical start-up – they do everything *on the run*, and just see how to muddle through/make it work, and I am not entirely sure how much this is strategy or just derives from the fact that they are disorganized/confused/dopey [*verpeilt*]' (Interview with Joseph, Neukölln, 25 May 2017, my emphasis).

In fact, many interviewees mentioned as a primary problem their difficulties in accessing relevant information for doing their work in the most beneficial way for them, and having access to reliable information. In a work setting in which the labour force is extremely mobile and not tied to a specific workplace, emails and WhatsApp messages became tools to disseminate rules and work directives. According to Joseph, the platform company tried to provide information on how to do the work as a rider as best as possible, and offered a FAQ page for workers on their website. However, when it came to providing information which benefitted workers in helping them to earn more money, the company was opaque: 'It is extremely difficult to access information about the kind of bonus payments there are, you would not find it anywhere on their official web page. You always need to ask someone', Joseph complained to me. The 'someone' Joseph mentioned here most likely does not indicate a boss or a company PR manager, but probably a co-worker. Such mouth-to-mouth information among workers requires chatting with people you hardly encounter.

All in all, regulations were not contradictory, but they were overlapping and referred to different timescales (the season, the work day, the biweekly rhythm of payment). For some interviewees, just as Joseph described, uncertainty was a matter of being deceived in their trust in the law, rather than the absence of legal regulations. There was too little legal certainty, because the regulations changed too rapidly. As Keebet von Benda-Beckmann suggests, in such situations, people

> no longer can have sufficient confidence that their conduct is in accordance with the valid law. In such cases, people may revert to 'selective trust' in personal networks … A viable legal order that elicits trust and allows actors to act with confidence has to find balance between continuity and adjustment. Too much stability stifles a legal order and too little generates a sense of uncertainty in which people feel they cannot rely on the law (Benda-Beckmann 2014, 13).

The fact that the companies changed the way they calculated the rules of payment very frequently shows that a work setting made up of a 'rapidly changing tangle of overlapping and often contradictory regulations of varying space and time scales' (Benda-Beckmann 2014, 13) requires workers to learn about the rules all the time. In Fordist companies, employees rely on the validity of their working contract and their monthly pay check. In the context of the platform companies, such trust in the legal contract was likely to deprive one of shifts and payments. Instead, the regulation of employment relations required a constant calculation and management of shifts and their remuneration. Such recommodification in employment relations has been summed up by the term '*Arbeitskraftunternehmer*' (Wilz 2005), which designates the transformation of employees into entrepreneurs of their own labour power, vested in self-control and the development of an enterprising self (cf. Skeggs 2004). Here, this meant assuming the responsibility to manage your own shifts and payment. Riders such as Wolfgang had to write their own bills if they wanted to make sure they were correct, and needed to carefully manage their time to organize their shifts and prepare bills.

Moreover, they needed to actively seek information about the rules and how to play with them, as routines in the work process did not exist. 'Things change, for better or worse is not the question here right now, but – they change and this is something you have to know', Ludwig, one of the interviewees stressed. This is why being updated is crucial. '[I]f you don't keep yourself updated and you are not aware of the fact that there are free slots to work opening again … just because you rely on your own experience that in spring time, there are no slots available', then you might be excluded. After two weeks of not picking up a shift, the system automatically excludes a worker from the distribution of shifts (see Interview with Ludwig, Köpenick, 17 August 2017). As such, experience alone was not enough – you had to 'engage with the job', as Ludwig said. Disadvantage here did not result from deregulation, but from a rapidly changing, and arbitrarily effective regulation, which recompensated those who were showing self-initiative and who had the possibility to play with the rules to their benefit.

For the gig workers, engaging with the job did not mean adhering to the work directives that the company issued via app, phone or email to the riders. But in all the different ways in which workers 'played the game' and used their margins to manoeuvre, law-like arrangements served as central legitimate 'structures of anticipation' against which rule transgression was identified or principles of action evaluated. Let us explore this configuration in more depth, by focusing on the sensing of the algorithm and statistical evaluations, and by looking more closely at the negotiation of ambivalence in roles in work relations.

Sensing the algorithm

Diffuse communication and inconsistency of rules was one way of producing uncertainty; the black-boxing of rules was another. Particularly the algorithmic dispatching of orders via app and the constant, automated evaluation of workers' performance presented a case for this black-boxing of rules.

Some of my acquaintances in the field tried to use the algorithm in ways that increased their likelihood to get new orders as riders, or to have less work to do (dependent on their contract the riders were paid per order or per working hour). In informal conversations with riders who were paid by the hour, I heard stories in which riders moved with their bikes during their shifts to sites that were in their work area, but at the same time so far away from restaurants that they were unlikely to get orders. This was fine for a while, but could become a problem, when monitors reported the riders' statistics of orders/hour to headquarters and decisions about the extension of working contracts were being made. But it also could be not a problem at all – what the rules were here was not clear, and in chat groups among riders, often a matter of speculation – and this created mistrust (not distrust) (Blokland and Nast 2014; Sztompka 1999) among the riders we encountered. They didn't know when or how the official tracking and evaluating of the workers' performances became effective for the distribution of orders or even exclusion from work.[3]

To use these black-boxed rules to their advantage, riders tried to 'sense' the algorithm, by trying to locate themselves most advantageously in the city, as the algorithm was supposed to also dispatch orders in relation to the rider's current location. The freelance rider Joseph hesitated between 'moving around' all the time, and sitting with other riders to gain more information about how things were working.

> I don't know exactly how the algorithm works, but it works, you sense that people who are closest to the restaurant get the order there. That means if you sit in one place with ten people, then you have ten per cent chance of getting a gig. But ... I live up at the top of Tempelhofer field and then I drive, I sometimes just chill at the front of the field: and then I actually know, whenever there's an order [for the] restaurant at the corner ... I know I'm usually the closest driver there [and will get it].

These 'small things', little pieces of information, which resemble guesses more than information, are crucial to earn money as a rider. To access this information, other riders matter – but at the same time, hanging too much together decreases the likelihood of getting orders dispatched via app. Riders are torn between 'playing it alone', and hanging around together in order to get a sense of the game. During one shift, for example, Joseph sat together with other riders at the public spot which served as a 'log-in' point for riders starting their shifts in that area of Berlin. And ironically, it was through this sitting around that he learned that making the most of the situation required constant movement, and not remaining still.

> Oh yes, that was quite interesting! That was exactly the point where I learned that if you want to earn money as a freelancer, you don't just sit around and wait – I could have guessed it, but I also like to sit around and chat, and ... well, we just chat and sat there and it was just relatively little going on and I talked about it ... I had worked for two hours at that time and had three gigs, orders so to speak, that is an hourly wage of 7 Euro or something. Then I chat with him (who had driven his seventh!): why did you get seven orders in a time when I got three? And then he said he doesn't know exactly ... he ran off, and then I talked to other people ... they said, well, one thing is you just sit here, then you just don't get any orders. (Interview with Joseph, Neukölln, 25 May 2017)

This sharing of assumptions about how the game was played helped riders to move along in their activity. Part of these assumptions turned around the black box 'algorithm'. The conversations about deciphering the algorithm among riders show that the technological set-up was an effective and legitimate source for regulating work practices and sociability at work.

Keeping at a distance

Alongside the algorithmic dispatching of orders, the technological set-up of the work as riders comprised the tracking of workers' location, velocity and reaction time to the app's instructions. So-called heads of riders were responsible for interpreting and reacting to the day-to-day statistics on riders' performances, deciding on sanctions, promoting riders etc. In our conversation with Ludwig, a head of riders, we learned that the belief, or the upholding of the *illusio*, of a separation of professional roles and personalized trust guided daily regulatory practices. Ludwig had been delivering food with his bike for more than a year, and was employed as a midi-jobber, an employment relation in which one can earn between €450 and €850 maximum per month, and where one is insured by the employer.[4] Besides undertaking regular shifts, he had been manager of the official meeting space for riders (to register, pick up their delivery boxes or hold office hours with the company) and the head of riders. The company did not assign any specific official professional role to Ludwig as head of riders, such as a special contract or list of tasks. What indicated his new position was the fact that he received extra pay, and that he was allowed to join a different chat group in which the manager of the riders was also a member. Ludwig explained to us that, when he began as head of riders, he didn't get any other directives except to monitor performance sheets and send them to the riders, and to be a contact person for the riders. He was supposed to diffuse the 'directives' of the company, in addition to the mails, contracts and messages sent regularly by the company to the riders. Twelve riders were under his supervision. He had also created a WhatsApp group with them in order to communicate important information concerning work processes.

He saw himself as a mediator between the company and the riders, as a broker of information: similar to a *bureaucrat*, Ludwig tried to interpret the measures indicated by the performance sheets and to reflect on their applicability to a given situation in which a rider was working. He gave one example in our conversation about a rider whose statistics were 'red' (red = score is problematic, green = good scores). According to him, it was important to understand what stood behind each number. Did the numbers correctly document what happened? Ludwig complained that some heads of riders wouldn't understand that a percentage of 100 in the variable measuring the frequency of delays in starting the shift was maybe the result of only one delay or late show-up. Ludwig stressed that he considered it important that the riders had the possibility to justify themselves for their no-shows. So that 'one can really see if he is making an effort, and if they are concerned by their situation, they care about it – or if they just do "not fancy doing it"' (Interview with Ludwig, 17 August 2017).

Ludwig wanted to give the riders the opportunity to explain their results, but the way he evaluated their explanations introduced another ranking system. The underlying evaluation scheme that he used to decide if he should impose sanctions for bad statistics or not depended on the answer to the question: are riders disciplined, entrepreneurial and willing to work? He enforced the same principle on which the statistical rankings were based – the rule that only the most motivated should remain in this job. Actually, Ludwig didn't neglect the numbers, but tried to ascertain if they fitted to the principle they were supposed to enforce. Interestingly, the expectation of good performance from workers, and also of what comprised good performance, was plausible to Ludwig and he did not question it; only the means of measurement and enforcement were debatable. The riders' opportunities to get along well within the employment setting were shaped by the evaluation of their character, specifically the evaluation of a rider's 'sportiness'. Moreover, openly doing favours for others was out of the question, and not the legitimate way of performing his role as head of riders or office manager. For example, no official rule defined how much, at what time and in what way he would be in contact with the riders he was 'responsible' for. Given this lack of clarity in the rules, Ludwig explained his reasoning for how to limit his availability: 'That you will somehow/at some point answer is natural, but if you are in a situation where you just can't answer right now, then it's their bad luck, and not my fault – I am not their "paramedic" [*Rettungssanitäter*]!' (Interview with Ludwig, Köpenick, 17 August 2017). He contrasted his role with that of a paramedic, a care professional, which suggests that Ludwig did not attempt to build care relations with his co-workers. Instead, he stressed that he 'keeps the rules' and didn't like 'to wipe the asses of others'. First of all, he felt that he shouldn't do this, as the company was vigilant about such things. Secondly, he didn't want to make life easier for random people, because if they made a mess of something they needed to assume responsibility for the consequences too. Ludwig did not interpret his mediating role between riders and main office employees as an opportunity to build trust relations that would function to authorize and legitimate transactions on the basis of kinning. Rather, he interpreted his role in terms of rule-making, with rules confirming the impersonal character of transactions and services between him and the riders. The forty-eight-hour rule is set, and instead of using this rule to organize an economy of distributing shifts based on relations of trust, Ludwig stuck to it and legitimized it morally as a means of educating the rider for their own benefit.

The productive use of the gap between company and street

Selling airtime was an activity that didn't involve many formalities to start it. Also, in their way of organizing their activity, airtime sellers seemed site-independent in terms of any constraints of public or contractual law. Airtime sellers sat at roadsides, with mobile phones in their hands or laid out on small tables that served as sales counters. Each call box was slightly different, as the tables and chairs were arranged differently, and the site often looked provisional, easily movable and adaptable to the circumstances. In the literature, the emergence of airtime sellers and phone boxes is discussed in terms of the ingenuity of residents of African cities. Annie Chéneau-Loquay, for instance, contends that 'there is a particular universe of the users of mobile telephony in Africa, which has generated a new informal economy in the cities' (Chéneau-Loquay 2012, 83). Others relate the emergence of airtime sellers to the expensive, malfunctioning telecommunications infrastructure in Côte d'Ivoire following its privatization in the early 2000s (Hamanys Broux de Ismael 2016, 200ff.). Yet the distinction between wage employment and entrepreneurial activities – a fundamental distinction that was previously used to define the informal sector (Hart 1973) – does not hold once one considers the place of airtime sellers in the system of distribution of airtime as a whole.

Juxtaposing the airtime seller activity against that of delivery riders in Berlin allows us to see something else: a form of attachment to the company that is neither employment nor self-employment, but something in between, an ambivalent status as micro-entrepreneur who at the same time is treated by the telecommunications firms as flexible manpower in the sale of airtime units.

Here, the technical infrastructure of a platform is crucial. In the case of the airtime sellers we spoke to, the platform 'RESUS'[5] was the central platform with which the telecommunications firm we focused on was able to connect the subcontracting firm of distribution (franchise) and the micro-entrepreneurs who sold airtime as call box workers on the street-level (Interview with the responsible manager of this platform, 8 April 2016).

What linked the airtime sellers to the company was their SIM card, through which they undertook their financial transactions, which were documented and configured by those providing the platform, the telecommunications firms. The airtime sellers received a percentage for every financial transaction, and similarly, the franchise bought the airtime units and received a discount back if they achieved a particular amount of sales in a month. These goals were set by the telecommunications firms on the basis of the purchasing power of the area of sales. On this basis, the firm created different zones, which all had an equivalent of 1 million FCFA turnover per month (Interview with franchise's director of distribution, Yopougon, 11 October 2017). RESUS registered all transactions between the SIM cards of micro-entrepreneurs, clients and dispatchers, and hence constituted a system that documented in real time how much airtime units were available in a particular area at a particular moment in time (Interview with franchise's director of distribution, Yopougon, 11 October 2017).

Now, the franchisee had the possibility, with the use of the RESUS platform, to follow up with the call box worker instantly and to know his/her financial transactions through the SIM card. On that basis, call box workers could be ranked and promoted or fired accordingly. The director of distribution explained that they used this classification in order to evaluate the value of the worker for his/her respective working zone, and in order to assess their seniority and commitment, as well as their presence on the spot. They could also know if, on the contrary, the worker was someone who was 'sleeping'.

> And on that basis, if the times are a bit difficult, if everyone is a bit out of tune at the end of the month, and you are a call box worker who is besides all that someone who knows how to stick out [*sortir ses epingles du jeu*], on that basis, we know how to congratulate you, how to make you loyal to us [*fidéliser*] … We will not give credit to someone who is just arriving, who has not yet proved anything. We will give credit to the one who has been here for five years, who has a turnover of 20,000 FCFA a day etc., etc. This one, we can accompany, the risk will be minor. Thanks to this classification [we can do this]! (Interview with franchise's director of distribution, Yopougon, 11 October 2017)

The ranking of the call box workers (or better put: the ranking of SIM cards attached to a particular person's ID) was one way of creating differentiated access to resources through the company.

The insights gathered at the franchisee in the formal interviews with high-ranked employees of the company, such as the director of distribution, did not match with the realities encountered while observing the daily activities of the dispatcher and monitors, nor while conversing with the phone box workers themselves. None of the interviewees spoke about their awareness of being ranked according to their turnovers, and none of the interviewees mentioned any experience with sanctions because they were not regularly at their spot. Apparently, the ranking of phone box workers according to their sales and commitment didn't seem to impact the way the workers organized their activity in the everyday – it had no apparent regulatory function for them.

More often, they were not selling airtime as individual entrepreneurs. Like Boris, who we introduced at the beginning of this chapter, many others of the young men we met sold airtime for someone else, or several actors were using the same SIM card registered with one personal ID, which was not necessarily their own, but borrowed from someone else. For Boris and his friend and colleague, the sale of airtime was based on mutuality and symmetrical interdependency. While Boris considered him and his friend to be on the same level, in other work arrangements similar relational mechanisms[6] legitimized unequal pairs in work relations. Here, the sharing of effort and profit was not as equal as that between Boris and his colleague. Luc, also in his mid-twenties, sold airtime at a phone box along with three other young men. They worked for 'a lady', as Luc put it. She had invested capital in the phone box, and gave Luc and his co-workers money at the end of the month, on the basis of the sales they had made that month. As an average, Luc mentioned 25,000 FCFA as a monthly share.[7] Even though Luc did not use kinship categories to describe his 'boss', as he called her, he still stressed that to make his relationship to her work, he showed respect towards her in order to consolidate a good reputation, as this enabled trust and continuous transactions. He showed through his acts that he did not steal money or mobile phones.

> It was a Sunday, Valentine's Day, and everything I had, the money, laptops and everything, I stored them and dropped them off [at a safe place]. But when I left, they couldn't call me [to see if everything went well] because my cell phone was dead. So she was scared – she thought I had run away. But she checked the notebook, it was all there, the cell phones were there. So they were surprised themselves. This example shows you how I am ... she thought I was going to run away but I dropped everything off. If you start to work somewhere, don't leave a bad trace there. They should talk about you [like this]: ah, he was such a thing, it was good! When it's like this, you always have God's blessing. (Interview with Luc, Yopougon, 23 February 2016)

Showing respect, and not taking the money he had made, but giving it to the investor in the call box, even though he had no legal working contract with her, was a means of building a good reputation and trust that enabled future shares for Luc. Given the fact that most of the interviewees were not selling airtime as individuals, it mattered more to them how to negotiate their shares and access to capital in these relations based on what Bourdieu calls the code of honour, than to work towards an increase of the quantity of their sales to improve their rank in the official statistics.

Creating complicity

Sales statistics were not only important in the speech of the director of the franchisee. He had also brought in middlemen who monitored the distribution. To do this, these middlemen also had access to the status of activity of the airtime sellers and supervised the dispatching of credit to them. In the franchise of one telecommunications firm we were able to get access to in more depth, each dispatcher had a specific zone they were responsible for. In this zone, they distributed airtime to the call box workers. Each day, they would wander from phone box to phone box with their motorbike, and dispatch airtime and receive money in return. Even though the call box workers were not contracted by the firms whose products they were selling, they depended on the dispatchers on an everyday basis: only through them could they gain access to airtime units, the product they sold to their customers.

Daniel had been working as a dispatcher for a while. He had developed a fixed route which he took each morning, that covered all the call box workers working in his zone. The zoning model split up urban areas on the basis of the purchasing power of the residents. The telecommunications firm developed their market by fixing sales objectives for each zone for their franchise, and using the platform technologies to keep the output of their call box workers under surveillance (Interview with director of distribution, Yopougon, 11 October 2017). Daniel would stop at the call box, ask the amount of money the seller wanted to top up in airtime, and then send a message via the RESUS system to order airtime to the call box worker's account; he would then take the money in cash from the worker in exchange. In fact, it was not evident that the dispatcher was always able to pass by in time, or to cover the call box workers immediately when they needed airtime. Daniel, whom I spent most time with, was regularly overwhelmed and exhausted by the daily tour of distribution, and had his own techniques for how to manage these (physical and temporal) resource constraints.

Call box workers and dispatchers were not tied to each other by any written contract. However, they made sure they had reliable business partners. For Daniel, this worked above all through the creation of familiarity.

> [W]e are helping each other where we can [*un peu un peu*]. This means that we are getting familiar with each other [*on se familiarise*] – we call this 'the family'. Because it's even not friendship any more, in the end we call each other brothers. We are sympathizing … So the difference from being an acquaintance and then becoming like a

> brother, it's that: if you have a problem, the other one will not let you down. They will help you, they will support you. This is how it is. And if they have a bit, and they see that you are in need, they can also share it together with you. Easy! If they want something, you as well, they can ask you. (Interview with Daniel, Yopougon, 13 October 2017)

Daniel connected with others so as to create familiarity and turn his work relationships into kin. This for Daniel comprised caring for each other – 'not letting each other down' in a situation of need, and 'supporting' each other. Becoming part of the 'family' thus secured him the right to a share and promised the circulation of resources as generalized reciprocities (Sahlins 1972) among those belonging together as kin: if someone was in need, the others would give as much as they could. Giving here referred not to a quantity of resources, but to the willingness to support with 'as much as you have'. The familiarity between Daniel and the airtime sellers secured the distribution of airtime and enabled the appropriation of labour without any legal contract. The continuity of exchange between dispatcher and airtime sellers was ensured through the establishment of care relations (cf. Thelen 2015) that were based on disinterested exchange – the creation of sympathy and familiarity, similar to Bourdieu's economy of faith (Bourdieu 1977).

In the concrete work setting, such mutuality consisted of transferring airtime in emergencies at any time. Emergencies could happen when airtime sellers ran out of airtime unit stock during the day or late at night, outside of the dispatcher's regular working hours, but had a customer that needed to top up their phone. Also, Daniel supported some of the call box workers with whom he became friends, by investing in their business. In our conversations, he often referred to them as brothers too, which further indicates how transactions of resources were based on (practices of) kinning, although in a way which was less fixed on the idea of 'unconditional solidarity'. As brother, he would give them capital to buy more airtime units, but still as a loan, which they would have to repay after making enough money.

Familiarity was not only binding, it also helped establish authority. Daniel later changed positions and became supervisor to those who dispatched airtime units to call box workers. Even if now his working contract instituted his status as superior vis-à-vis the dispatchers,

Daniel hesitated in calling himself a 'boss'. Asked about his tasks, he explained that 'the supervisor, he is the first responsible … for the dispatcher. He is, to a certain extent, to not call it their boss, but he is their boss' (Interview with Daniel, Yopougon, 13 October 2017).

> Interviewer: … So why do you hesitate?
>
> Daniel: Because I *am* their boss, but in order to not [be] doing this too much, in order to familiarize a bit, I am not keen to pronounce this word 'boss'. That's it.
>
> Interviewer: To familiarize in what sense?
>
> Daniel: In fact it would not be good if there is a distance between my dispatcher and me. On the contrary, it is important that there is complicity. It is in this complicity that you can work better … Maybe the dispatcher is going out today, he meets an airtime seller who behaved badly towards him. If I'm not too hard on him, he will call me 'Super' [Short version of *superviseur*, surveillant] … [It means] they liked the supervisor, t'at's why they call him 'Super'. [The dispatcher tells you:] That's what Richard [the airtime seller] did. And then I give him [the dispatcher] instructions: 'Ah if he did that, you have to understand it – but you have to act in this way, so that tomorrow, he himself can understand that, because what he did is not normal. [The airtime seller] comes to you, he apologizes, and you move on' (Interview with Daniel, Yopougon, *13.10.2017,* emphasis in original).

Daniel stressed the importance of creating complicity. His instructions reflect that instead of creating distance in order to acquire authority, he guides with advice that allows for apology and learning. Complicity arose further through speaking about non-work-related problems, and through the inclusion of needs and events outside of work into the organization of work relations. For example, once one of the dispatchers was worried about his nephew, who had disappeared in the city, and so Daniel, who was supervisor by then, allowed the dispatcher to go home earlier (Interview with Daniel, Yopougon, 13 October 2017). This flexibility was not in itself special, but Daniel brought up this example to show that maintaining authority was not possible only by reference to his official professional position in the company, but was made possible through the creation of complicity. He had to 'win' over the dispatcher personally, and had to 'create a bond between persons' (Bourdieu 1977, 190) in order to establish a 'socially recognized domination, in other words, legitimate authority' (Bourdieu 1977, 192).

Daniel contrasted the complicity of personal bonds to a situation in which conflicts at work were regulated via official procedures and relations based on professional status positions. If he did not build personal bonds at work with his co-workers, and something went wrong at work, his co-workers wouldn't tell him because they knew that negotiating a solution for the problem as 'brothers' would not be possible – instead, they might fear that Daniel would report the mistake or problem to his boss, who would send an email and enact sanctions (Interview with Daniel, Yopougon, 13 October 2017).

Complicity gave workers room to manoeuvre, and allowed Daniel to show gratitude, do favours etc., which increased his recognition and status as 'carer'. In Daniel's description of an ambiguous role as boss and carer, we see a moment in which juridically codified official roles, like the professional status one occupies in a firm, are used in the everyday not as a source of authority, but as a role through which one can create bonds with others to establish status, and hence authority. The official role still remains a possible repertoire for Daniel to use in order to regulate the relationship between him and the dispatcher he 'surveilled'. The possible practices emerging from here could perhaps be described as 'acting in light of [official] rules' (cf. Chiodelli and Moroni 2014), not as encompassing principles guiding interactions.

Daniel involved himself in the work setting in a particular mode of behaviour (cf. Hannerz 1980, 317). He was recruited into roles, bundles of norms which prescribe behaviours for occupants in particular social positions (Portes 2006, 238). As dispatcher, I expected Daniel to be acting in a role in which he avoided building any personal ties to those he supervised, in order to maintain his impartiality and to be able to enforce the official rules. But to him, being a boss meant also acting in the role of a carer, as someone who satisfied needs for those he had to supervise, and vice versa. He occupied an ambivalent social role with a 'cluster of norms and counter-norms', which enabled him to gain the trust of his co-workers, and through which he was able to monitor their work practices. As carer, he still used the legal rules as a sanctioning mechanism, however not to sanction deviance from the rule of law, but rather to re-actualize his status as carer and to define who belongs to his circle of responsibility and who, instead, was a stranger (cf. Newell 2006).

At the same time, the trust relations that were built through the distribution of airtime enforced unequal benefits and power positions. First, with (practices of) kinning came the possibility of sanctioning, particularly when someone refused to obey the 'rule to please'. This creates differential power positions, with the call box worker being dependent on the good faith of his patron. The privilege of receiving airtime any time when needed came with the pressure to maintain a 'good relationship' – that is, to do favours, as one of the call box workers called it. During one of our daily distribution tours in Yopougon, Daniel himself joked about the many invitations for lunch he received from the call box workers (Daniel, on the other hand, was all the time inviting *me* to lunch).

However, being able to bond with dispatchers or monitors from the company was beneficial for receiving deliveries in time, accessing credit or being supported in emergencies. This then also brought airtime sellers good official evaluations, and perhaps recompensation by the company. Economic practices of gifting and sharing combined with the market logic of recompensating those who had the best turnovers (dispatchers and airtime sellers alike). Together, this reproduced advantages for those airtime sellers and dispatchers who were able to create complicity in work relations.

Entangled regulatory practices in digital economies

This chapter analysed regulatory practices in hybrid employment systems beyond analytical distinctions between informal and formal rules. The delivery riders and the airtime sellers were both characterized by their loose attachment to the companies they worked for. Despite differences in contractual forms, they mostly all worked flexibly, temporarily and under legal precarity – their contractual status gave them few status rights. Such hybridization of employment systems is characteristic of digital capitalism (Staab and Nachtwey 2016). The firm as place of control and protection dissolves, and instead companies function as hybrids of firms and markets, organizations and networks (cf. Staab and Nachtwey 2016; see also Srnicek 2016). New technological tools, such as platforms, then allow for new possibilities for monitoring and regulating the transactions of riders and airtime sellers. But my analysis of the regulation of work relations shows that these technological tools are embedded within the relational work of actors at work, in 'intermediary zones of regulation' (Chauveau *et al.* 2001).

In Berlin, the monitor I interviewed who secured a mediating role between company and riders, brokered information and resources (shifts) to the riders. Ludwig's relational work consisted of ensuring rules, performing his role as monitor on the basis of its function for the labour process and not as a person that creates personal ties and engages in transactions following the principle of solidarity (gifting and sharing). Through his practices and in the interactions with the riders, a form of domination was recognized as legitimate, in which legal rules were supposed to be the register through which to make claims on others, ensure previsibility for future transactions and trust, or sanction their behaviour. The monitor interpreted the statistics and enacted their officially underdetermined roles at work by valuing certain cultural skills above others: self-motivation and self-discipline, as well as self-responsibility. Ludwig expected objective mechanisms, consecrated in law, to be valid – not necessarily 'right', but constituting the *illusio* of the game – the limits of what was sayable, or thinkable. Through this, a shared *illusio* was upheld, in which statistics and legal codes were valid, if interpreted correctly. These field dynamics reproduced the goal of the company to enforce work discipline through these tools of quantification.

The dispatcher, monitor and airtime sellers in Abidjan filled the gap between the company and the street by establishing relationships based on personal trust. These were regulated by the code of honour, that is, their relationship was guaranteed by loyalty and not by an abstract discipline, rigorous contracts or specific sanctions (Bourdieu 1977, 190). Creating complicity in personalized relations was an example of this. To create complicity, ambivalence of professional roles was productive, as it allowed for an actualization of who belonged to the circle of those under protection – the monitor Daniel saw himself not as a 'boss' only, but also as a 'carer', and could benefit from personal bonds with airtime sellers as much as they could be sure to be supported by him. The interviewees shared the *illusio* in which building reputation in personalized relations was a socially recognized form of domination (cf. Bourdieu 1976). This form of domination alludes to a more generalized mechanism of social reproduction in Côte d'Ivoire, documented in the concept of the 'big man' (Médard 1992) or in the analysis of state elites (Fauré and Médard 1982). Accumulation of resources and privileges is not objectified in political titles or professional roles: 'the attainment of big-man status is rather the outcome of a series of acts which elevate a person above the common herd and attract about him a coterie of loyal, lesser men ... it is but an acknowledged standing in interpersonal relations (Sahlins 1963, 298).

Evaluations of individual work efficiency in statistics and official roles did not have the same weight in constituting the legitimate authority to define status positions in work relations. This recalls Mbembe and Roitman's analysis (1995) on the *normalcy* of improvisation of efficacious action in contexts of crisis – that is, acting at the same time inside and outside of bureaucratic procedures and legal rules, as following formal rules and conventional procedures did not necessarily lead to the prescribed results (Mbembe and Roitman 1995, 342). Yet inequalities were reproduced through the combination of the importance of symbolic capital and the tools of recompensation that the company used to enforce the logic of the market: creating bonds with the dispatcher or monitors of the company on the basis of a code of honour could increase turnover (as the dispatcher/monitor would be more available to deliver new airtime credit, goods to sell) – efforts that were then officially registered and could be recompensated by the company. Second, the dispatchers, too, were most keen to keep airtime sellers who had large turnovers, because the dispatchers' bonus payments from the company were based on airtime sellers' turnovers. As a result, they preferred to support those airtime sellers who had good turnovers. In this way, advantages are reproduced, and those who have less capital lose even more (see, more generally, Vuarin 1994).

In Berlin, the provisionality and overlapping of official rules was not a *situational normalcy*, but was productive in relations of domination too. It produced uncertainty and mistrust among the riders and made them responsible for actively seeking to enforce the rules of the game. I interpret this as commodification of work – workers need to be self-managers of their labour. This comprised an active monitoring of one's work and non-paid labour as accountant (cf. Wolfgang) – time that one needed to be able to afford as a rider!

– and self-discipline and competition. Riders were caught between competing with each other over orders and sharing information about how to get resources at work (cf. Joseph) – which relates back to Chapter 3, where I showed the importance of social capital and processes of closure.

Relational work differed between the two cases, and in particular, in how actors were recruited into roles and how different roles were combined (cf. Hannerz 1980, 174). This became clear when looking at the 'relational packages' (Zelizer 2012) that were socially recognized as legitimate to organize the labour process. The airtime sellers I interviewed in Abidjan used the role as friend and the set of norms that this implied as the convention for regulating business relations – like Boris and his friend, for example. He established the call box with a 'friend', or 'brother', he had known for a long time, and hence they trusted each other to not destroy the business or renege on the commitment to share profits. Interviewees earmarked the monetary transactions not as gifts, however, but understood them as payments that *compensated* for work done as 'brother', or 'bon petit'. The pay did not consist of a salary calculated on working hours, in which efforts had a fixed price and turned into a commodity, but yet co-workers concluded fixed amounts of compensation. Work was done not because written legal work contracts prescribed how work would be remunerated as labour, but because of personal bonds and trust. Similarly, Daniel used the ambivalence of his roles as monitor and dispatcher to create personal bonds in which he could establish authority as a carer, and not as a superior based on his professional status only.

Among the riders in Berlin, however, authority was established through the discretionary space riders obtained through their professional status as monitors. The monitor Ludwig also drew on symbolic economies – he and his colleague evaluated the riders on the basis of their fit to an ideal of a motivated worker – but upheld a separation between a professional role and the role of carer, earmarked by different forms of transactions (gifting and compensating, cf. Zelizer 1996). While in Abidjan interviewees maintained the ambivalence in social roles in organizing the labour process, in Berlin interviewees upheld the idea of a labour market in their practices – writing bills, presenting attests, interpreting statistics – separately from the acquaintances and friendships they established at the work setting, even though these personal ties mattered for accessing job positions and information at work (see, e.g., the rider Ludwig).

Both role constellations, however, enabled the appropriation of labour through mechanisms that establish authority in other ways than the working contract. In Abidjan, it was the creation of personal bonds that made the gap between company and street productive. In Berlin, it was the legal uncertainty that incited self-enterprising practices and self-discipline. At the same time, airtime distribution and platform-based services are economies that use legal forms to their benefit and create working contexts that are recognized as legitimate and compliant with legally coded norms. In both settings, the state is present through its absence in enforcing rules that would ensure the riders' entitlement to payment, or produce a work setting in which the airtime sellers could rely on a durable occupation even during slow and irregular flows in sales. Instead, official rules, such as the contract between franchise and telecommunications firm, are set in ways that guarantee beneficial conditions to the latter.

Notes

1 For a similar discussion on ambivalence for theorizing informality in comparative perspective, see Alena Ledeneva (2018).
2 By 'they', Joseph probably refers to the company for which he works as a delivery rider, but from whom and when exactly he got this information was not discussed in the interview.
3 As I was part of these chat groups but didn't have permission to quote from them, I cannot give more detailed quotations.
4 see Arbeitsvertrag.org 2022.
5 Anonymized.
6 See Tilly (2001, 365): '[R]elational [mechanisms are those social mechanisms] involving shifts in connections among social units.'
7 Luc said: 'she divided the benefit and gave them money' (Interview with Luc, Yopougon, 23 February 2016). He did not posit himself as receiving a wage or remuneration for his work. (For a discussion on models of work arrangements outside wage labour, see Viti 2013.)

5

Organizing care: distributive labour across private and public realms

Séverin was 25 years old and lived in Koumassi, Abidjan, along with his father. We met at his selling spot, close to a main road of the district, with a lot of circulation, which was beneficial for Séverin's business to sell airtime. The selling spot was barely remarkable, as Séverin literally embodied the phone box, and no other material support identified it: he sat on a bench, with a few mobile phones on his lap, and wore a fancy shoulder bag to store the money and other paraphernalia he needed to work. The casual character of the selling performance reflected the ephemerality of his identification with the airtime sales as income-generating activity. Séverin wanted to play football, and had begun to pursue a professional football career – against the expectations of his father. The latter not only stopped giving him money for the daily necessities because Séverin was too old, he was also displeased with the fact that Séverin had not pursued a career as a public servant (a policeman, to be precise). Séverin had tried to enter public administration too, but had not been successful so far. Caught between his personal desires, for which he did not get support, and the expectations of his father and his brothers, who had all become 'someone' by entering the civil service, he had to look for a way to keep going.

In this situation, Séverin could get support through one of his neighbours, a 33-year-old lady who had attained higher education qualifications (BTS, i.e. *Brevet Technique Supérieur*), and was currently a housewife. 'It was because she trusted that she wanted to help me', Séverin explained. The lady gave Séverin the opportunity to show that he was reliable: she entrusted him with an envelope containing money and asked him to keep it for her. After a couple of months, she asked for the money back – and Séverin still had all the money together. This created trust, and with that, support. While establishing trust, she had considered Séverin as her junior [*pétit frère*]. They lived in the same building, and she was married to a man who made a good revenue, according to Séverin. They shared the same ethnicity – which created an alliance based on ethnic categories. But Séverin also stressed that his relational work, 'his character', mattered for creating a care relation as junior–senior with her. He never disrespected her, and he could always call her, and she would always respond to his needs.

> So when I have a little problem I call her: Ah! Old mother [*La veille mère*], your junior [*ton pétit*] there is in trouble you know, you have to give [a part of your resources to others as a gift]! [She says] okay, there's no problem, come and see me. What I need, she takes away [from what she has and she gives it to me.] Well, I can call her like a mother! (Interview with Séverin, Koumassi, 3 March 2016)

The neighbour became like a mother to Séverin 'because mothers are those who do this for their children ... The one you are going to call ... to ask for a favour ten times is going to render the service to you ten times. It's rare' (Interview with Séverin, Koumassi, 3 March 2016). The reliability of her support was something that qualified her as a mother. She had helped him financially with the entrance fee for the public administration exam, and gave Séverin the starting capital of 60,000 FCFA as a gift, that enabled him to take care of himself alone [*se défendre tout seul*] instead of calling her to ask her for money.

Séverin's situation shows the importance of organizing support relations as young men in Abidjan. It also introduces us to the particular setting of the airtime sales: as informalized forms of entrepreneurship, selling airtime required access to capital, one's own working tools such as the mobile phones and an attractive selling spot. Starting from here we can see connections to the situation of the delivery riders: they needed to organize support relations too, as their work arrangements required them to use private working tools.

When Sam wanted to start work with the food delivery platform, he needed a new mobile phone. His old one had been damaged during a trip to South America. At first sight, this need was a banality to Sam, as he was simply given his father's old phone. When asked how this transaction came about, Sam laughed, maybe because to him this question seemed trivial. He said: 'I had to ask. Or I just told my parents that I need a mobile phone and that I even want to get a smartphone, because I realized that it was not that bad [after all to have mobile Internet on my phone].' Sam went to his father's house for a visit, and they were sitting in the garden. His father was an industrial assembler (*Industriemonteur*) with a secondary school leaving certificate, like his wife, who was self-employed and ran a kennel for dogs. '[A]nd well, I approached [my father] and he said, ok, let's see, and he had just bought a new one and he said, ok, just take my old one.' I wanted to know more about how he convinced his father to give him the phone, and Sam simply replied: 'I think he didn't need to be convinced, it was just like – ok *the boy needs something*, let's think about organizing something.' Even if it seemed easy to receive support from his parents, as long as he didn't ask for complete 'nonsense [*Blödsinn*]', he also stressed that his 'own feeling' was mostly that he wanted to 'work it out himself'. 'And only if I really don't have any money, because just too much falls apart, then I ask [for money]' (Interview with Sam, Wedding, 15 February 2017, my emphasis).

We could read Sam's story as a success story, in which the organization of support for doing gig work as a delivery rider seems to be frictionless, natural. However, bringing Sam's experiences into dialogue with those of airtime sellers like Séverin incites new questions: how does such a 'sacred space of the family' – that is, the naturalized transactions between Sam and his father – work, and what kind of expectations and conditions bring such sacredness about?

Sam and Séverin are both 'doing kinship' – by conversing, paying attention, building trust, they use kinning as an important practice to organize support. Both stories also show the importance of the social environment in which the young men started to sell airtime, or to deliver food. In other words, the gig work cannot be fully grasped without looking at the context: the economic and social context in which people are doing this work. This is particularly true because gig work relies so much on external, private resources – it is not made to be sustainable work for constructing livelihood. We will have a closer look at the ways in which deservingness in support relations is constructed, and how these norms also reproduce inequalities for young men in precariousness. By doing so, this chapter advances analytical tools to assess social support in urban theory comparatively, beyond measuring networks of support through fixed, categorical definitions of family members and friends. Rather, we can explain variation in the ways in which kin and friendship ties are used to confront socio-material insecurities by contextualizing how, historically, a particular separation of the public and domestic spheres has been institutionalized and used in mechanisms of secondary exploitation (Dörre and Haubner 2018).

Entanglements of market-work and care

Precarization concerns distributive as well as productive work, paid and unpaid work: in other words, social realms of work and of care. As Nancy Fraser points out, those two realms are entangled and the 'boundaries delimiting "economy" from "society", "production" from "reproduction", and "work" from "family"' are contested sites of struggle (Fraser 2016). For the analysis of experiences of precarity, this means to decentre from the realm of work to follow the actors into their organizing of resources in their relations with kin, friends and other urban dwellers outside of the actual work*place*. One way of looking at the entanglement of market-work and care is to enquire about the social relations around work that turn paid work into such a crucial element for access to protection against insecurities, against the vulnerabilities of life.

The notion of care has replaced the older debate on social reproduction (see Fraser 2016; Thelen 2015). By care, we think of all social-reproductive activities done in 'homes, neighbourhoods, civil-society associations, informal networks, and public institutions' (Fraser 2016). They range from 'activities of provisioning, care-giving and interaction that produce and maintain social bonds, although it accords them no monetized value and treats them as if they were free' (Fraser 2016). From a relational perspective, care is an

> open-ended process which ... connects a giving and receiving side in practices aimed to satisfy socially recognized needs. [It draws] our attention to the connection between persons, instead of turning the spotlight solely on the carer ... [T]hese relationships result from care practices (not the other way around). Thus, practices, and not presupposed relationships, form the point of departure for research. (Thelen 2015, 508)

Care practices are various. They include paid care in institutional settings like elderly care or childcare; or care can consist of emotional and material resources. In the following, care practices that contribute to making a living as airtime sellers and food delivery riders are at the focus. Expanding on Thelen's approach to care, we take care practices as the starting point rather than 'specific types of relations', which allows for a consideration of 'care outside of kinship relationships or in areas that encompass both private and public domains' (Thelen 2015, 510). Care practices can bring into being different categories of relationship, i.e. friendship, patron–client relations and professional care relationships. Furthermore, speaking of care practices detaches care from the place of residence. Forms of cohabitation then do not necessarily overlap with care relations and the sharing or redistributing of resources (cf. Seekings 2008). Also, a dichotomous distinction in regard to the quality of care can be overcome. '[C]are provided by relatives is often viewed as "warm and real", in contrast to substitute care offered by cold institutions' (Thelen 2015, 510).[1] Spinning this perspective further, we will look at the *doing of kinship* in care relations, and speak of it as *kinning*. Kinning comprises the mutualization of resources (gifting, sharing or redistributing on the principle of mutuality), caregiving and care receiving, and *can* imply drawing on categories of kinship in the relational work.

In the following, we will have a close look at the ways young men working in the digital economies of Abidjan and Berlin establish need and deservingness of support. I show that the actors use the sale of airtime and delivery of food in negotiating deservingness in care relations, and at the same time, they rely on care practices in order to be able to sell and deliver. I discuss how they organize material resources, like working tools or a place to work, financial resources like starting capital or income other than through market exchange. I analyse how actors earmark these transacted goods as gifts or a share and establish relationships accordingly (Zelizer 2012). I analyse to what extent their activity is part of their distributive labour,[2] which means that the activity is 'in fact less about producing goods and services … than it is about securing distributive outcomes. It is in large measure, that is, about accessing or making claims on the resources of others' (Ferguson 2015, 93). Ferguson argues, based on his work on distributive labour in Southern Africa, that,

> rather than striving to escape, cast off, or struggle against relations of hierarchical subordination (as the emancipatory liberal mind would

> expect and approve), [actors] are putting extraordinary energies into seeking them out. What are we to make of these pursuits of subordination, these (as I will call them here) 'declarations of dependence'? (Ferguson 2013, 224)

I compare how the interviewees identify the socially recognized as legitimate balance of individual responsibility and need of help by others – individual actors or collectives. More precisely, I look at the role of kinning in the distributive labour of my interviewees, and how kinning stretches across 'public', 'parochial' and 'private realms' (Lofland 1998, 10).

Realms are characterized by a distinctive relational form: 'An *intimate* relational form indicates the existence of a private realm, a *communal* relational form suggests a parochial realm, and a *stranger* or *categorical* relational form corresponds with a public realm' (Lofland 1998, 14, quoted in Kusenbach 2006, 280). In other words, what is the 'radius of responsibilities' for support, '[w]ho accepts responsibilities for whom and under which circumstances … [and how are] respective responsibilities of state, kin and "community" (i.e. neighbours) … demarcated' (Seekings 2008, 5)? Legitimizing access to support is also embedded in gendered expectations, i.e. in roles as providers. That said, in the knitting of relations of care and in the construction of household memberships, actors also make sense of their activity as a way to prevent them from being seen as idle, or too dependent on others. Furthermore, the organization of care is embedded in broader histories of welfare and how it is spatially organized: the historical separation of the public and domestic spheres in the context of Berlin, and the blurring of these spheres in the context of Abidjan, also affects how kinship and intergenerational relations unfold in practice. In different ways, care relations build on impersonalized relations with state representatives and personal relations in the private and public space, and these boundaries can be linked to the way in which care relations are organized through and by the state, I argue.

Maintaining control

At first glance, relationships with parents did not play a role for the young riders in Berlin. It was only when I asked them directly how they organized their bicycles and mobile phones or how they cushioned the effects of financial bottlenecks, and who they would ask, that family relationships came into the picture. As we learned in the introduction to this chapter, Sam laughed at me, surprised by my interest in his father's gifting of an old smartphone. Instead, the more prominent narrative consisted of the riders presenting themselves as self-reliant and autonomous. In the following, we will show how this self-representation is interwoven with the negotiation of the radius of responsibility in support relations.

Sam was not the only rider I met who upheld the *illusio* of the family as a sacred space of uninterested exchange. On the contrary, it was a shared idea among the young men I got acquainted with. Samuel was a rider's captain who began at the company after finishing his master's in neuroscience. He described his parents as 'very supportive' and 'really quite open' to any kind of projects he had. As an example of the protection he received from his family, he mentioned their support of his studies, during which he was fed by them, without any obligation to repay the support. 'My parents were always willing to take care of it, and I think I never really asked. I think it just was offered to me and I accepted it' (Interview with Samuel, Kreuzberg, 7 June 2017). Samuel said the only thing he needed to do in order to maintain support, was to visit his parents regularly at home, and to write them messages. Establishing need in these relations was not perceived by Samuel or others as 'hard social work', even though it was predicated on the fact that the young men kept intact the *illusio* of uninterested exchange in practices of kinning.

Relying on care relations in a family in which material support worked 'without question' enabled some riders to maintain a self-presentation as self-sufficient: 'I have never been in trouble. I have never asked for any help from anybody. I am able to sort things out on my own', Torben explained to me in our interview. He helped others, nevertheless, because he liked doing so, and hoped that in this way he would be helped in return. Understanding himself as someone with the possibility to 'go it alone' rested on the security that Torben's father sent him money quite regularly, even though not predictably. Torben had grown up in London with his parents and brother. His father was French and his mother Portuguese. Both had attended university; his father was employed as a salesman, and his mother worked as medical staff at a hospital. From time to time, without being asked, his father transferred between €300 and €1,000 to Torben's bank account, and gave him cash when the bank account was blocked once. Torben didn't feel any need to justify his father's support of a German language class: 'for educational issues, parents are always ready to pay, right?', he asked rhetorically (Interview with Torben, Prenzlauer Berg, 15 June 2017). The *ability* to pay was not mentioned once in our conversation. Through his parents' social capital, Torben found housing in Berlin very easily and cheaply. A member of his parents' circle of friends offered him a room at her apartment. He only had to pay symbolic rent: cooking with the tenant he shared the apartment with, doing grocery shopping from time to time, and chatting. Torben felt 'at home' there. Torben and his parents' friend both established a care relation through practices of kinning (doing grocery shopping for each other, asking if the other needs something).

This was a powerful perspective, as it made the problematization of scarcity and neediness difficult. Joseph describes this dilemma as a strange silence around money he experiences in his everyday life in Berlin. Joseph had moved from a middle-sized town in the North of Germany to Berlin to begin studying computer sciences, after he had finished his commercial apprenticeship and had been unemployed for some time.

> In his social environment in his hometown, a middle town in the North of Germany, '… [the people in] my environment … had no money, were not academic people and such things. It was commonplace that most of the people just had problems with money, and money was always a topic … [M]y environment in [my hometown] consisted of, I would almost say working-class children, actually. It was only in Berlin when I realized, somehow nobody talks about money, all people *have* money somehow. (Interview with Joseph, Neukölln, 25 May 2017)

In contrast to a dominant (middle-class) *perspective*, in which material support through kinning was a naturalized transaction, Joseph very carefully balanced out dependencies on others, also on support from his mother. He avoided asking his mother for money, even though he knew, when there was an emergency, he could ask her for help. But he didn't like to do this, as he knew she had no money (Interview with Joseph, Neukölln, 25 May 2017). Joseph's mother was an employee at a department store, who had commenced law studies at university but did not graduate as she worked full time and was the only carer for three children. Also Joseph points to the *illusio* of the sacred unit of the family, in which a generalized reciprocity structured the relations of exchange, but as a family with limited assets to share, the negotiation of support did not work 'without question' as portrayed by riders with more privileged family backgrounds.

To Joseph, Torben or Sam, it was important to be able to do it alone. That this required resources was not for all openly discussed as need and as provided for through interdependencies with others, but was 'naturalized' as given in the dominant *perspective* of those who could rely on assets, i.e. through family bonds.[3] They reproduced the idea of the family as a 'separate social universe' by boundary work that idealized the interior of the family almost as a 'sacred space' (Bourdieu 1993b, 33):

> [As a] universe where the ordinary laws of the economic world are suspended, the family is the place of trusting and giving – as opposed to the market and the exchange as tit-for-tat ... [It is a place] where interest in the narrow sense of the term, as the search for equivalence in exchanges, is put in suspense. (Bourdieu 1993b, 33, my translation)

This *illusio* was paired with the idea of being able to do it alone, and those who were struggling to play this game realized the extent of the power of the myth of the independent person.

The credo of 'being able to do it alone' was indeed a shared perspective among all the young men I got to know in the food delivery platform economy in Berlin. Not only were they attracted by the promise of 'independence' as gig workers, some of the riders also problematized material scarcity as something they had to deal with on their own and stressed their ability to discipline themselves in consumption and the management of their money. Dennis, for example, a full-time delivery rider who grew up in Spain, spoke of himself as someone able to 'control his money'. He just had turned 30 when we met, and to him, his age made the ability to discipline his spending in order to have some financial backup even more pressing. The only person he would ask for resources was his father, but he didn't want to rely on his support any more even if he could, '[b]ecause we're old, you know. Actually, we should be independent, so I always go to work' (Interview with Dennis, Mitte, 24 February 2017). Positioning himself in a group of 'old' residents to explain his reluctance to rely on support implies that age categories are not separate categories, but relational ones: age is constituted in intergenerational relationships, and age categories enable relationships across space and time (Cole and Durham 2007, 3). For Dennis, his role in intergenerational relations had changed – from being the dependent child of his father, he now felt the urge to demonstrate a status as an independent adult. Dennis saw in labouring his way towards independency, which also reflected gendered expectations of growing into adulthood. As a way of demonstrating his independence, he disciplined his consumption, which allowed him to maintain some control in a context in which establishing need in his social relations would be risky or shameful. Also borrowing or lending money to others was something he avoided, as he expected not to be repaid. In particular, he didn't want to introduce monetary transactions among friendships, as to him money didn't belong there. He wouldn't borrow money from someone or lend money to friends. He is hesitant: 'as soon as money comes in, real friendship ends' – and it could be risky, 'because then you won't get the money back', he explained. Money would mess up principles of friendship, in his view: 'with money, I think you won't have any real friends' (Interview with Dennis, Mitte, 24 February 2017). By differentiating social ties and their corresponding forms of payment (Zelizer 1996), Dennis excluded financial interdependencies among friends, and limited the entitlement for support to his father, 'his family'. Care practices of sharing and reciprocating belonged for him to bonds in the private realm (cf. Blokland and Noordhoff 2008; on bonds see Blokland 2003). Friendships, however, were not to be contaminated by monetary exchanges, and interdependencies that involved unpaid debts would risk the relationship.

Feelings of unbalance and inappropriate debt in intimate relationships are embedded in gendered expectations of roles as provider. Joseph's situation shows this very well. As a freelance rider in Berlin, he felt that he constantly lacked money to get by. In difficult situations, he tried to avoid borrowing money from others. In our conversations, he explained this also by the fact that he had accumulated debts over the life course: official ones recorded by the SCHUFA,[4] a public–private organization, and private debts with his girlfriend. And hence he tried not to ask others for money, as they might create even more obligations and commitments that he didn't want to deal with in his social relations (cf. Blokland and Noordhoff 2008). The fact that he had to borrow money from his girlfriend made him feel uncomfortable.

> As I said, it's an unpleasant interpersonal relationship … As I said for me money and power are very, very, very tightly connected, which means it's also a very strange relationship for me to know that my girlfriend just has money, she inherited it once and so on, and I won't. And … to borrow something from her is also somehow [depressing] because it [creates] a strange commitment that I actually don't want to have within an interpersonal relationship. (Interview with Joseph, Neukölln, 25 May 2017)

The loan he had taken from his girlfriend trapped him in an unbalanced interdependency: it created power relations that did not fit to gendered roles of carer and solicitor of help. This contributed to his feeling of non-deservingness as a man in romantic partnerships of support from the partner.

All in all, the norm to maintain control and self-discipline reinforced a boundary that relegated kinning to the private realm. To ask for support there was legitimate, although shaped by the temporal structuration of intergenerational interdependencies, and depended on the sense that in the family there were enough resources to share. Moreover, self-sufficiency was a norm that most of the interviewees stressed as important for them. While for some, 'doing it alone' was possible because material support through kinning was veiled as a naturalized entitlement in intergenerational bonds, others restricted their entitlement to support through bonds to emergencies, aware of the neediness of parents, or feeling that they were too old to ask for support as 'youth'. In this situation, resorting to other social ties for support, such as to friends or partners, was complicated. Joseph and Dennis didn't like to become interdependent in these ways, as it made it difficult to maintain honour and a feeling of control (cf. Blokland and Noordhoff 2008). These feelings of honour were embedded in expectations that came with age and gender roles: their positionality as young adult men accentuated the pressure to change roles in intergenerational relations towards more financial independence. This also meant that they had to provide for the working tools and costs of maintenance that the company had outsourced to the workers, in market exchange relations – a further pressure, given their limited financial resources.

Having a plan

The negotiation of legitimate interdependencies does not only relate to relations as kin, neighbours or friends in the private realm. Care practices also comprise support by professional agents and institutionalized mechanisms of provision of social security. Indeed, the mechanisms by which a society organizes care for those in need can be various: 'It may be more or less institutionalized and institutions may play a stronger or a weaker role in providing social security' (Benda-Beckmann 2015, 326; see also Vuarin 2000, 12). The German welfare state is a strongly institutionalized setting of care, which is the product of a collectivization of care in the context of changing relations of production (cf. de Swaan 1988). In the history of the German welfare state, the combination of increased security for the workforce – through social insurance and employment law – with the consolidation of the nation-state, is the fruit of a historic compromise between capital and labour (Zimmermann 2006, 33). The state became the constitutive Outside of the market, which made capitalist development in Western Europe possible (cf. Polanyi 1944). While the state provides for its citizens, it also promotes the self-propelling individual who ideally should provide for themselves autonomously, and solidifies the boundaries of the family as a sacred unit of support and care. The interactions of the young men with state agents to access public support illustrate this.

The entitlements to welfare programmes in general, and funds to study, insurance for young workers, unemployment benefits and subvention for professional training programmes, in particular, were not only tied to particular categories of employment or family status, age and nationality, but also required relational work (Zelizer 2012). This depended on the ability of the potential recipient to know how to 'play the game' (Bourdieu 1994, 155) in their interactions with state agents. Such knowledge comprised the literacy to understand the meaning (in its literal, but also symbolic sense) of bureaucratic forms and formulas. As a young person, presenting oneself as someone who cared, and who invested in a coherent career and knew what he or she wanted, seemed to be one of the rules of the game in establishing need and deservingness in care relations with state agents.

Salomon was almost 25 years old when we met, and lived at his mother's place in Berlin Hellersdorf. He had been seeking to move out for a while, but did not force it either, as financially it was quite tough to find something affordable in Berlin. Furthermore, his friends, with whom he wanted to move in, did not put much effort into the search for an apartment, and this discouraged Salomon. His mother was fine with letting him stay at her apartment, even though he felt that sooner or later he needed to find something of his own. Until then, his mother had received child benefits for him from the state, but with him starting to work, and turning older than 25, his mother would not be eligible for these benefits any longer.[5] After obtaining a college degree, he commenced professional training as an elderly carer, but quit to get his *Abitur* (A-levels), which he received in 2016. Since then, he had relied on his work as a delivery rider, a midi-job that consisted of twenty-four hours per week, earning €800 including tips per month. He had many encounters with the Jobcentre and the street-level bureaucrats working there. Also, after his A-levels, he went there to ask for help to find a suitable university study programme. During our discussion about his experience with state support programmes, he critically reflected that these programmes created a situation in which receiving money was 'always dependent on some kind of conditions. And this often somehow has a downside, it is most of the time very exhausting. Most of the times, they want to push you into some kind of profession that you don't want to get into.' And this is why he tried to be 'convincing' to them, by pretending that he knew exactly what he wanted:

Salomon: [A]nd in general, it was always quite easy for me to talk to the Jobcentre's state agents. I'm in general, or used to be, a person who was very good at talking very intensely and appearing convincing to people. I always talked in such a way that at the end of a session, for example, they were always fully convinced by me and left me alone again for half a year. That's how I always went through with it [*durchgezogen haben*]. I somehow could always tell myself that I have everything under control. So although that was mostly not the case at all – I was perhaps a bit manipulative. Yes …

Interviewer: What did they want to hear?

Salomon: Pfff. That I – they just wanted to know that I had a real plan. They just wanted me to say, 'Here, this and this is what interests me, this and this is what I want to do, and I did this and this now – without showing anything. (Interview with Salomon, Friedrichshain, 22 August 2017)

Salomon played the game by presenting himself as a self-accruing actor who had goals, and accumulated experiences and competencies (cf. Skeggs 2004). In this way, he could go to the Jobcentre and ask them for advice about his studies, tell them that he had already found a temporary half-time job at a delivery service, and still receive the child benefits, which would have been cut if he was not in school or was already working full time.

Salomon's story shows us the way in which 'institutional logics' (Blokland and Feltran forthcoming) define the distribution of resources in public institutions – entitlements to support operated with clear-cut status categories about youth transitions, such as age limits or status of activity (in training). Ideals of transition to adulthood were connected to norms about intergenerational interdependency and care relations as kin. Once in employment, the child became independent from the family, and parents would not receive any benefits as carers. Salomon understood this game and found a way of dealing with the ways in which state agents operated. Although he did not fit into any of the categories, as he was neither seeking employment nor in professional training, he could provide 'proof' that he intended to remain in the system of career building. He argued that he was currently waiting to begin his studies, even though he had not registered, nor even decided what kind of studies he wanted to pursue.

The strong emphasis on individual efforts in constructing entitlements to public support is part of the activation policy that characterizes the contemporary German welfare state:

> Activation is primarily understood as the strengthening of human capital, in particular through education and qualification policies. Central keywords here are personal responsibility, help for self-help or employability, whereby the 'marketability' of individuals is always the point of reference. In order to make better use of the efficiency

> advantages of markets also in the production of social services, social citizens should be made fit for the market – not only with regard to their material resources, but also with regard to the necessary cognitive abilities and their motivation (willingness to be active). (Ullrich 2004, 146, my own translation; cf. Lessenich 2012, 123–8).

These policies foster norms of deservingness that promote people, on the condition that they show the ability to help themselves and the willingness to be active, self-accruing individuals. Reforms of the unemployment benefits scheme in the mid-2000s instituted a policy of 'demanding and promoting', known as the 'Hartz reforms' (cf., e.g., Konle-Seidl *et al.* 2007). They cemented the idea of unemployment as something self-inflicted, and were a response to public discourse on welfarization. Those depending on social benefits as a result of being out of formal employment would become passive 'social parasites' [*Sozialschmarotzer*] that needed activation instead of care. The Hartz IV reforms reduced benefits, and also introduced more rules and sanctions in their procedures (see Butterwegge 2007, 188). The activation policies hence indicate a shift towards the recommodification of a welfare state that had constituted the Other, outside of the market (e.g. Dörre 2012; Polanyi 1944).

Besides the rules of the game that actors needed to know in order to successfully receive support through public care relations, the increase in regulations and sanctions created feelings of entrapment in interdependencies that constrained agents' control and freedom, and accentuated a feeling of loss of honour so long as one relied on welfare. In some of the stories as to why riders ended up in the delivery job, we see that assistance from welfare state agencies was either difficult to get or avoided, as the expectation of being able to do it alone was strong. As Blokland and Noordhoff (2008, 112) have argued, people who are 'located in positions of structural dependency … [as] they depended on bureaucracies, and their rules and regulations, that curtailed their possibilities to live their lives differently' may try to avoid engaging in further interdependencies, to be able to assert their independence. Victor, for example, ended up as a full-time rider in Berlin after he migrated to Germany from Spain through the mobility programme 'Mobipro'. As Mobipro didn't offer Victor the professional training he wanted, he had contacted an employment agency near where he lived, in Lichtenberg, a district in the former East Berlin, to find information about his professional training options. But the bureaucratic procedures at the agency put him off – in particular, they couldn't communicate with each other as he didn't speak German and the agents weren't able to speak English. But he also looked for unskilled jobs instead of further training, as he didn't want to ask the Jobcentre for a job or any help:

> at the beginning I was searching for [further qualifications], but then after a while and thinking, I just decided it is better to work … [I] t's, this is really funny, because it is about my, *me myself, being proud*, and – *I don't want to ask the job from the Jobcentre. The help.* You know that one for German classes, rent paid, everything. I don't want to ask for that, because I want to do it for myself. (Interview with Victor, Friedrichshain, 3 April 2017, my emphasis)

Theoretically, Victor could get support from a public institution, the Jobcentre in Lichtenberg – but he wanted to 'do it for himself'. For him, it was a matter of pride: he wanted to show that he could do it without the help of institutions, no matter how difficult it was, as he had been helped by them a lot already, like the counsellors in the MobiPro programme or the employees at the Spanish Embassy that gave him information about the education system and social assistance in Germany. Victor expressed in this discourse the imaginary of personhood as the independent individual (Skeggs 2004), which state policies that promote self-sufficiency valorize too. Applying for unemployment benefits, then, appeared to some of my interviewees to be a failure, or like 'giving up' (Interview with Ludwig, Köpenick, 17 August 2017). Against this background, making money as a rider was one way of demonstrating his capacity to get along without help from others.

The situations of Ludwig, Victor, Dennis and Joseph indicate how the recommodification of the welfare state and the ideology of self-sufficiency pushed them to organize their livelihoods through exchange relations. Earning money as delivery riders was fundamental to their survival. The outsourcing of maintenance costs in the platform economy and the cutbacks to entitlements for care derived from work (i.e. paying health insurance as a freelancer in Joseph's case) were risks that riders had to compensate for through their private resources. The norms of deservingness, and feelings of unbearable interdependency in social networks for some of them, pushed them to rely on individualized resources.

By contrast, others, like Torben, introduced earlier in the chapter, or Salomon, played the game and used 'the system' but did not depend on it. They were people who could step in and out of the 'system', as they were not in a situation of structural dependency. Torben, for example, used the job as a delivery rider to obtain the status to gain access to statutory health insurance, instead of paying for private insurance with high fees – he used the job to get entitlements to a share, institutionalized in the healthcare system. Healthcare in Germany is based on the principle of solidarity and organized as statutory health insurance. According to their employment status, residents become entitled to healthcare whose costs are shared between employee and employer.[6] As such, for Torben his activity was distributive labour; it was 'in fact less about producing goods and services ... than it [was] about securing distributive outcomes. [It enabled] accessing or making claims on the resources of others' (Ferguson 2015, 93).

In sum, we see how the orientation towards a side job is for young adults also shaped by their experiences with institutions that could support their transition from school to work and growing up. Redistributive politics like child benefits etc. reproduce the idea of the family as a 'separate social universe' (Bourdieu 1993b, 33). And the recommodification of the welfare state accentuates the importance of privatized care relations. All in all, the maintenance of a sphere of 'non-market' relations, even though not as public welfare institutions, remains fundamental for capitalist accumulation. Workers are not exploited for their labour power only, but companies capitalize on their care relations to ensure the reproduction of their labour power/working tools at low cost, with important consequences for the role of access to private assets and practices of kinning in reproducing inequalities.

Bearing good testimony

You could top up your phone with airtime at the call boxes that popped up across the city of Abidjan. At the same time, the call boxes functioned as advertising platforms for the telecommunications companies. Often, you would find call boxes with sun umbrellas in the colours of the company providing shade to clients and service providers. Or there were billboards and small tables used as sales counters with logos and the corporate design of the company printed on them. This paraphernalia was distributed as 'compensation' (Zelizer 1996): those who had the highest sales, according to the director of the franchise of distribution, would be compensated for their efforts with these working tools. They were not a basic entitlement of all due to their status as airtime sellers, but became a tool used to increase competition among workers and, from the start, only some call box workers had access to them.

It was not surprising that almost all of the airtime selling research participants provided for their working tools privately – similar to van der Linden's (2008) description of 'subaltern workers' who were in between self-employed workers and employees. They owned elements of the means of production,[7] but at the same time depended on price regulation and distribution policies of the telecommunications firms, which were able to regulate their activity through instantaneous control of their sales, as we have seen in the last chapter. Their position in the organization of airtime distribution was such that all risks fell on their own shoulders as workers. They were only selectively provided with working tools that were functional, and none of them were insured against loss; they didn't receive any payment in case of sickness, or insurance that would fund them when they lost their capacity to work (old age), or lost their activity (unemployment).

But the privatization of risks did not individualize their risks. Instead, the airtime sellers built and maintained relationships that provided them with tools, a place and capital to sell – through transactions in which these things were not only commodities, but turned into gifts or objects of barter. Transactions were possible as agents built relationships of a different kind: things circulated between persons that interacted as kin or friends, which made the price and ownership of things negotiable and the time gap between giving and receiving more flexible. As workers, they not only accrued individual capital in the form of individually owned working tools and work spaces, but they tried to get it as a share from others, and kinning was an important practice for establishing legitimate needs.

Séverin, the young man who sold airtime on the pavement of a street in Koumassi, Abidjan, depended on the support of a neighbour who became like a mother to him, as we learned at the beginning of this chapter. The lady's starting capital enabled him to begin selling airtime – and as a gift, Séverin was not expected to pay the capital back in equal terms, like a loan (Interview with Séverin, Koumassi, 3 March 2016). As co-residents, Séverin and the lady emulated categories of kinship to establish care relations: she became a 'mother' through the gifts she gave to Séverin, and through her availability to respond to his needs. These gifts were transactions that tied Séverin and the neighbour in an interdependent relationship in which the expectation of reciprocity was not 'stipulated by time, quantity, quality: the expectation of reciprocity [was] indefinite'. As 'generalized reciprocity', the time and worth of reciprocation was also based on the need and the possibilities the recipient had to give back (Sahlins 1972, 194). Still, it was a hierarchical relationship. Séverin was the lady's junior, and showed her respect and built a good reputation as someone reliable and trustworthy. Kinning encompassed the private realm of intimate relations, to become an important practice for organizing resources by resorting to relations with neighbours. But the intimacy between Séverin and the lady was not a 'pure relationship' in the modernist, bourgeois sense of the term intimacy, defined by 'equality between the parties, a shared sense of self-disclosure and a contribution on an equal footing to the relationship' (Jamieson 1999, 478). Nor was the lady's gift to Séverin only parochial helpfulness addressing a particular situational constraint, such as giving a cup of sugar to a neighbour if they run out temporarily.[8] Séverin received support from the lady beyond a concrete situational constraint. Her help was meant to support him to realize himself, to grow into adulthood, with no concrete beginning or end to the care.[9]

Care relations based on categories of kin and personal dependency extended beyond the private realm of intimate relations. The parochial realm served as a space in which interdependencies as kin were established through practices of care.

Gaining trustworthiness and reputation mattered for Séverin to access relations beyond direct kin: he had to prove that he was reliable to be able to become 'the *bon petit*' of his neighbour. The call box was part of this economy of symbolic goods, in which reputation was an important good to accumulate and maintain, as it enabled the organization of resources through securing distributive outcomes. This is how another seller, Laurent, was able to sell airtime, not only to earn money to increase his individual financial/ economic capital, but also to maintain a status as 'bon petit' in the social relations with his neighbours.

The trustworthiness of someone was also informed by institutionalized categories, such as the status as student, and their willingness to contribute and invest in relationality. David ran a call box together with a friend in Koumassi, in front of his residence. Previously, he had happened to manage a call box for his neighbour, who had been looking for someone and agreed when David presented himself and told him that he would like to manage the call box. He agreed, as he knew that David lived in the neighbourhood and enjoyed a good reputation. David explained to me what made people know whether they could trust someone to manage a call box or other business: 'Well you need to know what the person is like, whether the person is not a villain [*bandit*], as you cannot entrust your meat to a dog, because he would eat it [laughs].' He continued:

> You are in the neighbourhood, you are young, you are a student, you are a bit at school, and you are doing [this] just as a means to get a bit of cash for your own pockets ... But if you are doing nothing, you are in the neighbourhood, you don't do anything – [someone] cannot give you a call box to manage ... Or you can behave well with people. If that is the case, there's no problem – so on the other hand, I don't have a problem with someone, like [you know] I was kind of a good person. So when I went to see him, he told me, no, there's no problem, as we know you, I know you live somewhere over there. (Interview with David, Koumassi, 13 October 2017)

A person's value was defined according to their 'good sociability' with others. David framed it as 'behaving well with people'. He mentioned being seen as a student as a status that facilitated trustworthiness and added to the symbolic capital, so was fundamental to accessing opportunities to organize livelihood. This shows how classification schemes instituted through the (post)colonial state served as a reference point to establish a person's worth in relations of care in the neighbourhood.

After independence, Côte d'Ivoire had invested extensively in the education of its population (Cooper 2002, 212; Crook 1989,

209). As with other governments in sub-Saharan Africa, education was used as a symbol of national progress. It also fit with the development policies of the former colonial regimes in the 1940s, which understood their role as developers who stabilized an (urban) labour force, which remained always partial: in 1988, the modern wage labourer represented only 8 per cent of the labour force in Africa, according to the International Labour Organization (ILO) (see Cooper 2002, 229). In Côte d'Ivoire, Bazin and Gnabéli note an increase in wage labourers from 181,000 people in 1961 to 470,000 in 1980, but 'despite the strong growth from the 1950s to the end of the 1970s, wage employment … remain[ed] the privilege of a minority … particularly in urban areas' (Bazin and Gnabéli 1997, 693, my translation). This minority was for the main part constituted of men.

David's reference to using his position as a student to work on his reputation in his living area shows how powerful the expectation of social mobility through education, with the ultimate goal of ensuring a position as a wage labourer, still was circulating in middle-class areas in Abidjan. This expectation was closely related to the realization of manhood. The social relations established around work were gendered: work was accessible within moral categories of being hard working, decent and gentle. And working was a fundamental way for men to gain a valuable presence in public and domestic spaces, given the 'deeply held and long-standing links between wage labour and a social order premised on the "male-breadwinner"' (Dawson and Fouksman 2020, 236).

The accounts of the airtime sellers I interviewed show, furthermore, a detachment from their work as airtime sellers: they were not lazy, but still not really working either. Taking this position was functional for securing distributive income. They spoke of themselves as having 'no activity', and as jobseekers, to maintain the support relations as 'good unemployed youth', while youth here mainly referred to young men. Maintaining a status as being in education legitimized social support in neighbourhoods where the majority of residents belonged to the lower middle class that had held, at least in previous generations, close relations to the state as employer (cf. Manou-Savina *et al.* 1985). Hence, they saw attending school as the most important activity for social mobility.

Selling airtime further increased David's good reputation, which he calls bearing 'good testimony':

> Well, it had a positive impact. They know, you are not stealing. This is one point. And you know, they know that you are 'hustling', because the fact that you sit down, you sell the airtime units, this means that you are courageous. This is because in order to do it, you must be patient. This is also a good reputation [*temoignage*] … [W]hile waiting, because you didn't get so much yet, and you didn't get work yet, or you didn't get anything to do, this [activity] is helping you. For example, if someone has a store or stuff like this, he can call you to manage it. The people know that you are earning very little, and they will tell you, Ah! *Mon petit*, as you are earning little here, come and manage my store, you will get a bit more. You see, this is also advantageous. (Interview with David, Koumassi, 13 October 2017)

People[10] who saw David sitting at the call box selling airtime helped him by telling him about opportunities for work. They saw that he was 'earning very little' – was in need – but still, he was actively seeking to make the best of his situation, by being 'courageous' and 'patient'. To David, what was good about the phone box was the social ties. 'Because if you are managing a call box, you build more relationships', he explained. Sitting at a corner of the neighbourhood, people passed by, and he was able to do favours in the form of 'parochial helpfulness' (Kusenbach 2006): keeping their keys, money, passing money over to their family members when they were in town. These small favours, practices of neighbouring, served to build a positive image, or reputation. It turned into symbolic capital, 'because [as a consequence,] if there was an opportunity, someone was able to do you a favour, someone was able to help you', according to David (Interview with David, Koumassi, 13 October 2017). For instance, he received some meals for free, prepared by neighbours. Building a good reputation enabled relations of interdependency in which David also accessed work opportunities. To establish a legitimate need, the interviewees needed to be seen as 'decent', 'trustworthy' and 'entrepreneurial' (not as thieves, but rather as patient and courageous). But in this investment in reputation, many interviewees tried to maintain the legitimacy of being 'in need'. David also needed to remain 'junior', that is, a jobseeker, but without stable work. Otherwise, his status in relations of care would change, and he would be approached as the one who others solicit for support. His position legitimized access to a share; hence, managing the call box was also distributive labour, in which the call box activity was less about earning money than about 'securing distributive outcomes' as a young man in Abidjan's lower middle-class neighbourhoods.

Staying a member of a household

Managing a call box was not only a way to establish and maintain relationships with others, a means of building *entregent* (Vuarin 1994) or a web of interdependencies crucial for making claims on rights for support, as the last section has shown. To the young men I got acquainted with, it was also part of their distributive labour to maintain their right of a share as members of a household. Most of the interviewees did not live alone, and most of them did not pay for their shelter through rent or live in a privately owned place. Nor did they provide for their daily meals primarily by buying groceries at the supermarket, in monetarized market-exchange relations. They organized these resources by becoming members of a household as kin. The most recurrent expression for this was to 'live in family', even though their living arrangements did not reproduce those of a nuclear family (cf. Seekings 2008). Households are social projects, and imply norms that regulate membership (Seekings 2008). They are not 'static, unitary and egalitarian' but 'porous, in that individuals are often members of more than one household in the same area, eating with or sleeping under the same roof as or sharing their own resources with more than one other residentially-rooted group of people or "household"' (Seekings 2008, 3). Against this background, how do young men use the selling of airtime as a means to negotiate their household membership?

Boris sold airtime in Yopougon, and lived with his 'kin' [parents], by which he referred to the ten people he lived with, including 'nephews, dad, mum, step-mother'. In the course of our conversation, it turned out that Boris was semi-orphaned, as he had lost his father, which was why at that moment he was staying with his uncle.[11] Boris adored his uncle. To him, he was a respectable man, because of his simplicity (he ate at the same table and not separately from

Boris and the other children), and humility. He greeted everyone, even though he had stable work and hence had obtained a status that allowed him to distance himself from others not of his level, if he chose to. Boris described the relationship to his uncle as one of mutual consideration and respect:

> Well, we get along fine! … he considers me, he respects me, I respect him too … I am major, but at the moment I live under his roof, I will do what he asks me to do … I know where I go, where I can put my feet, this motivates him … Because today, a young man who has nothing like me, he has nothing, but regardless, he has children. I have nothing, so I put myself in the shoes of someone who has nothing. (Interview with Boris, Yopougon, 8 March 2016)

The idiom of kinship here expresses relations of domination, by reformulating them as personalized relations of dependence. 'Material circulation (money, goods) mediates emotional investments: assistance considered satisfactory will be translated into terms of consideration and love … Power and authority are essentially based on an ability to provide assistance' (Bazin 1999, 3). That the need for support could become a burden, and in particular for young men between the ages of 20 and 30, was something that Boris explained further, after I asked him to provide details about the ways that he and those he shared a roof with organized living together as a family. Confronted with my question about these arrangements, Boris was ill at ease. I tried to explain why I wanted to understand better how he contributed to the household, and after a discussion between us, in which I also asked him if he felt upset by my question, he explained:

> I am not getting upset. We[12] are aware of it already, when you live with parents, first of all, if you are in an age of maturity, it is already a shame to go asking the parents for a useless thing. I mean: 'Dad give me hundred francs, give me five hundred francs', you understand, don't you? … We, in this situation, this is what has 'boosted' me to do something, because two or three times like that, it happened already that they refused [to give me money]. So … this is when it did 'click', and I ask myself: what is necessary to do in order to satisfy the parents? So, [as] … the parents have already paid the schooling of their children, up to – well I can say – up to Cocody [where the university is situated], up to the level of university, they pay the schooling of the children. You are enrolling in an elite university, and still, your parents are in charge! So this is already a weight for the

> parents. So what can the child do in order to take something at home? (Interview with Boris, Yopougon, 8 March 2016, my emphasis)

Boris felt he did not contribute enough to the household and couldn't satisfy the parents with whom he lived together. They had paid for his schooling as a gift (Mauss 1954), and Boris felt indebted because he was not giving back. Boris had become old enough to begin working and earning resources to redistribute in the household, to 'bring something back home'. To maintain a bonding relation, Boris felt the obligation[13] to 'do something'. Boris's sense of obligation to give instead of receiving only, made him feel ashamed to ask for resources that exceeded basic daily needs (such as shelter or food). Robert Vuarin (2000, 150) considers shame a regulating principle, and a norm that prevents people from asking generally and permanently for support (see also Marie 1997). Shame affects feelings of worth and a person's status, expressed as a loss of their social honour (cf. Neckel 1991). It shows that establishing need was difficult when it generated a loss of honour, as we discussed in relation to the riders in Berlin earlier.

Boris and other young airtime sellers I met faced this feeling of shame at being in a relation of interdependency in which they had accumulated too much debt and felt an outstanding obligation, by showing, at least symbolically, their willingness to contribute. At times, this obligation was felt very explicitly. Luc, who I met at a call box at a public square in Yopougon, lived at the place of someone he called his brother. The latter lived together with his wife and their three children. Luc aspired to become a footballer in the future. He had left secondary school at the level of the lower secondary school leaving certificate (*troisième*), before graduating. His father had passed away at that time, which was why he left school. While he had begun playing football in his childhood, after leaving school it became his 'project' and he started to play in competitions. But in 2010 he developed health problems, having been injured in football training. This changed his status as a contributor and the support he received at the place he lived. He describes that

> [i]n the beginning, when [the brother] came at home, we chatted ... But over time, at a certain moment, you know, a man, if you are not working because you are injured, even the small gestures at home,

> you can't make them, so I am not doing anything else than sitting around ... This is when they see things differently, they will say that I am lazy, that I am like this and that, so ... this is what made me start working, because they will think that I am lazy, even though it is because I am injured that I can't work ... In Africa, like this ... you can be strong in school, but as you don't have enough resources, people will reject you. This is why for me, my goal is to have money in order to help the family, because a family, it is not only one person who makes a family. If everyone has a bit of money, then the family grows. (Interview with Luc, Yopougon, 23 February 2016)

As Luc was unable to make 'small gestures' that would actualize his legitimate membership of the household, the other members (he refers to a 'they' without specifying) started to make him feel that he was not meeting his obligations to contribute. They called him 'lazy', which Luc took as a rejection. Small gestures of contribution became a valuable good in an economy of symbolic goods and legitimized access to care, to establish need when injured.

Boris and Luc were particularly careful not to put additional weight on the kin relations that provided them with support, which consisted not of their direct parents, but the extended family (uncles or brothers). Luc contrasted his current situation with the time he lived with his father, in which the support, according to him, was unconditional and endless:

> [When] my dad was [still] there, I didn't do anything ... if I needed something ... once I called [him], it [the support] came. I was there, I'm the youngest, I'm the last one in the family. So my dad was in the military, so all I asked for he gave it to me, as I was junior. I slept at my dad's until 2010 [... And even when] I was old ... I knew where he kept his money! And if there was a lot of [money] he wanted to send it to me. He said: Ah it's a sign, you have to take it ... [H]e trusted me so much. If I need money, I'll talk to him, if I only cry it'll come. (Interview with Luc, Yopougon, 23 February 2016)

This indicates that the claims for support interviewees could make on their kin depended also on the radius of responsibilities within kin networks, in which actors differentiated between close and distant kin (cf. Seekings 2008). Luc didn't need to ask, often his father just sent him money, or he would 'cry' and successfully establish his need in this way. This shows that maintaining relations of support required specific performances. In that, what was valued as a contribution that the interviewees had to make in order to maintain the caring relations in the household reproduced imaginaries of success and manhood. The majority of my interviewees had a family background in which investing into formal education and the respective ideals of (male) adulthood, like finding stable employment in public administration or in the service sector more generally, were symbolic resources to become entitled to support as household members. Many of my interlocutors stressed therefore their status as 'students', and experienced the cut in support by kin when they didn't continue educational training, even though the resources to pay for school fees were available in principle.

The call box was, then, a way of managing the relations of debt and expectations around work and male adulthood, as it presented an opportunity to show willingness to contribute to a household economy, while at the same time airtime sellers could still present themselves as aspiring students (Schilling and Dembélé 2019). And it was also a way to avoid asking for support from members of the household or others, and to respond to the increasing economic pressure on households in the context of broader processes of commodification in Côte d'Ivoire. Residents depended more and more on market relations to make a living. Households were constrained to use market exchanges and income-generating activities with the hope of increasing resources to redistribute among household members (cf. Akindès 2000).

Indeed, many of the interviewees started their call box, like Luc, at a moment when the households they were members of faced social or material hardships – the loss of a provider, father, mother, uncle; difficulties to make ends meet and pay for the school fees for the pupils in the household. Since 1985 the poverty rate in Côte d'Ivoire has increased, and between 2008 and 2015 urban poverty rates rose from 29.5 to 35.9 per cent (République de la Côte d'Ivoire 2015, 21). The steady impoverishment of households in Abidjan over the last twenty years combines with social policies which invest in seed funding for projects, encourage individual entrepreneurship among youth and focus on the improvement of young residents' competences to fit the labour market (cf. Kouakou and Koba 2015). But access to these funds is highly competitive and near-impossible, given the disproportion in supply and demand. To the interviewees, this situation was particularly pertinent. They could not change their status as youth or their roles as contributors to households, as they had difficulty in accessing employment that would enable this. In this context of social and symbolic pressure on unemployed graduates, starting to sell airtime was a chance to keep going and accessing entitlements to a share as members of households by sticking to the *illusio* of transitioning through access to public service work. For the companies, it was a situation they could exploit, by using the young residents' cheap labour power and their investment in building *entregent* (see Schilling and Dembélé, 2019). The political support of micro-entrepreneurialism which normalizes informal work arrangements (cf. Meagher and Lindell 2013) further encourages this commodification of labour and labour power.

Distributive labour across public and private realms

Care practices were the starting point in this chapter for studying processes of commodification and the reproduction of inequalities: I studied the role that young men's activity as sellers and riders played in their 'distributive labour', that is, the 'securing of distributive outcomes' outside of their labour-relation (Ferguson 2015, 93). Both activities, food delivery and the sale of airtime, require workers to organize the means of production outside of the companies that use their labour power for producing value. For many interviewees, their risks in case of sickness, work accidents or loss of work are not collectivized and shared with the telecommunications firms, their subcontractors or the delivery platforms. While there are important differences in the contracts of the young workers who participated in the research in Berlin and Abidjan, the situation of these workers is an example of work arrangements in which the status as employee provides few social rights to state welfare. In this situation, care practices need to be studied differently than through a focus on formal entitlements only.

In Berlin, kinning was legitimate as building and maintaining bonds (Blokland 2003) within the private realm. Kin as nuclear family, that is parents, extended perhaps to grandparents (see Samuel), were the most frequently mentioned relational categories through which young workers accessed material support in the form of sharing or gifting (a mobile phone, a place to stay for free). Interdependencies beyond family bonds were difficult to resort to, as friendships were thought to be 'money-free' relationships (Dennis) – which is an example of the demarcation of differentiated fields of market, family and state. Another barrier to interdependencies beyond family bonds was that interviewees like Joseph felt it was important to keep social honour by maintaining a status as independent individuals (cf. Blokland and Noordhoff 2008, 114f.). Accumulating debts created asymmetrical interdependencies that first of all devalued people who were not performing as equal self-accruing individuals (Skeggs 2004), and second, accentuated the feeling of loss of control in the organization of livelihood (Blokland and Noordhoff 2008, 114). These politics of valuation of certain practices of personhood were embedded in gender and intergenerational relations. So particularly from the perspective of young men in Berlin, it was important to acquire a particular form of independency from parents through work. These expectations evoked imaginaries of manhood as breadwinners and providers.

At the same time, kinning through family bonds was a crucial asset, especially against the background of the companies' outsourcing of risks to the workers themselves. This worked not so much as exchange relations between children and parents, i.e. as an exchange of gifts, but as sharing of goods among members of a family. The sharing of resources as kin was an expression of love and mutual attachment, the family turned into a sacred private space, with strong boundaries towards other social realms. The centrality of this kind of kinning through family bonds reproduced inequalities – framed as sharing, it also meant that riders whose communities (families) had few assets to share would risk becoming stuck with fewer resources, and relations of support that bridged private and public realms.

In Abidjan, only the transaction – the sale of airtime – was remunerated to the sellers of airtime (for the transfer of 10,000 FCFA, the seller receives between 4 and 6 per cent of the sum on their cell phone as phone credit). The rest of their efforts – waiting for clients, maintaining the workplace and the working tools, covering the losses and risks of robbery and erroneous transactions – were not compensated by those who benefit from the sales (telecommunications companies and subcontractors, franchises). In such an exploitative context of work, how can we explain why airtime sellers made all these efforts without direct monetary compensation? This chapter has shown that we find answers by considering the selling of airtime also as a means to secure distributive outcomes.

This distributive work fundamentally also comprised the realm of the neighbourhood. Here, interdependencies based on the principle of seniority secured distributive outcomes for the young men who participated in my research. The radius of responsibility, that is, the question of 'who accepts responsibilities for whom, under what circumstances, on what conditions' (Seekings 2008, 5), did not delimit a clear boundary around the nuclear family as the only entity responsible for care. Even though responsibilities for support were distributed gradually between close and more distant kin, interviewees did not delimit kinning to family bonds in the private realm. Kinning in the parochial realm of the neighbourhood was an important way to organize resources to establish and maintain a call box. Getting a share implied here taking on a role as junior, and building a good reputation around that status as someone who was in need of support from those who had more. These asymmetrical interdependencies between elders and juniors required them to build a specific reputation as 'junior', and particularly for the young men under question: in the neighbourhoods of the lower middle classes, expectations of social mobility through education still worked as symbolic capital, and were closely related to gendered norms of becoming adult. For men, it was above all important to gain a legitimate presence in the street as decent, hard-working and non-violent (Schilling and Dembélé 2019), against the background of their widespread problematization as a threat to the public sphere (Cohen 1972; Collignon and Diouf 2001). Through work at the call box, the young men could accumulate such symbolic capital and consolidate their reputation as people worthy of support, because they were trustworthy, courageous and not lazy. For the interviewees, securing distributive outcomes required establishing personal care relations across private and public spaces, in which interdependencies were based on economies of debt that maintained obligations as bonds on which to rely in the future.

Returning to the reproduction of social inequalities, let me conclude by pointing to a core mechanism through which advantages are reproduced in the two contexts. In Berlin, the idea of self-sufficiency, the symbolic value of individual independence from other people or the state as well as the importance of equality in interdependencies, creates difficulties for actors who have fewer resources through family bonds: the sacred space of the family becomes the crucial realm to compensate against the platform companies' outsourcing of risks to the workers. But also in Abidjan, the importance of the principle of seniority in kinning, as a means to establish authority and status, enables asymmetrical interdependencies and care relations in which redistribution takes place, but makes it difficult to transform the status as junior and to access power and resources in a way that would put in danger the monopoly of power and resources of those 'elders' in Côte d'Ivoire.

Notes

1 Also parts of Zelizer's (earlier) work (Zelizer 1994, 2000) risk reifying this particular separation of economic worlds, while she focuses 'on domestic transactions, the bestowing of gifts, and charity', which reifies the idea that 'real care' is situated in families – while in fact, we could ask more openly in what way care relations are important for any other form of social organization (Thelen 2015, 503).

2 Here I keep the word 'labour', to refer to the original concept developed by James Ferguson. In my understanding, however, it would be more correct to call it distributive work.

3 I use family bonds to refer to Blokland's definition of bonds: 'Emotions determine the contents of bonds, although emotions are intrinsically connected to interactions. People bond with unique individuals who are not universally interchangeable. All bonds are interactive and are relatively long-lasting' (Blokland 2003, 73).

4 SCHUFA stands for Schutzgemeinschaft für allgemeine Kreditsicherung (General Credit Protection Agency). It is a credit bureau which provides, for example, proofs about the creditworthiness of consumers who want to rent a flat. The agency holds credit rating information, which it issues via reports to private and corporate customers. On its website, their activity is described as 'work [that] makes it convenient and quick for people to perform transactions and for companies to trust them without knowing them personally' (SCHUFA 2022).

5 Child benefits are a monthly allowance of around €200 per child, transferred by the state for each of the applicant's children (including adopted), step children and foster children until the age of 18,

or 25, on the condition that the child is undertaking training for an occupation. See the Child Benefits Leaflet by the Office of the Family Benefits of the Federal Employment Agency: Bundesagentur für Arbeit 2019.

6 As Reinhard Busse *et al.* (2017, 893) explain in more depth: 'Statutory health insurance is mainly financed through a contribution of 14.6 per cent of wage-related income, which is divided equally between the employee and the employer.' To be health-insured is obligatory if you are a registered resident in Germany, independent of your nationality. Employed citizens and pensioners, and individuals earning less than €57,600 per year (in 2017), have a mandatory statutory health insurance (through their wage or past contributions to social insurance while employed), and their non-earning dependants are insured free of charge. For all those who don't fit into these categories, the individual purchase of private health insurance is possible (see Busse *et al.* 2017, 892f.), or the public health insurance may be paid on one's own. This explains Torben's attempt at attaining formal employment to be insured again through the statutory insurance, as he didn't want to pay for very expensive private or public health insurance.

7 The airtime sellers owned phones as instruments of labour. The mobile phones were means of production and distribution, as these devices allowed connection via radio masts to technological platforms through which airtime was circulated as a commodity.

8 Parochial helpfulness is 'any kind of assistance that does not cost the giver much yet may mean a lot to the receiver because of a particular situational constraint. Actual examples of parochial aid range from small services – such as accepting a package delivery, transferring someone's clothes into the laundry room dryer, or holding an emergency set of keys – to larger ones such as safeguarding a neighbour's plants, home, pets, and even children for a limited period of time' (Kusenbach 2006, 291).

9 Also, it didn't imply she did it because of 'good sentiments' for Séverin.

10 David did not specify who, but used a generalized 'they'.

11 Author's note: this shows that categories of kin did not necessarily indicate, nor overlap with, biological affiliations. Boris explained he lived with a bunch of kin, among them a dad, but presented himself also as semi-orphaned.

12 Referring to his situation as sharing with others, even though they were not specified, turned it into a normal situation, which might alleviate a loss of status that my questions had produced in the interview situation.

13 See here the close etymological relationship between 'obligation' and 'bonding': '"Obligation" derives from Latin ligare, to bind. Bond is an

Anglo-Saxon/Old English term ... Both obligation and bond can imply constraint and captivity, but both can also imply an act one performs on oneself ... In English, "bond" is used for feudal dependency ... whereas in the participle-noun of "bonding" it has become reciprocal and implicitly equal' (Guyer 2012, 493). This further stresses that through his feeling of obligation, Boris maintained the bonding relationship as kin, and was not excluded from it (see Roth 2007).

Not just of symbolic value: work to make oneself living

The last chapters have given voice to the lives of young men who try to make a living through gig work and entrepreneurial activities in the digital economy. Their making of livelihood consisted of accessing resources in different economies – in redistributive economies, in price-making markets, or in economies of gift and debt (reciprocities). The young men drew on relations in and outside of work, and to them, work mattered in different kinds of relations, had different value here, and their making do implied multiple forms of value making. Young men, in exercising a particular activity, i.e. sale of airtime or food delivery, used the activity as members of households, or as citizens in relation to the state. Their practices show that inequalities were reproduced at the intersection of these diverse economies.

The sale of airtime and the delivery of food are also activities that make up urban infrastructures of communication and logistics. The everyday economies of residents like Séverin, Marian or Sam can thus be discussed in their role in contemporary platform urbanisms. Telecommunications and food delivery platforms are distinct socio-technical assemblages. There exist a range of platforms, and in all their heterogeneity there is a shared concern: the attempt to turn platforms into indispensable infrastructures of the everyday (Altenried *et al.* 2021, 13). As a consequence of this endeavour, the platformization of urban life exceeds the 'platform economy', and this is what makes an in-depth analysis of the everyday so fruitful and important. Companies externalize as much of the costs and risks as possible, and at the same time feed our interactions as data points into their calculations and use this information to accrue value. Often, these projects are veiled under narratives of sharing, and praise of the users of platforms. But rather than emancipating urban citizens from commodity exchange and market concentration, this also allows the companies to capture value from populations. 'Urban settings have become especially appetible for platform economies thanks to their unique condensation of cooperative relations, affectivities, and socially diffused knowledges, thus forming the "social factory" of contemporary capitalism' (Rossi 2020, 1107, quoting Negri 2018).

How did the everyday practices of the airtime sellers and food delivery riders feed into the value making of platform companies? We look now at the ways in which entangled economies matter in extractive operations of capital in digital economies, and focus on the relevance of symbolic capital.

Symbolic economies and extractive practices

The young urban residents I met in this research made money as riders and airtime sellers to keep going in their everyday life in Berlin or Abidjan. But as sellers and riders, they not only bought and sold goods and services. Work was more than that. Airtime and shifts were not only transacted as market exchanges or dispatched following the application of the rule of most efficient allocation – airtime and shifts circulated as gifts or shares too. And work was a symbolic resource, a setting in which one could perform practices of cultural distinction. Symbolic investments, like spending time with others and gifting, were important to build reputation, and hence turned into intangible assets, or 'symbolic capital' (Bourdieu 1977). For example, Ludwig, a rider in Berlin, familiarized with his co-workers at the riders' office by drinking beer with them. This disinterested exchange enabled him to build symbolic capital as a 'passionate' rider, motivated and available. This worked, as he conformed to the *perspective* in which certain cultural resources, e.g. a passion for bikes, was legitimized as cultural capital (closure and domination). It enabled Ludwig to get shifts easily, and to access monetary resources to make a living. But also presenting oneself as someone with a 'plan', as the rider Salomon did, provided symbolic resources which conformed to the logic of the field at state organizations like the Jobcentre. The economy of symbolic goods also hindered traffic in interactions – maintaining control and self-reliance were honourable, and riders in Berlin wanted to avoid losing honour in interdependencies where they could accumulate too many debts. In Abidjan, bearing 'good testimonies' (David) through practices of keeping money for others, or being available to them if they needed services, constituted part of an economy of symbolic goods. The sale of airtime turned into such a symbolic good, bestowing airtime, proving your reliability and trustworthiness. At the same time, this economy of symbolic goods hindered traffic when actors did not fit the *situational normalcy*, as in Adou's case. He felt 'doomed' in the neighbourhood as he tried to 'be strict' in selling airtime, and transacted the communication credit as a commodity with a fixed price and as a market exchange.

In short, symbolic capital mattered in work relations and shaped the role of work in organizing livelihood as a young male urban resident. The importance of the symbolic corresponds to some of the characteristics of the digital economy. The digital economy relies on artefacts, immaterial economies, such as the circulation of information, whose value is also a matter of collective recognition and intersubjective validation. The discussion around new forms of prosumption and free labour (Ritzer 2015; Ritzer and Jurgenson 2010; Terranova 2000) in the digital economy stresses the blurring of the boundaries of production and reproduction (see also Knaus *et al.* 2021). Users of platforms contribute, share and read content of other users in a perspective of consumption. Implicitly, however, through their consumption, they produce data that presents value for companies to exploit. These symbolic economies that inform mundane exchange practices as gifts or shares, like writing a message to a friend or liking the new picture of a family member, can be discussed as similar to the economic practices with which the young airtime sellers and food delivery riders organize their livelihoods. The latter participate in the digital economy, with their own calculations and needs – not necessarily compatible with the logic of the firms which exploit them. Hence, commodification is not an encompassing project that subsumes all subjectivities under its logic, but there is a world of sociality that operates with distinct ideas about value and wealth. At the same time, hinges exist between commodified realms and symbolic economies, and different circuits of resources come together. At their intersections, keeping economies incommensurable was beneficial. In this way, labour power could be exploited at a cheap price.

In Abidjan, actors maintained an economy of reciprocity and redistribution in the sale of airtime. The business of mobile telephony could benefit from these economies – it could capitalize on their distributive labour and investment in relationality, without the airtime sellers following principles of market exchange in their transactions. In Berlin, labour power could be used by seizing on an economy of symbolic goods and reputation, as well as on practices of distinction based on different economic practices than those of market exchange. At the same time, these practices were used by the companies to sell their products by reducing the remuneration to those who provided the service – seeing biking as fun and framing it as a challenge to win the next race, and selling airtime as a way to build a positive reputation as an unemployed student looking for work contributed to sustaining these working conditions. Commodification of work did not imply the introduction of an encompassing logic of the market, but was possible because of non-market economies at work, and imaginaries of personhood that did not follow a liberal credo.

The young men in Abidjan used the sale of airtime to develop relationships based on non-market transactions. They seized the possibilities that came with these relationships: organizing a workplace, a store and clients to sell mobile phones. Investing in relationality, in time and energy for others, through 'uninterested' relational work and gifting, was key. Sitting together at bars or in public spaces was a means of passing time together, showing oneself to be in a 'good mood', and being someone able to create a good atmosphere. These turned into valuable skills to build status and value as a person. The companies that monopolized the airtime economy did not offer stable working contexts that could provide the continuous revenues that one would require in order to make a living through investing in market transactions, only based on commodified transactions. The example of Adou indicated this problem. In other words, those who were not investing in relationality, in being and spending time with others, were more exposed to the risk of being marginalized. This way of constructing personhood was a normalcy that worked in institutional settings too. Gérard pointed to this by noting that relationships and money were prerequisites for getting good grades to pass the exam to enter the civil service.

This non-commodified work of relating and spending time together was beneficial to the companies, who seized on this social capital to expand their markets. They maintained the loose attachment of their workers to the companies: airtime sellers were self-entrepreneurs, but through the new technologies, their activities could be surveilled and sanctioned – they were not independent workers. The companies' incentives to create competition among airtime sellers to increase their sales was in principle a technique to further commodify labour. In practice, however, monitors and airtime sellers created work relations in which symbolic economies mattered more than objectified principles of evaluation. Dispatcher and monitor Daniel used the ambivalence of professional roles to create complicity in personalized relations as a means to establish relations of domination. He saw himself not as a 'boss', but also as a 'carer', and could benefit from personal bonds with airtime sellers as much as they could be sure to be supported by him. The young airtime sellers I met shared the *illusio* of the work setting in which loyalty ensured a good reputation, a symbolic capital that had more weight than evaluations of individual work efficiency in statistics. The relational packages were legitimate for organizing the labour process in which categories such as friend, brother, and the bonds that these implied, were matched with transactions that were not gifts (as in Zelizer's typology [1996]), but compensations for work done regulated on the basis of conventions, even though labour here was not a commodity.

Selling airtime was a means to secure distributive outcomes, as a form of distributive labour. It was often an answer to economic hardships of households the interviewees were members of. In this sense, the young men's resort to the sale of airtime was an indicator for a further commodification of their labour power. In an employment-scarce environment like Abidjan, the young men simply were inclined to go and sell their labour power, as part of their strategy to pluralize sources of income as households. At the same time, establishing a call box was also distributive labour – a means to secure distributive outcomes, outside of market transactions. This labour extended from kinning as members of households, to the realm of the neighbourhood in which relations based on the principle of seniority secured distributive outcomes for interviewees. Becoming a member of a household came with obligations to contribute and norms of transition into adulthood. Contributions were not only tied to the status of activity, but also to investment in the right cultural resources that could be transformed into symbolic capital: pursuing school training, or engaging in a career in public service were such ideals of transition into adulthood that those interviewees had to follow who negotiated their membership in households with middle-class backgrounds (see Séverin; Timo). Selling airtime was a way of ensuring the rights to a share as a member of a household, or in care relations beyond the household.

From there, to look at the Berlin context renders visible the importance of the 'non-commodified' spheres and the non-market transactions in shaping the experiences of the work on the ground. Similarly, these were beneficial to the companies too: riding a bike in Berlin as gig worker was not *only* labour, but also a way of gaining prestige: equipping oneself with biker accessories, approaching the job as a game, consuming the 'hip' places of Berlin, were practices of distinction. This attitude towards cycling, the work on your body, as well as language skills, enabled relationships and resourceful transactions among the riders. These cultural resources were exchangeable and valuable as symbolic capital. In a difference from the airtime selling in Abidjan, labour was further commodified in the delivery platform work. The riders were allocated with maximal efficiency in the labour process: shifts were calculated and distributed on the basis of in-time demand, which meant that riders sometimes had shifts cancelled that they had signed up for a week earlier. Furthermore, the workers' contracts were temporary, so they did not have the assurance of being continuously employed by the company. Even though workers had working contracts, the provisionality and overlapping of official rules created a situation of ambivalence. This ambivalence produced uncertainty and mistrust in the rules of the game among the riders, and made them responsible for actively enforcing the rules of the game. This comprised an active monitoring of one's work and non-paid labour as accountant (see Wolfgang) – time that one needed to be able to afford – as well as self-discipline and competition. This demonstrates that a lot of extra work was needed, i.e. unpaid waiting time, doing accounting work, organizing shifts through social capital, in order to undertake the labour. Riders were caught between competing with each other over orders and sharing information about how to get resources at work (see Joseph). These field dynamics reproduced the goal of the company to enforce labour discipline through these tools of quantification.

The companies decreased costs for the reproduction of their labour force by privatizing the responsibility for maintenance work and care. Processes of recommodification of state care and the ideology of self-sustainability as individuals pushed actors to sell their labour power, as we have seen in the stories of Ludwig, Joseph and Victor. But at the same time, some of the young men I met began delivery work also to secure distributive outcomes, like Salomon when he kept his status as youth in search of educational training thanks to his 'in-between work' as a rider.

In both settings, we see that commodifications of labour and labour power were not encompassing. Non-market transactions, like gifts and the struggle for reputation and legitimate relations of interdependencies, were important. For a discussion of precarity in digital economies, we should consider gifts and gift-like bargains, as well as symbolic capital, as central for capitalism, and particularly in digital capitalism (cf. Fourcade and Kluttz 2020): on the one hand, they are central in new extractive operations, in which the frontiers of capital expand towards spaces and subjects constructed as marginal and peripheral (Gago and Mezzadra 2017, 579). In this context, '[w]e are faced with capitalist actors who do not directly organize the social cooperation that they exploit' (Gago and Mezzadra 2017, 579). On the other hand, these symbolic and non-market economies organize the access to resources in social interactions, and as such, become a crucial dimension in relational mechanisms to reproduce inequalities among workers in the digital economy. We will turn to this aspect now.

Entangled economies and inequalities among youth

I have shown that symbolic economies are important for the maintenance of exploitative labour contexts. Taking symbolic economies as a starting point for studying precarity among young men complements an analysis of extractive operations in the political economy of platform urbanisms. At the same time, this focus also innovates how we look at the mechanisms that reproduce inequalities among workers. The different positionalities of the workers to each other are paradigmatic in this labour context, as gig work attracts all kinds of urban dwellers. We should take inequalities among young workers seriously and study them as a pivotal aspect for explaining enduring precarity in youth transitions. Hence, the diverse economic practices are conceptualized as diverse but should also be contextualized in fields of struggle that make certain transactions more plausible than others – with important consequences for access to resources. The starting point to study economic practices was the assumption that in order to access resources, actors interact with each other in roles and relational categories that define the plausibility of certain exchange practices. Zelizer's economic sociology helps us to see these matching processes (Zelizer 2012). However, this research shows the importance of ambivalence in roles: sometimes, relational packages were not consistent. To access resources, delivery riders and airtime sellers needed to be able to play with this ambivalence and have a sense for the ways in which combinations of economic exchange and roles were appropriate in a given context.

For some of my interlocutors in Berlin, asking for support from anyone other than close kin was an action they perceived as risky, as it might place them in inadequate interdependencies. Among the airtime sellers in Abidjan, however, the radius of responsibility in kinning stretched beyond parents and grandparents – co-residents became kin through care practices in which trustworthiness and respect for the principle of seniority were key. In both cases, inequalities were reproduced – in Berlin, those with access to the assets of a 'nuclear family' were further advantaged. The young men in the research drew a strong boundary between private and public relations of care. Family bonds bound to the private realm and that reproduced the idea of a nuclear family, extended perhaps to grandparents (see Salomon), were the most frequently mentioned relations through which young workers accessed material support (a mobile phone, a place to stay for free). Interdependencies beyond family bonds were difficult to resort to, as friendships were thought to be 'money-free' (Dennis), or interviewees like Joseph felt it was important to keep their social honour by maintaining a status as independent individuals. The idea of self-sufficiency, the symbolic value of individual independence from other people or the state, as well as the importance of equality in interdependencies, made it difficult for actors who have fewer resources through family bonds to use other ties to access resources. Maintaining margins for manoeuvre was particularly difficult for interviewees who were, or feared to be back again, in a situation of structural dependency, that is, in need of support through public institutions. In Abidjan, the interviewees' status as youth risked being further perpetuated. The importance of the principle of seniority in kinning, as a means to establish authority and status, enabled asymmetrical interdependencies and care relations in which redistribution took place, but also made it difficult for the young men to transform their status as junior or to access power and resources in a way that would enable them to grow into adults.

This insight expands Zelizer's (2012) conceptual framework on relational work: first, relational packages varied between the cases, depending on the way areas of economic practice were entangled and on the 'role constellations' (see Hannerz 1980, 174) that were legitimate. Second, relational packages consisted of relational categories, forms of transactions and media that were in tension with each other, as contradicting normative expectations, and this was a tension that actors like Daniel maintained in order to uphold positions of power or access to resources more generally. Moreover, the comparative analysis puts into the foreground the context of economic practice and urges us to consider more extensively the rules of the game that make certain transactions plausible. Most importantly, we expanded our view about rules and the construction of legitimacy: rules are not only legally codified; rather, practices become legitimate as they fall in line with what is sayable, thinkable, not necessarily 'right', but legitimate. Legitimacy refers to, first, the validity of rules and, second, the appropriateness of an action or a transaction. Both dimensions are captured in Bourdieu's notion of doxa. Bourdieu's praxeological approach conceives rules as improvisations: 'No game can be understood simply by grasping the rules that define it. It requires not just following rules, but having a sense of the game, a sense of how to play' (Calhoun 2008, 275, on Bourdieu).

In the context of the gig economy, this analytical perspective helps to decentre from the legal regulations and technological law-like arrangements (i.e. algorithmic management) to the ways in which rules were valid over time for the daily practices, and to the ways these were made public or not (black-boxing the dispatching algorithm, for example). I have shown that in Berlin, although platforms were strongly regulated by German labour law, rapid changes in the organization of the labour process, and the companies' black-boxing of the operational rules, generated uncertainties among workers. The interviewees' uncertainty was a matter of being deceived in their trust in the law, rather than the absence of legal regulations. There was too little legal certainty, because the regulations changed too rapidly. Moreover, the young riders in Berlin recognized written rules and statistical numbers as valid, even though they needed to be interpreted and played out in improvised ways in practice. Ludwig, for example, held an ambiguous position as a monitor: his role was not clearly defined. Against this background, he interpreted workers' performance data on the basis of personal evaluations, but restrained from care practices in his role as monitor, as the rules of the game in the field he was working in made it a professional duty to demarcate a boundary between support as mutualizing resources and caring (he speaks of solidarity), and equal treatment of all riders as monitor.

Ambivalence in professional roles, and the fragmentation of legal regulations, was revealed to be productive in the reproduction of relations of domination at work. In contrast, my observations in Abidjan show actors who used ambivalence to reproduce relations of domination, but here through personal bonds and the creation of complicity in the light of the law. Consequently, we see that written rules, legal codes and objectifying numbers had a different weight in constructing legitimate authority to regulate work relations. This was certainly also related to the different weight law and law-like arrangements had in organizing the labour process as such (sale of airtime was not coordinated as much through applications as the platform-based delivery of food). The construction of legitimacy is not referable to the belief in legitimacy of an individual actor, but part of the rules of a game in the particular work setting. To acknowledge this broadens the perspective beyond new surveillance technologies: these alone do not explain discipline at work, but instead the legitimacy of rules, and the regulatory practice of actors that results from them, makes these technologies productive for relations of domination.

Part of this broader perspective is to look at the organization of livelihood beyond the work setting as such. Also here, access to resources is embedded in struggles about the rules of the game. When we look at the young actors' distributive labour, the legitimacy of a claim to get a share is key. It defines the appropriateness of the demand. Remaining a member of the household in Abidjan required making valuable contributions, and what legitimized access to a share of a meal and a place to sleep was embedded in (gendered) imaginaries of personhood: as a young man, one shouldn't be idle, but should strike out to bring something home. Maintaining a status as youth entitled to support by the state in Berlin similarly required knowing how to play the game – including self-presentation as someone who knows what he wants, as in Salomon's case. The process through which claims become appropriate needs further explanation and comparative research, to give a fuller account of how ideas of the state and imaginaries of personhood are produced as doxa of a field, and legitimize or define what is appropriate and valid practice – and eventually become a norm.

Studying the legitimacy of rules at work and the appropriateness of demands in distributive relations complements analyses that stress the heterogeneity of experiences of workers across and within platforms (Cansoy *et al.* 2021; Drahokoupil and Piasna 2019). We can grasp marginalization processes in heterogeneous work settings such as the gig economy, by embedding the gig work in the broader organization of livelihood, which can consist of multiple activities and forms of economic practices. In addition, this shows how relational mechanisms such as social closure create further disadvantage for those workers who mostly depend on their income through platform work. This accumulation of disadvantage, or risk of remaining caught in enduring precarity as gig workers, also points to the temporality as a structuring dimension of inequalities in and through work. We will now look at the ways in which temporality becomes an organizing logic and what this means for belonging and storing of resources.

Becoming in times of permanent temporariness

The focus on the entanglement of economic practices not only helps us to see extractive operations and the appropriation of everyday life by platform companies and telecommunication firms. The fragmentation of work in the digital era also politicizes the role of work for becoming a person of value. To be able to capture this, I conceived work as constituted by diverse sets of economic practices, and thought work through the everyday – that is, focused on 'the ways in which it is experienced and understood in everyday life; its entanglement with other activities, relations and projects' (Monteith *et al.* 2021, 11). What the chapters have shown, each in their own way, is that the young men used their activity as delivery riders or airtime sellers also as a means to construct their social existence in the two cities. They did not always understand their activity in terms of work and professional identity. In Berlin, for example, riders gained prestige through displaying sportiness and individualized style, calling the delivery fun and treating the job as a game. In Abidjan, investing in time and energy for others helped airtime sellers to build 'wealth in people'. The young men I met were able to gain a reputation as active, trustworthy and engaged youth, to become entitled to make claims on their relations as kin or neighbours.

Bringing into dialogue the experiences of workers in Berlin and Abidjan helps us to discuss more openly the roles and performances that give actors value as persons and make them count in interactions. Performing an enterprising self was important in Berlin: correct remuneration and access to shifts and bonus payments at work required self-responsibility of the riders (see the story of Wolfgang) and the possibility to invest time in this extra-work. As a monitor, Ludwig evaluated riders for showing self-motivation. For the riders I met, accruing cultural resources as an individual was a shared *perspective* that gave them access to resourceful social relations at work. At the same time, maintaining an image as a self-reliant individual hindered some of the young men in asking for a share from others when needed, particularly for those in structural dependencies.

As such, the comparative analysis provincializes the possessive individual as a particular form through which actors bring themselves into existence in their webs of relations. At the same time, it reveals similar mechanisms in both settings: for young men in Abidjan and Berlin, organizing resources required both distancing from others to accumulate resources for themselves as individuals, and familiarizing with others in order to stay in the game. Riders found routes far away from other riders to increase their likelihood of getting orders, and airtime sellers saved their profits made at the call box to pay for the next *concours*. But also spending time drinking beer with other riders or waiting with them at a public square were valuable practices in Berlin. They allowed riders to become familiar with other riders and helped them become someone who has weight and who matters, as they got recognized by others and acquired knowledge in how to play the game in a work arrangement characterized by temporariness, deinstitutionalized professional status positions, and rapid changes in the rules of the game. Airtime sellers, too, made themselves known as valuable persons, by hanging out with others in restaurants, taking the time to chat, offering services 'for free', without expectation of remuneration. This familiarity created 'complicity' (Daniel) and a shared history which could serve to access a share in the future.

Looking at imaginaries of personhood and *perspective*s enables a common frame of analysis: we can carve out how particular ideals of 'individuality' and 'communality' structure inequalities and figurations of interdependencies and the relational packages in economic practice to make a living in Abidjan and Berlin. I did this by situating these ideals historically, and as (re)produced in state practices (e.g. the activation policies in Germany). These ideals are sustained through institutional practices, and imply notions of masculinity. Figurations of interdependencies are as such deeply gendered. Ideas about laziness, as put forward by one young man in Abidjan, pointed to when discussing his investment into airtime selling, or expectations about financial autonomy, as in the case of a young rider in Berlin, show that economic practices are enmeshed in the doing of masculinity. The delivery job and the airtime selling are both areas of activity in which young men are particularly visible, and in which certain practices of masculinity, such as physical performance, speed and competition, or presence in the public space, day and night, structure the spaces of work. The few conversations with women in both fields show their struggles to fit into this culture of work, with marginalizing effects, which again feed into gendered experiences of precarity.

Last but not least, both activities, airtime selling and delivering food, were ways to make money temporarily. The interviewees conceived of the activities as temporary sources of income; they were in a situation of transition to adulthood. In this temporariness, how do actors transform resources into value over time, or transfer them into other forms of value? Bourdieu's sociology of different sorts of capitals (see his typology of social, cultural and economic capital [1983]) becomes difficult to maintain as a common frame of analysis, when comparing the contexts of riders and airtime sellers. Obtaining a bachelor's degree or a professional qualification as an electrical engineer did not ensure access to labour and status positions as an employee in Abidjan. Objectified mechanisms of social reproduction, that is, the reproduction of positions through institutional titles and capitals, did not work as expected. Value was not stored as institutional capitals, but rather through building *entregent*, a standing in interpersonal relations which could serve as credit and which attributed value as a person (i.e. in the concept of the big man or wealth in people). As the story of the dispatcher Daniel showed, as a co-worker, he did not rely on his professional role of dispatcher and supervisor to attribute resources, but used kinship roles to maintain work relations and economies of distribution at work. This did not make diplomas and professional roles obsolete: they served as symbolic goods to transfer into social capital to access material resources. Airtime sellers kept the image of their status as students to access rights to a share in households and neighbourhoods. This implied the hoarding of opportunity through boundary work which emulates institutionalized categories of cultural stratification (as language competencies in French and level of formal education). The 'game' to reproduce social positions through access to formal education and access to salaried work seems to remain intact, while the transversion of cultural capitals into labour positions was not working accordingly. This contrasts to the context of young men in Berlin, where the norm of flexibility of work and seeing the job as a side activity which was 'fun' to do, risked entrapping in enduring material and social insecurity those who were not able to acquire institutionalized cultural capital – that is, formal qualifications – in parallel. Consequently, a sociology of unstable work in digital economies should broaden the perspective to other forms of storing of value.

At the same time, the temporality of the work is an example of how time turned into a structuring dimension of reproducing inequalities. Companies in both case studies could attract young residents with flexible work conditions, but at the same time, in this discourse on convenience and flexibility among the interviewees, a long-term perspective on the making of livelihood as a delivery rider or airtime seller was absent. The temporariness of the *now* was liveable, as the promise of change in the future was for many interviewees still tangible, although less so in Abidjan, but definitely in Berlin. Here, the idea that it didn't matter what you become, unless you become who *you* want to be, made a permanent temporariness a valuable situation, to which making money as a rider fitted.

Flexibility was liveable in the long term only from a particular starting point and position. In Berlin, being positioned as a young, male, white student was advantageous to convert and reuse cultural capital throughout the life course and reproduce one's own privileges in that way. Similarly, in Abidjan, even though institutional cultural capital was not directly transferrable into work positions and economic capital, being a student constituted symbolic capital that was important to building relations that would eventually help to gain access to economic resources and social status.

These processes of closure, the detachment from the work as professional status and the temporal character of the activity also made it difficult to build viable alliances for protest. The tension between the temporary and the long term did not only unfold in processes of closure at work among riders. Also relations of exploitation of airtime sellers and riders built on the tension in capitalist accumulation between time-spaces of production and reproduction. Capitalism needs reproductive activities, and the drive towards unlimited accumulation stands in contradiction to the time needed to reproduce the resources and capacities to keep production going (Fraser 2016). The digital economies I studied use the labour power of young residents in a highly flexible manner. For many interviewees, their risks in case of sickness, work accidents or loss of work were not collectivized and shared with the telecommunications firms, their subcontractors or the delivery platforms. This turned the organization of care to crucial practices through which inequalities were reproduced. Those privileged in capital through close kin were further advantaged. The interviewees who had to rely on other care relations either maintained a status as junior, as Séverin did in Abidjan, or the traffic of resources was blocked when the ideal of a self-reliant individual made it difficult to use ties outside of close kin, as in the case of Joseph in Berlin. The introduction of market logics into welfare programmes in both countries made access to care in private or parochial realms even more important.

Future research on the reproduction of inequalities in processes of commodification should elaborate further on this tension between the temporariness in the everyday organization of the livelihoods of young residents and social reproduction in the *longue durée*. The analysis showed interviewees' making of livelihood not in stable, differentiated fields. This invites a further exploration into what gives actors faith to endure in cities (Simone 2018) where situations of permanent temporariness become generic (cf. Schilling *et al.* 2019).

Epilogue

While finishing this book, the sale of airtime and the deliveries for Foodora and Deliveroo have changed their guise. The logos of Orange, Moov and MTN continue to plaster the street sides in Abidjan. The telecommunication companies have expanded their services, turning into digital banks and platforms to enrol for financial products such as insurance or subscriptions for electricity. New urban practices have emerged, such as the uberization of the transport industry and the digitalization of informal trade, with the help of platforms like Jumia Food and Glovo (see Akindès and Kouamé 2019). Prepaid communication is increasingly being replaced by subscriptions paid via mobile money, which makes the sale of communication credit in the street a less lucrative business. Young urban dwellers might hence move on to new activities and repurpose the call box, which remains an important urban hub for exchange and sociality.

In Berlin, the delivery riders changed their uniforms, several times, since we met in the streets in 2017: in 2018, the company Takeaway took over the German brands Foodora, Pizza.de and Lieferheld. The Berlin company Delivery Hero received more than €1 billion for its three German delivery services.[1] In 2020, the lockdown policies in Berlin and elsewhere in the world due to the Covid-19 pandemic made 'stay at home' or 'work from home' industries even more attractive: the stock value for these industries rose remarkably, and the 'delivery platforms, from Takeaway.com to Amazon, also grew exponentially' (Altenried *et al.* 2020, 2). New and old actors compete for the market, and each one outdoes the other for its speed in delivery. In this context, the struggles around working conditions as delivery riders gained new momentum in Berlin, as the strikes at the new platform Gorillas show (cf. Bovermann *et al.* 2021).

The dynamic and expanding field of the gig economy brings along with it temporary working positions. The ephemerality of the activities makes it even more important to study social reproduction at the entanglement of different economic fields, where the status of employment is only a starting point from which to reach out to better understand the making of livelihoods in contemporary cities.

Note

1 See an article in Businessinsider (Ksienrzyk 2019).

References

Abbink, J., and I. van Kessel (eds) (2005), 'Being young in Africa. The politics of despair and renewal', in *Vanguard or Vandals: Youth, Politics and Conflict in Africa* (Leiden and Boston: Brill), pp. 1–34.

Abbott, A. (2005), 'Sociology of work and occupations', in N. J. Smelser and R. Swedberg (eds), *The Handbook of Economic Sociology* (New York: Princeton University Press), pp. 307–30.

Abidjan.net (2016), 'Les gérants de cabines téléphoniques de Côte d'Ivoire annoncent "une grève le 15 décembre pour réclamer 10% de bénéfice"', https://news.abidjan.net/articles/605747/les-gerants-de-cabines-telephoniques-de-cote-divoire-annoncent-une-greve-le-15-decembre-pour-reclamer-10-de-benefice [accessed 24 July 2019].

Abrams, P. (1988), 'Notes on the difficulty of studying the state (1977)', *Journal of Historical Sociology*, 1:1, 58–89.

AGEPE (2014), *Enquete nationale sur la situation de l'emploi et le travail des enfants (ENSETE 2013): Rapport déscriptif sur la situation de l'emploi: Rapport final* (Côte d'Ivoire: Agence d'Etudes et de Promotion de l'Emploi).

Akindès, F. (2000), 'Inégalités sociales et régulation politique en Côte d'Ivoire', *Politique Africaine*, 2:78, 126–41.

Akindès, F. (2003), 'Côte d'Ivoire: Socio-political crises, "Ivoirité" and the course of history', *African Sociological Review / Revue Africaine de Sociologie*, 7:2, 11–28.

Akindès, F. (2004), *Les Racines de La Crise Militaro-Politique En Côte d'Ivoire* (Dakar: CODESIRA).

Akindès, F. (2008), 'Racines des crises socio-politiques en Côte d'Ivoire et sens de l'histoire', in J.-B. Ouédraogo and E. Sall (eds), *Frontieres de la citoyennete et violence politique en Côte d'Ivoire* (Oxford: African Books Collective), pp. 25–62.

Akindès, F. (2017), '"On ne mange pas les ponts et le goudron": Les sentiers sinueux d'une sortie de crise en Côte d'Ivoire', *Politique Africaine*, 148:4, 5–26.

Akindès, F., and S. Y. Kouamé (2019), 'L'immixtion "par le bas" des technologies digitales dans la vie urbaine africaine', *Afrique Contemporaine*, 269–70:1–2, 87–107 (I–XX).

Alonso, M. F. (2012), 'Social support networks in Spain: The factors that determine models of choice', *International Sociology*, 27:3, 384–402.

AlSayyad, N. (2003), 'Urban informality as a new way of life', in N. AlSayyad and A. Roy (eds), *Urban Informality: Transnational Perspectives from the Middle East, Latin America and South Asia* (Lanham, MD: Lexington Books), pp. 7–29.

Altenried, M., S. Animento and M. Bojadžijev (2021), 'Plattform-Urbanismus. Arbeit, Migration und die Transformation des urbanen Raums', *Sub/urban Zeitschrift für Kritische Stadtforschung*, 9:1/2, 73–92, https://doi.org/10.36900/suburban.v9i1/2.605.

Altenried, M., M. Wallis and M. Bojadžijev (2020), 'Platform im/mobilities: Migration and the gig economy in times of Covid-19', *Routed: Migration & (Im)mobility Magazine*, 10:June, https://www.routedmagazine.com/platform-immobilities [accessed 4 October 2022].

Altvater, E., and B. Mahnkopf (2001), *Globalisierung der Unsicherheit – Arbeit im Schatten, Schmutziges Geld und informelle Politik* (Münster: Westfälisches Dampfboot).

Animento, S., G. Di Cesare and C. Sica (2017), 'Total eclipse of work?', *PROKLA: Zeitschrift Für Kritische Sozialwissenschaft*, 47:187, 271–90, https://doi.org/10.32387/prokla.v47i187.145 [accessed 4 October 2022].

Antoine, P., A. Dubresson and A. Manou-Savina (1987), *Abidjan 'Coté Cours'* (Paris: Karthala et Orstom).

Arbeitsvertrag.org (2022), 'Midijob – Was müssen Arbeitnehmer hier beachten?', https://www.arbeitsvertrag.org/midijob/#Midijob_Definition_Was_ist_das_eigentlich [accessed 1 October 2022].

Archambault, J. S. (2013), 'Cruising through uncertainty: Cell phones and the politics of display and disguise in Inhambane, Mozambique', *American Ethnologist*, 40:1, 88–101, https://doi.org/10.1111/amet.12007 [accessed 4 October 2022].

Archambault, J. S. (2017), *Mobile Secrets* (Chicago: University of Chicago Press), https://www.press.uchicago.edu/ucp/books/book/chicago/M/bo25681045.html [accessed 10 March 2020].

Arnaut, K. (2012), 'Social mobility in times of crisis. Militant youth and the politics of impersonation in Côte d'Ivoire (2002–2011)', MICROCON Research Working Paper 58.

ARTCI (2015), *Données Statistiques Du Secteur Des Télécommunications En Côte d'Ivoire: Troisième Trimestre 2015* (Côte d'Ivoire: Autorité de régulation des télécommunications/TIC de Côte d'Ivoire).

Ayimpam, S. (2014), *Economie de la débrouille à Kinshasa: Informalité, commerce et réseaux sociaux* (Paris: Karthala Editions).

Ball, S., M. Maguire and S. Macrae (2000), *Choice, Pathways and Transitions Post-16: New Youth, New Economies in the Global City* (London: Routledge/Falmer).

Bamba, N., B. Contamin, K. Diomandé and M. Koulibaly (1992), 'Crises economique et programmes d'ajustement structurel en Côte d'Ivoire', in GIDIS-CI (ed.), *Crises et Ajustements En Côte d'Ivoire: Les Dimensions Sociales et Culturelles* (Petit-Bassam, Abidjan: Orstom), pp. 10–23.

Banégas, R. (2007), 'Côte d'Ivoire. Les jeunes "se lèvent en hommes". Anticolonialisme et ultranationalisme chez les Jeunes patriotes d'Abidjan', *Les Etudes Du CERI*, 137, 1–52.

Banégas, R. (2011), 'La politique du "gbonhi". Mobilisations patriotiques, violence milicienne et carrières militantes en Côte-d'Ivoire, Summary', *Genèses*, 81, 25–44, https://doi.org/10.3917/gen.081.0025 [accessed 4 October 2022].

Banégas, R. (2012), 'Reconstruction "post-conflit" violence et politique en Côte d'Ivoire' [White Paper] (CERI Sciences Po).

Barbier, J.-C. (2005), 'La précarité, une catégorie française à l'épreuve de la comparaison internationale', *Revue française de sociologie*, 46:2, 351–71, https://doi.org/10.3917/rfs.462.0351 [accessed 4 October 2022].

Barchiesi, F. (2006), 'Commodification, economic restructuring, and the changing urban geography of labour in post-apartheid South Africa: The case of Gauteng Province, 1991–2001', *Urban Forum*, 17:2, 93–124, https://doi.org/10.1007/s12132-006-0001-z [accessed 4 October 2022].

Baumann, E. (2003), 'Marché du travail, réseaux et capital social', in F. Leimdorfer and A. Marie (eds), *L'Afrique Des Citadins* (Paris: Karthala Editions), pp. 219–92.

Bayat, A. (2013), *Life as Politics: How Ordinary People Change the Middle East* (Stanford, CA: Stanford University Press).

Bazin, L. (1999), 'La parenté: Miroir et enlisement des hiérarchies en Côte-d'Ivoire', *Journal Des Anthropologues*, 2–3:77–8, 193–215, https://doi.org/10.4000/jda.3061 [accessed 4 October 2022].

Bazin, L. (2014), 'Le travail. Un phénomène politique complexe et ses mutations conjoncturelles', *Politique Africaine*, 1:133, 7–33.

Bazin, L., and R. Y. Gnabéli (1997), 'Le travail salarié, un modèle de décomposition?', in B. Contamin and H. Memel-Fote (eds), *Le Modèle Ivoirien En Questions: Crises, Ajustements, Recompositions* (Paris: Karthala Editions), pp. 689–705.

Bear, L. (2014), 'Doubt, conflict, mediation: The anthropology of modern time', *Journal of the Royal Anthropological Institute*, 20:S1, 3–30. doi: 10.1111/1467–9655.12091.

Beck, U., W. Bonss and C. Lau (2003), 'The theory of reflexive modernization: Problematic, hypotheses and research programme', *Theory, Culture*

& Society, 20:2, 1–33, https://doi.org/10.1177/0263276403020002001 [accessed 4 October 2022].
Becker, H. S. (1998), *Tricks of the Trade* (Chicago: Chicago University Press).
Benda-Beckmann, K. von (2014), 'Trust and the temporalities of law', *Journal of Legal Pluralism and Unofficial Law*, 46:1, 1–17, https://doi.org/10.1080/07329113.2014.894743 [accessed 4 October 2022].
Benda-Beckmann, K. von (2015), 'Social security, personhood, and the state', *Asian Journal of Law and Society*, 2:2, 323–38, https://doi.org/10.1017/als.2015.13 [accessed 4 October 2022].
Benton, L. (1994), 'Beyond legal pluralism: Towards a new approach to law in the informal sector', *Social & Legal Studies*, 3:2, 223–42, https://doi.org/10.1177/096466399400300202 [accessed 4 October 2022].
Bernt, M., B. Grell and A. Holm (2013), *The Berlin Reader: A Compendium on Urban Change and Activism* (Bielefeld: Transcript).
Biaya, T. K. (2000), 'Jeunes et culture de la rue en Afrique urbaine: (Addis-Abeba, Dakar et Kinshasa)', *Politique Africaine*, 80:4, 12–31, https://doi.org/10.3917/polaf.080.0012 [accessed 4 October 2022].
Bilgen, A., A. Nasir and J. Schöneberg (2021), 'Why positionalities matter: Reflections on power, hierarchy, and knowledges in "development" research', *Canadian Journal of Development Studies / Revue canadienne d'études du développement*, 42:4, 519–36, https://doi.org/10.1080/02255189.2021.1871593 [accessed 4 October 2022].
Blokland, T. (2003), *Urban Bonds* (Cambridge, UK and Malden, MA: Polity Press).
Blokland, T. (2012), 'Blaming neither the undeserving poor nor the revanchist middle classes: A relational approach to marginalization', *Urban Geography*, 33:4, 488–507, https://doi.org/10.2747/0272-3638.33.4.488 [accessed 4 October 2022].
Blokland, T. (2017), *Community as Urban Practice* (Malden, MA: Polity Press).
Blokland, T. and G. Feltran (forthcoming) 'How institutional and everyday logics reproduce urban inequalities', *Tijdschrift voor Economische en Sociale Geografie (TESG)*.
Blokland, T., C. Giustozzi, D. Krüger and H. Schilling (2016), *Creating the Unequal City: The Exclusionary Consequences of Everyday Routines in Berlin* (Farnham: Routledge).
Blokland, T., and J. Nast (2014), 'From public familiarity to comfort zone: The relevance of absent ties for belonging in Berlin's mixed neighbourhoods', *International Journal of Urban and Regional Research*, 38:4, 1142–59, https://doi.org/10.1111/1468-2427.12126 [accessed 4 October 2022].
Blokland, T., and F. Noordhoff (2008), 'The weakness of weak ties: Social capital to get ahead among the urban poor in Rotterdam and Amsterdam',

in M. Savage and T. Blokland (eds), *Networked Urbanism* (Farnham and Burlington, VT: Ashgate Publishing, Ltd.), pp. 105–25.

Blokland, T., and M. Savage (eds) (2008), *Networked Urbanism* (Farnham: Ashgate).

Boeck, F. de, and A. Honwana (2005), *Makers and Breakers: Children and Youth in Postcolonial Africa* (Oxford: James Currey Publishers).

Bourdieu, P. (1976), 'Les modes de domination', *Actes de la recherche en sciences sociales*, 2:2, 122–32, https://doi.org/10.3406/arss.1976.3456 [accessed 4 October 2022].

Bourdieu, P. (1977), *Outline of a Theory of Practice*, trans. R. Nice (Cambridge and New York: Cambridge University Press).

Bourdieu, P. (1983), 'Okonomisches Kapital, kulturelles Kapital, soziales Kapital', in R. Kreckel (ed.), *Soziale Ungleichheiten: Soziale Welt, Sonderband 2* (Göttingen: Otto Schwarz & Co.), pp. 183–98.

Bourdieu, P. (1993a), 'Esprits d'etat', *Actes de La Recherche En Sciences Sociales*, 96:1, 49–62, https://doi.org/10.3406/arss.1993.3040 [accessed 4 October 2022].

Bourdieu, P. (1993b), 'A propos de la famille comme catégorie réalisée', *Actes de la recherche en sciences sociales*, 100:1, 32–6, https://doi.org/10.3406/arss.1993.3070 [accessed 4 October 2022].

Bourdieu, P. (1994), *Die Feinen Unterschiede* (Frankfurt am Main: Suhrkamp).

Bourdieu, P. (1997), 'Le champ économique', *Actes de la recherche en sciences sociales*, 119:1, 48–66, https://doi.org/10.3406/arss.1997.3229 [accessed 4 October 2022].

Bourdieu, P. (1998), 'The economy of symbolic goods', in *Practical Reason: On the Theory of Action* (Stanford, CA: Stanford University Press), pp. 92–124.

Bourdieu, P. (2000), 'Making the economic habitus. Algerian workers revisited', *Ethnography*, 1:1, 17–41.

Bourdieu, P. (2003), *Méditations Pascaliennes* (Paris: Editions du Seuil).

Bourdieu, P. (2005), 'Principles of economic anthropology', in N. J. Smelser and R. Swedberg (eds), *The Handbook of Economic Sociology* (Princeton, NJ: Princeton University Press), pp. 75–89.

Bovermann, P., S. Hurtz and M. Kläsgen (2021), 'Streiks beim Lieferdienst Gorillas', *Süddeutsche.de*, https://www.sueddeutsche.de/politik/gorillas-lieferando-lieferdienste-lebensmittel-investoren-1.5390049 [accessed 3 October 2021].

Breman, J. (2013), 'A Bogus Concept?', *New Left Review*, 84:2, 130–8.

Breman, J., and M. van der Linden (2014) 'Informalizing the economy: The return of the social question at a global level', *Development and Change*, 45:5, 920–40. https://doi.org/10.1111/dech.12115 [accessed 4 October 2022].

Bröckling, U. (2007), *Das unternehmerische Selbst: Soziologie einer Subjektivierungsform* (Frankfurt am Main: Suhrkamp Verlag).

Bröckling, U. (2015), *The Entrepreneurial Self: Fabricating a New Type of Subject* (Thousand Oaks, CA: SAGE).

Bruijn, M. de, F. B. Nyamnjoh and I. Brinkman (2009), *Mobile Phones: The New Talking Drums of Everyday Africa* (Oxford: African Books Collective).

Buckley, M. (2018), 'Labour and the city: Some notes across theory and research', *Geography Compass*, 12:10, e12400, https://doi.org/10.1111/gec3.12400 [accessed 4 October 2022].

Bundesagentur für Arbeit (2019), *Financial Support*, https://www.arbeitsagentur.de/en/financial-support [accessed 27 April 2019].

Burawoy, M. (2015), 'Facing an unequal world', *Current Sociology*, 63:1, 5–34, https://doi.org/10.1177/0011392114564091 [accessed 4 October 2022].

Burchardt, H.-J., S. Peters and N. Weinmann (2013), 'Prekarität und Informalität. Eine Annäherung in globaler Perspektive', in H.-J. Burchardt, S. Peters and N. Weinmann (eds), *Arbeit in Globaler Perspektive: Prekarität Und Informalität: Eine Annäherung in Globaler Perspektive* (Frankfurt and New York: Campus Verlag), pp. 9–28.

Burrell, J. (2009), 'The field site as a network: A strategy for locating ethnographic research', *Field Methods*, 21:2, 181–99, https://doi.org/10.1177/1525822X08329699 [accessed 4 October 2022].

Busch, M., J. Jeskow and R. Stutz (eds) (2010), *Zwischen Prekarisierung und Protest: Die Lebenslagen und Generationsbilder von Jugendlichen in Ost und West* (Bielefeld: Transcript).

Businessinsider Lexikon (2019), 'Startup', *Businessinsider*, 1 January, https://www.businessinsider.de/gruenderszene/lexikon/begriffe/startup/?interstitial [accessed 5 July 2019].

Busse, R., M. Blümel, F. Knieps and T. Bärnighausen (2017), 'Statutory health insurance in Germany: A health system shaped by 135 years of solidarity, self-governance, and competition', *Lancet*, 390, 882–97.

Butler, J. (2009), *Frames of War: When is Life Grievable?* (London and New York: Verso).

Butterwegge, C. (2007), 'Rechtfertigung, Maßnahmen und Folgen einer neoliberalen (Sozial-)Politik', in C. Butterwegge, B. Lösch and R. Ptak, *Kritik des Neoliberalismus* (Wiesbaden: VS Verlag für Sozialwissenschaften), pp. 135–220, https://doi.org/10.1007/978-3-531-20006-4_3 [accessed 4 October 2022].

Butz, D., and K. Besio (2004), 'The value of autoethnography for field research in transcultural settings', *Professional Geographer*, 56:3, 350–60, https://doi.org/10.1111/j.0033-0124.2004.05603004.x [accessed 4 October 2022].

Calhoun, C. (2008), 'Pierre Bourdieu', in G. Ritzer (ed.), *The Blackwell Companion to Major Contemporary Social Theorists* (Malden and Oxford: John Wiley & Sons), pp. 274–309.

Cansoy, M., S. Eddy, I. Ladegaard and J. B. Schor (2021), 'Homines diversi: Heterogeneous earner behaviors in the platform economy', *Sociologica*, 14:3, 143–65, https://doi.org/10.6092/ISSN.1971-8853/11508 [accessed 4 October 2022].

Carroll, T. (2014), 'Introduction: Financialisation and development in Asia under late capitalism', *Asian Studies Review*, 38:4, 533–43.

Castel, R. (1995), *Les métamorphoses de la question sociale: Une chronique du salariat* (Paris: Fayard).

Castel, R. (2003), *L'Insecurité sociale: Qu'est-ce qu'être protégé?* (Paris: Seuil).

Castel, R., and K. Dörre (2009), *Prekarität, Abstieg, Ausgrenzung: Die soziale Frage am Beginn des 21. Jahrhunderts* (Frankfurt am Main: Campus Verlag).

Castro Varela, M. (2005) 'Prekarität Für Alle?!: Zur Differentiellen Symbolischen und Faktischen Deklassierung von "Migrantinnen". Eine Transnationale Perspektive', *Armut Und Geschlecht*, Bulletin Texte, 16:29/30, 90–102.

Chauveau, J.-P., M. Le Pape and J.-P. O. de Sardan (2001), 'La pluralité des normes et leurs dynamiques en Afrique: Implications pour les politiques publiques', in G. Winter (ed.), *Inégalités et politiques publiques en Afrique: Pluralité des normes et jeux d'acteurs* (Paris: IRD), pp. 145–62, http://www.documentation.ird.fr/hor/fdi:010024542 [accessed 11 November 2017].

Chen, S.-H. (2011), 'Power relations between the researcher and the researched: An analysis of native and nonnative ethnographic interviews', *Field Methods*, 23:2, 119–35. https://doi.org/10.1177/1525822X10387575 [accessed 4 October 2022].

Chéneau-Loquay, A. (2004), 'Comment les NTIC sont-elles compatibles avec l'économie informelle en Afrique?', *Annuaire Francais de Relations Internationales*, 5, 345–63.

Chéneau-Loquay, A. (2010), 'L'Afrique au seuil de la révolution des télécommunications. Les grandes tendances de la diffusion des TIC', *Afrique Contemporaine*, 2:234, 95–112.

Chéneau-Loquay, A. (2012), 'La téléphonie mobile dans les villes africaines. Une adaptation réussie au contexte local', *L'Espace Géographique*, 41:1, 82–93.

Chiodelli, F., and S. Moroni (2014), 'The complex nexus between informality and the law: Reconsidering unauthorised settlements in light of the concept of nomotropism', *Geoforum*, 51, 161–8, https://doi.org/10.1016/j.geoforum.2013.11.004 [accessed 4 October 2022].

Cleaver, F. (2002), 'Reinventing institutions: Bricolage and the social embeddedness of natural resource management', *European Journal of Development Research*, 14:2, 11–30, https://doi.org/10.1080/714000425 [accessed 4 October 2022].

Cohen S. (1972), *Folk Devils and Moral Panics* (London: MacGibbon and Kee Ltd).

Cole, J., and D. Durham (eds) (2007), *Generations and Globalization: Youth, Age, and Family in the New World Economy* (Bloomington: Indiana University Press).

Collignon, R., and M. Diouf (eds) (2001), 'Les jeunes. Hantise de l'espace public dans les sociétés du Sud?', *Autrepart*, 18.

Colomb, C. (2012a), 'Pushing the urban frontier: Temporary uses of space, city marketing, and the creative city discourse in 2000s Berlin', *Journal of Urban Affairs*, 34:2, 131–52, https://doi.org/10.1111/j.1467-9906.2012.00607.x [accessed 4 October 2022].

Colomb, C. (2012b), *Staging the New Berlin: Place Marketing and the Politics of Urban Reinvention Post-1989* (London and New York: Routledge).

Comaroff, J., and J. Comaroff (2000), 'Réfléxions sur la jeunesse. Du passé à la postcolonie', *Politique africaine*, 80:4, 90–110

Comaroff, J., and J. Comaroff (2012), 'Theory from the south: Or, how Euro-America is evolving toward Africa', *Anthropological Forum: A Journal of Social Anthropology and Comparative Sociology*, 22:2, 113–31.

Connell, R. W. (1995) *Masculinities.* (Berkeley: University of California Press).

Contamin, B., and H. Memel-Fote (eds) (1997), *Le Modèle Ivorien En Questions: Crises, Ajustements, Recompositions* (Paris: Karthala et Orstom).

Cooper, F. (2002), *L'Afrique Depuis 1940* (Paris: Payot & Rivages).

Corbin, J., and A. L. Strauss (1990), 'Grounded theory research: Procedures, canons and evaluative criteria', *Zeitschrift Für Soziologie*, 19:6, 418–27.

Costey, P. (2005), 'L'illusio chez Pierre Bourdieu. Les (més)usages d'une notion et son application au cas des universitaires', *Tracés: Revue de Sciences Humaines*, 8, 13–27, https://doi.org/10.4000/traces.2133 [accessed 4 October 2022].

Crook, R. C. (1989), 'Patrimonialism, administrative effectiveness and economic development in Côte D'ivoire', *African Affairs*, 88:351, 205–28, https://doi.org/10.1093/oxfordjournals.afraf.a098161 [accessed 4 October 2022].

Cupers, K., and M. Miessen (2002), *Spaces of Uncertainty* (Wuppertal: Müller & Busmann).

Cutolo, A. (2015), 'Giovani, cadetti et vieux pères. Guerra e riproduzione sociale in Costa d'Avorio', *Anthropologia*, 2:1, 61–84.

Cutolo, A., and R. Banégas (2012), 'Gouverner par la parole: Parlements de la rue, pratiques oratoires et subjectivation politique en Côte d'Ivoire', *Politique Africaine*, 127:3, 21–48.

Dawson, H. J., and E. Fouksman (2020), 'Labour, laziness and distribution: Work imaginaries among the South African unemployed', *Africa: The Journal of the International African Institute*, 90:2, 229–51.

De Broux, Ismael. 2016. *La Téléphonie Mobile à Abidjan: Usagers, Usages et Représentations* (Saarbrücken: Editions universitaires européennes).

De Haan, Leo. J. (2012), 'The livelihood approach: A critical exploration', *Erdkunde*, 66:4, 345–57.

Deliveroo (2017), *Du entscheidest, wann du arbeitest. Mit Deliveroo erhältst du eine hohe Flexibilität, die dir ermöglicht, deinen Tag nach deinen Regeln zu gestalten*, https://deliveroo.de/en/apply [accessed 8 November 2017].

Dembélé, O. (2009), *Migration, Emploi, Pression Foncière et Cohésion Sociale en Cote d'Ivoire* (Geneva: OIM Organisation Internationale pour les Migrations).

Dery, I. (2020), 'Negotiating positionality, reflexivity and power relations in research on men and masculinities in Ghana', *Gender, Place & Culture*, 27:12, 1766–84, https://doi.org/10.1080/0966369X.2020.1748578 [accessed 4 October 2022].

Dietrich, H., and A. Patzina (2018), 'Bogus self-employment in Germany. Also a question of definition' (IAB-Forum), https://www.iab-forum.de/en/bogus-self-employment-in-germany-also-a-question-of-definition [accessed 24 July 2019].

Diewald, M. (1991), *Soziale Beziehungen: Verlust oder Liberalisierung?: Soziale Unterstützung in informellen Netzwerken* (Berlin: Edition Sigma).

Diouf, M. (2003), 'Engaging postcolonial cultures: African youth and public space', *African Studies Review*, 46:2, 1–12, https://doi.org/10.2307/1514823 [accessed 4 October 2022].

Doorn, N. van, and A. Badger (2020), 'Platform capitalism's hidden abode: Producing data assets in the gig economy', *Antipode*, 52:5, 1475–95, https://doi.org/10.1111/anti.12641 [accessed 4 October 2022].

Dörre, K. (2010), 'Die Selbstmanager. Biographien und Lebensentwürfe in unsicheren Zeiten', in A. T. Bolder, R. Epping, R. Klein, G. Reutter and A. Seiverth (eds), *Neue Lebenslaufregimes – Neue Konzepte Der Bildung Erwachsener?* (Wiesbaden: VS Sozialwissenschaften), II, 139–46.

Dörre, K. (2011), 'Capitalism, Landnahme and social time régimes: An outline', *Time & Society*, 20:1, 69–93, https://doi.org/10.1177/0961463X10394965 [accessed 4 October 2022].

Dörre, K. (2012), '*Landnahme*, das Wachstumsdilemma und die "Achsen der Ungleichheit"', *Berliner Journal für Soziologie*, 22:1, 101–28, https://doi.org/10.1007/s11609-012-0176-1 [accessed 4 October 2022].

Dörre, K., and T. Haubner (2018), '*Landnahme* through tests: A useful concept for the sociology of work', in K. Dörre, N. Mayer-Ahuja, D. Sauer and V. Wittke (eds), *Capitalism and Labor: Towards Critical Perspectives* (Frankfurt and New York: Campus Verlag), pp. 71–112.

Doucet, A., and N. Mauthner (2008), 'Qualitative interviewing and feminist research', in P. Alasuutari, L. Bickman and J. Brannen (eds), *The SAGE Handbook of Social Research Methods* (Thousands Oaks, CA: SAGE), pp. 328–34.

Drahokoupil, J., and A. Piasna (2019), 'Work in the platform economy: Deliveroo riders in Belgium and the SMart arrangement', ETUI Working Paper 01.

Eichhorst, W. (2015), *Der Wandel Der Erwerbsformen in Deutschland* (Bonn: Forschungsinstitut zur Zukunft der Arbeit).

Emirbayer, M., and J. Goodwin (1999), 'Network analysis, culture, and the problem of agency', *American Journal of Sociology*, 99:6, 1411–54.

England, K. V. L. (1994) 'Getting personal: Reflexivity, positionality, and feminist research*', *Professional Geographer*, 46:1, 80–9, https://doi.org/10.1111/j.0033-0124.1994.00080.x [accessed 4 October 2022].

Eurofound (2019), 'Individual employment relations', https://www.eurofound.europa.eu/country/germany#individual-employment-relations [accessed 27 April 2019].

Fanon, F. (2008), *Black Skin, White Masks* (New York: Grove Press).

Fauré, Y.-A., and J. F. Médard (1982), *Etat et bourgeoisie en Côte-d'Ivoire: Etudes* (Paris: Karthala).

Federal Government Commissioner for Migration, Refugees and Integration Office for the Equal Treatment of EU Workers (Federal Government Commissioner) (2022), '*Special Forms of Work*', https://www.eu-gleichbehandlungsstelle.de/eugs-en/eu-citizens/information-center/special-forms-of-work/special-forms-of-work-1894218 [accessed 1 October 2022].

Federici, S. (2012), *Revolution at Point Zero: Housework, Reproduction, and Feminist Struggle* (Oakland, CA: PM Press).

Feld, S. L. (1981), 'The focused organization of social ties', *American Journal of Sociology*, 86:5, 1015–35.

Ferguson, J. (2013), 'Declarations of dependence: Labour, personhood, and welfare in southern Africa', *Journal of the Royal Anthropological Institute*, 19:2, 223–42.

Ferguson, J. (2015), *Give a Man a Fish: Reflections on the New Politics of Distribution* (Durham, NC and London: Duke University Press).

Ferguson, J., and T. M. Li (2018), 'Beyond the "proper job": Political-economic analysis after the century of labouring man', PLAAS Working Paper Series, 51.

Fincham, B. (2008), 'Balance is everything: Bicycle messengers, work and leisure', *Sociology*, 42:4, 618–34, https://doi.org/10.1177/0038038508091619 [accessed 4 October 2022].

Foodora (2017), 'Apply as partner courier with Foodora', https://kurier.foodora.de/en/?utm_medium=ats&utm_source=greenhouse&utm_campaign=foodora.contents [accessed 8 November 2017].

Fouksman, E. (2020), 'The moral economy of work: Demanding jobs and deserving money in South Africa', *Economy and Society*, 49:2, 1–25, https://doi.org/10.1080/03085147.2019.1690276 [accessed 4 October 2022].

Fourcade, M., and D. N. Kluttz (2020), 'A Maussian bargain: Accumulation by gift in the digital economy', *Big Data & Society*, 7:1, 1–16, https://doi.org/10.1177/2053951719897092 [accessed 4 October 2022].

Fraser, N. (2016), 'Contradictions of capital and care', *New Left Review*, 100, 99–117.

Freudenschuss, M. (2013), *Prekär Ist Wer?: Der Prekarisierungsdiskurs Als Arena Sozialer Kämpfe* (Münster: Westfälisches Dampfboot/PRO).

Furlong, A. (2009), *Handbook of Youth and Young Adulthood: New Perspectives and Agendas* (London and New York: Routledge).

Gago, V., and S. Mezzadra (2017), 'A critique of the extractive operations of capital: Toward an expanded concept of extractivism', *Rethinking Marxism*, 29:4, 574–91, https://doi.org/10.1080/08935696.2017.1417087 [accessed 4 October 2022].

Gawa, F. (2014), 'Le coupé décalé en Côte d'Ivoire: Sens et enjeux d'un succès musical', *African Sociological Review / Revue Africaine de Sociologie*, 18:1, 112–26.

Go, J. (2013), *Decentering Social Theory*, New edition (Bingley: Emerald Publishing Ltd).

Graham, S., and S. Marvin (2002), *Splintering urbanism: Networked infrastructures, technological mobilities and the urban condition* (Abingdon: Routledge).

Granovetter, M. (1973), 'The strength of weak ties', *American Journal of Sociology*, 78:6, 1360–80.

Granovetter, M. (1974), *Getting a Job: A Study of Contacts and Careers* (Cambridge, MA: Harvard University Press).

Granovetter, M. (1985), 'Economic action and social structure: The problem of embeddedness', *American Journal of Sociology*, 91:3, 481–510.

Guyer, J. (1993), 'Wealth in people and self-realization in equatorial Africa', *Man*, 28:2, 243–65, https://doi.org/10.2307/2803412 [accessed 4 October 2022].

Guyer, J. (1995), 'Wealth in people, wealth in things. Introduction', *Journal of African History*, 36:1, 83–90, https://doi.org/10.1017/S0021853700026980 [accessed 4 October 2022].

Guyer, J. (2004), *Marginal Gains: Monetary Transactions in Atlantic Africa* (Chicago: University of Chicago Press).

Guyer, J. (2012), 'Obligation, binding, debt and responsibility: Provocations about temporality from two new sources', *Social Anthropology*, 20:4, 491–501, https://doi.org/10.1111/j.1469-8676.2012.00217.x [accessed 4 October 2022].

Hahn, H. P., and L. Kibora (2008), 'The domestication of the mobile phone. Oral society and new ICT in Burkina Faso', *Journal of Modern African Studies*, 46:1, 87–109.

Haid, C. G. (2017), 'City life in limbo: Globalizing urban informality and (in)stabilities in informal practice'. Unpublished dissertation, Humboldt-Universität zu Berlin, Berlin.

Hamanys Broux de Ismael, K. (2016), *La Téléphonie Mobile à Abidjan: Usagers, Usages et Représentations* (Saarbrücken: Editions universitaires européennes).

Hanappi, D. (2014), 'Revisiting field theory. On taking Bourdieu to envisioned futures', in A. Christoforou and M. Lainé (eds), *Re-Thinking Economics: Exploring the Work of Pierre Bourdieu* (Abingdon and New York: Routledge), pp. 161–73.

Handelsblatt (2018), 'Delivery Hero verkauft Lieferheld, Foodora und Pizza.de an Takeaway.com', https://www.handelsblatt.com/unternehmen/handel-konsumgueter/lieferdienst-delivery-hero-verkauft-lieferheld-foodora-und-pizza-de-an-takeaway-com/23789062.html [accessed 4 September 2021].

Hann, C. (2018), 'Economic anthropology', in H. Callan (ed.), *The International Encyclopedia of Anthropology* (Oxford: John Wiley & Sons), pp. 1–16, https://doi.org/10.1002/9781118924396.wbiea2194 [accessed 4 October 2022].

Hannerz, U. (1980), *Exploring the City: Inquiries Toward an Urban Anthropology* (New York: Columbia University Press).

Hansen, K. T. (2005), 'Getting stuck in the compound: Some odds against social adulthood in Lusaka, Zambia', *Africa Today*, 51:4, 3–16.

Hansen, K. T., and A. L. Dalsgaard (2008), *Youth and the City in the Global South* (Bloomington: Indiana University Press).

Hart, K. (1973), 'Informal income opportunities and urban employment in Ghana', *Journal of Modern African Studies*, 11:1, 61–89.

Heer, B. (2019), *Cities of Entanglements: Social Life in Johannesburg and Maputo: Through Ethnographic Comparison* (Bielefeld: Transcript Verlag).

Hentschel, C. (2015), 'Postcolonializing Berlin and the fabrication of the urban', *International Journal of Urban and Regional Research*, 39:1, 79–91, https://doi.org/10.1111/1468-2427.12193 [accessed 4 October 2022].

Hepp, R.-D. (2012), *Prekarisierung und Flexibilisierung* (Münster: Westfälisches Dampfboot).

Hilbrandt, H. (2017), 'Everyday urbanism and the everyday state: Negotiating habitat in allotment gardens in Berlin', *Urban Studies*, 56:2, 352–67, https://doi.org/10.1177/0042098017740304 [accessed 4 October 2022].

Hillcoat-Nallétamby, S., and J. E. Phillips (2011), 'Sociological ambivalence revisited', *Sociology*, 45:2, 202–17, https://doi.org/10.1177/0038038510394018 [accessed 4 October 2022].

Hillenkamp, I., F. Lapeyre and A. Lemaître (eds) (2013), *Securing Livelihoods: Informal Economy Practices and Institutions* (Oxford: Oxford University Press).

Huws, U. (2016), 'Logged labour: A new paradigm of work organisation?', *Work Organisation, Labour & Globalisation*, 10:1, 7–26, https://doi.org/10.13169/workorgalaboglob.10.1.0007 [accessed 4 October 2022].

Huws, U., N. H. Spencer and M. Coates (2019), *The Platformisation of work in Europe: Highlights from Research in 13 European Countries* (Brussels and Hatfield: FEPS; UNI Europa; University of Hertfordshire).

Jamieson, L. (1999), 'Intimacy transformed. A critical look at the pure relationship', *Sociology*, 33:3, 477–94.

Jan, A. (2018), 'Livrer à vélo … En attendant mieux', *La Nouvelle Revue du Travail*, 13:July, https://doi.org/10.4000/nrt.3803 [accessed 4 October 2022].

Jansen, D. (2003), *Einführung in die Netzwerkanalyse* (Opladen: Leske + Budrich).

Jansen, A. (2020), *Wachsende Graubereiche in der Beschäftigung: Ein interdisziplinärer Forschungsüberblick über die Entstehung und Entwicklung neuer Arbeits- und Beschäftigungsformen in Deutschland* (Düsseldorf: Hans-Böckler-Stiftung), http://hdl.handle.net/10419/217242 [accessed 4 October 2022].

Jeffrey, C. (2010), 'Geographies of children and youth I: Eroding maps of life', *Progress in Human Geography*, 34:4, 496–505, https://doi.org/10.1177/0309132509348533 [accessed 4 October 2022].

Jörg, S., W. Konrad, B. Andreas, F. Sybille, M. Angela, M. Philipp, *et al.* (2016), *Beware of Smart People! Redefining the Smart City Paradigm towards Inclusive Urbanism: Proceedings of the 2015 'Beware of Smart People!' Symposium* (Berlin: Universitätsverlag der TU Berlin).

Jungwirth, I., and K. Scherschel (2010), 'Ungleich Prekär – Zum Verhältnis von Arbeit, Migration und Geschlecht', in A. Manske and K. Pühl (eds), *Prekarisierung zwischen Anomie und Normalisierung* (Münster: Westfälisches Dampfboot), pp. 110–32.

Kamga, O. (2012), 'Digital technologies and imaginary of uses in the developing world: Mobile phone inroads in the Côte d'Ivoire's social fabric', in V. Kumar and J. Svensson (eds), *Proceedings of M4D 2012*

28–29 February 2012 New Delhi India (Karlstad: Karlstad University Studies), 377–81.

Katz, C. (1994), 'Playing the field: Questions of fieldwork in geography', *Professional Geographer*, 46:1, 67–72, https://doi.org/10.1111/j.0033-0124.1994.00067.x [accessed 4 October 2022].

Katz, C. (2001), 'Vagabond capitalism and the necessity of social reproduction', *Antipode* 33:4, 709–28, https://doi.org/10.1111/1467-8330.00207 [accessed 4 October 2022].

Kendall, J., B. Maurer, P. Machoka and C. Veniard (2012), 'An emerging platform: From money transfer system to mobile money ecosystem', *InnovaTions*, 6:4, 49–64.

Kidder, J. L. (2011), *Urban Flow: Bike Messengers and the City* (Ithaca, NY: Cornell University Press).

Kiyindou, A., K. Anaté and A. Capo-Chichi (eds) (2015), *Quand l'Afrique Réinvente La Téléphonie Mobile* (Paris: L'Harmattan).

Klauser, F., T. Paasche and O. Söderström (2014), 'Michel Foucault and the smart city: Power dynamics inherent in contemporary governing through code', *Environment and Planning D: Society and Space*, 32:5, 869–85, https://doi.org/10.1068/d13041p [accessed 4 October 2022].

Knaus, K., N. Margies and H. Schilling (2021), 'Thinking the city through work: Blurring boundaries of production and reproduction in the age of digital capitalism', *City*, 25:3–4, 303–14, https://doi.org/10.1080/13604813.2021.1939966 [accessed 4 October 2022].

Köhler, C., S. Schröder and S. Weingärtner (2017), 'Arbeitsmärkte. Wirtschaftssoziologische Perspektiven', in A. Maurer (ed.), *Handbuch Der Wirtschaftssoziologie* (Wiesbaden: Springer Fachmedien Wiesbaden), pp. 275–305.

Kohlhagen, D. (2005), 'Frime, escroquerie et cosmopolitisme: Le succès du "coupé-décalé" en Afrique et ailleurs', *Politique Africaine*, 100:4, 92–105, https://doi.org/10.3917/polaf.100.0092 [accessed 4 October 2022].

Kohli, M. (2002), 'Der Institutionalisierte Lebenslauf: Ein Blick Zurück Und Nach Vorn', in J. Allmendinger (ed.), *Entstaatlichung und soziale Sicherheit: Verhandlungen des 31. Kongresses der Deutschen Gesellschaft für Soziologie in Leipzig 2002* (Opladen: Leske + Budrich), pp. 525–45.

Kollmann, T., S. Hensellek, P. B. Jung and L. Kleine-Stegemann (2018), *Deutscher Startup Monitor 2018* (Berlin: Bundesverband Deutsche Startups e.V.).

Kollmann, T., P. B. Jung, L. Kleine-Stegemann, J. Ataee and K. de Cruppe (2020), *Deutscher Startup Monitor 2020* (Berlin: Bundesverband Deutsche Startups e.V.), https://deutscherstartupmonitor.de/wp-content/uploads/2020/09/dsm_2020.pdf [accessed 20 August 2021].

Konaté, Y. (2002), 'Génération zouglou', *Cahiers d'Etudes Africaines*, 42:168, 777–96, https://doi.org/10.4000/etudesafricaines.166 [accessed 4 October 2022].

Koné, G. (2015), *Les jeunes patriotes ou la revanche des porteurs des chaises en Côte d'ivoire* (Côte d'Ivoire: Les Classiques Ivoiriens).

Koné, H. (1999), 'The Ivory Coast (Côte d'Ivoire)', in E. Noam (ed.), *Telecommunications in Africa* (Oxford: Oxford University Press), pp. 141–62.

König, B. (2014), 'Les économies occultes du broutage des jeunes Abidjanais. une dialectique culturelle du changement générationnel', *Autrepart*, 71:3, 195–216.

Konle-Seidl, R., W. Eichhorst and M. Grienberger-Zingerle (2007), 'Activation policies in Germany. From status protection to basic income support', IAB Discussion Paper 6.

Kouakou, C. K. (2011), *Urban Youth Labour: Supply and Employment Policy in Côte d'Ivoire* (Kenya: African Economic Research Consortium).

Kouakou, C. K., and A. T. Koba (2015), *L'emplois Des Jeunes En Côte d'Ivoire: Une Étude Diagnostique* (Ottawa: Centre de recherches pour le développement international).

Krämer, K. (2014), 'Prekarisierung', *Soziologische Revue*, 37(4), 437–44, https://doi.org/10.1515/srsr-2014-0072 [accessed 4 October 2022].

Ksienrzyk, L. (2019), 'Kein Pink mehr auf den Straßen: Foodora ist jetzt Lieferando', *Businessinsider*, 18 April, https://www.businessinsider.de/gruenderszene/food/foodora-lieferando-integration/?interstitial [accessed 15 July 2019].

Kusenbach, M. (2006), 'Patterns of neighboring: Practicing community in the parochial realm', *Symbolic Interaction*, 29:3, 279–306, https://doi.org/10.1525/si.2006.29.3.279 [accessed 4 October 2022].

Ladd, B. (2012), 'Staging the New Berlin: Place marketing and the politics of urban reinvention post-1989', *Planning Perspectives*, 27:3, 478–9, https://doi.org/10.1080/02665433.2012.680284 [accessed 4 October 2022].

Laffont, J.-J., and T. N'Guessan (2002), *Telecommunications Reform in Côte d'Ivoire*, Policy Research Working Paper 2895 (Washington, DC: World Bank), https://doi.org/10.1596/1813-9450-2895 [accessed 4 October 2022].

Lamont, M., and V. Molnár (2002), 'The study of boundaries in the social sciences', *Annual Review of Sociology*, 28, 167–95.

Lanz, S. (2007), *Berlin Aufgemischt: Abendländisch, Multikulturell, Kosmopolitisch?: Die Politische Konstruktion Einer Einwanderungsstadt* (Bielefeld: Transcript Verlag), https://doi.org/10.14361/9783839407899 [accessed 4 October 2022].

Lanz, S. (2013), 'Berlin diversities. The perpetual act of becoming of a true metropolis', in M. Bernt, B. Grell and A. Holm (eds), *The Berlin*

Reader: A Compendium on Urban Change (Bielefeld: Transcript Verlag), pp. 207–22.

Larkin, B. (2013), 'The politics and poetics of infrastructure', *Annual Review of Anthropology*, 42:1, 327–43, https://doi.org/10.1146/annurev-anthro-092412-155522 [accessed 4 October 2022].

Laruffa, F., and H. Schilling (2016), 'Work and inequality revisited: A global socio-historical perspective and its political implications', *Sociologia Del Lavoro*, 144, 85–100, https://doi.org/10.3280/SL2016-144006 [accessed 4 October 2022].

Le Pape, M. (1997), *L'energie sociale à Abidjan: Economie politique de la ville en Afrique noire, 1930–1995* (Paris: Karthala Editions).

Ledeneva, A., A. Bailey, S. Barron, C. Curro and E. Teague (eds) (2018), *Global Encyclopaedia of Informality, Volume 1: Towards Understanding of Social and Cultural Complexity* (London: UCL Press), http://www.jstor.org/stable/j.ctt20krxh9 [accessed 4 April 2018].

Lefebvre, H. (1991 [1974]), *The Production of Space* (Oxford: Blackwell).

Lessenich, S. (2012), *Theorien Des Sozialstaats: Zur Einführung* (Hamburg: Junius Verlag).

Levine, D. N. (2006), 'Merton's ambivalence towards autonomous theory: And ours', *Canadian Journal of Sociology / Cahiers Canadiens de Sociologie*, 31:2, 235–43, https://doi.org/10.2307/20058698 [accessed 4 October 2022].

Lewek, M. (2016), 'Spaces of fear and their exclusionary consequences: Narratives and everyday routines of sub-Saharan immigrants in Berlin', in T. Blokland, C. Giustozzi, D. Krüger and H. Schilling (eds), *Creating the Unequal City* (Farnham: Ashgate), pp. 31–52.

Linden, M. van der (2008), *Workers of the World: Essays toward a Global Labor History* (Leiden and Boston: Brill).

Lofland, L. H. (1998), *The Public Realm: Exploring the City's Quintessential Social Territory* (New York: Aldine de Gruyter).

Lont, H. B., and O. Hospes (2004), *Livelihood and Microfinance: Anthropological and Sociological Perspectives on Savings and Debt* (Utrecht: Eburon Uitgeverij B.V.).

Lorey, I. (2010), 'Prekarisierung als Verunsicherung und Entsetzen. Immunisierung, Normalisierung und Neue Furchterregende Subjektivierungsweisen', in A. Manske and K. Pühl (eds), *Prekarisierung Zwischen Anomie Und Normalisierung* (Münster: Westfälisches Dampfboot), pp. 48–81.

Lorey, I. (2017), 'Becoming common: Precarization as political constituting', *E-Flux*, 17:June/July, 1–10.

Loukou, A. F. 2005. 'Télécommunications et développement en Côte d'Ivoire à l'ère de la société de l'information et de la mondialisation'. Dissertation, Université Montpellier.

Loukou, A. F. (2013a), 'Les techniques d'information et de communication (TIC) et l'évolution de l'économique africaine: Vers une hybridation des activités', *Les Enjeux de l'Information et de la Communication*, 14:1, 103–16.

Loukou, A. F. (2013b), 'Les mutations dans le secteur des télécommunications en Côte d'Ivoire et leurs implications', *Revue FRANÇAISE des SCIENCES de l'Information et de la Communication*, 3:July, http://rfsic.revues.org/660 [accessed 1 October 2022].

Lourenço-Lindell, I. (2001), 'Social networks and urban vulnerability to hunger', in A. Tostensen, I. Tvedten and M. Vaa (eds), *Associational Life in African Cities: Popular Responses to the Urban Crisis* (Uppsala: Nordiska Afrikainstitutet), pp. 30–45.

Lourenço-Lindell, I. (2002), *Walking the Tight Rope: Informal Livelihoods and Social Networks in a West African City*, Acta Universitatis Stockholmiensis 9 (Stockholm: Almqvist & Wiksell International).

Lyster, C. (2016), *Learning from Logistics. How Networks Change our Cities* (Basel: Birkhäuser).

Mackert, J. (2004), 'Die Theorie sozialer Schliessung. Das analytische Potential einer Theorie mittlerer Reichweite', in J. Mackert (ed.), *Die Theorie Sozialer Schliessung: Tradition, Analysen, Perspektiven* (Wiesbaden: VS Verlag für Sozialwissenschaften), pp. 9–24.

MacLean, L. M. (2010), *Informal Institutions and Citizenship in Rural Africa: Risk and Reciprocity in Ghana and Côte d'Ivoire* (New York: Cambridge University Press).

MacLeod, J. (1995), *Ain't No Makin' It: Aspirations and Attainment in a Low-Income Neighbourhood* (Boulder, CO, San Francisco and Oxford: Westview Press).

Mahieu, R. (1989), 'Principes de l'économie africaine', *Tiers-Monde*, 30:120, 725–53.

Mains, D. (2007), 'Neoliberal times: Progress, boredom, and shame among young men in urban Ethiopia', *American Ethnologist*, 34:4, 659–73, https://doi.org/10.1525/ae.2007.34.4.659 [accessed 4 October 2022].

Mains, D. (2012), *Hope is Cut: Youth, Unemployment, and the Future in Urban Ethiopia* (Philadelphia, PA: Temple University Press).

Mains, D. (2013), 'Friends and money: Balancing affection and reciprocity among young men in urban Ethiopia', *American Ethnologist*, 40:2, 335–46, https://doi.org/10.1111/amet.12025 [accessed 4 October 2022].

Manou-Savina, A., P. Antoine, A. Dubresson and A. Yapi Diahou (1985), 'Les en-haut des en-bas et les en-bas des en-haut. Classes moyennes et urbanisation à Abidjan (Côte d'Ivoire)', *Revue Tiers Monde*, 26:101, 55–68.

Manske, A., and K. Pühl (eds) (2010), *Prekarisierung zwischen Anomie und Normalisierung* (Münster: Westfälisches Dampfboot).

Marcelli, E., C. C. Williams and P. Joassart (eds) (2010), *Informal Work in Developed Nations* (New York: Routledge).

Marchart, O. (2013), *Die Prekarisierungsgesellschaft: Prekäre Proteste: Politik Und Ökonomie im Zeichen der Prekarisierung* (Bielefeld: Transcript).

Marie, A. (1997), 'Individualisation. Entre communauté et société l'avènement du sujet', in A. Marie and R. Vuarin (eds), *L'Afrique Des Individus: Itinéraires Citadins Dans l'Afrique Contemporain* (Paris: Karthala), pp. 407–3.

Marquardsen, K. (2012), *Aktivierung und Soziale Netzwerke: Die Dynamik Sozialer Beziehungen unter dem Druck der Erwerbslosigkeit* (Wiesbaden: VS Verlag für Sozialwissenschaften).

Masquelier, A. (2005), 'The scorpion's sting: Youth, marriage and the struggle for social maturity in Niger', *Journal of the Royal Anthropological Institute*, 11:1, 59–83, https://doi.org/10.1111/j.1467-9655.2005.00226.x [accessed 4 October 2022].

Masquelier, A. (2019), *Fada: Boredom and Belonging in Niger* (Chicago: University of Chicago Press).

Massey, D. (2005), *For Space* (London: SAGE).

Matlon, J. (2014a), '"Elsewhere": An essay on borderland ethnography in the informal African city', *Ethnography*, 16:2, 145–65, https://doi.org/10.1177/1466138113513527 [accessed 4 October 2022].

Matlon, J. (2014b), 'Côte d'Ivoire. The symbolic capital of the mobile phone', *Global Dialogue*, 4:1, 33–4.

Matlon, J. (2016), 'Racial capitalism and the crisis of black masculinity', *American Sociological Review*, 81:5, 1014–38, https://doi.org/10.1177/0003122416658294 [accessed 4 October 2022].

Maurer, A. (ed.) (2017), *Handbuch der Wirtschaftssoziologie* (Wiesbaden: Springer Fachmedien Wiesbaden).

Mauss, M. (1954), *The Gift: Forms and Functions of Exchange in Archaic Societies* (New York: W. W. Norton).

Mayer-Ahuja, N. (2012), 'Arbeit, Unsicherheit, Informalität', in K. Dörre, D. Sauer and V. Wittke (eds), *Kapitalismustheorie Und Arbeit: Neue Ansätze Soziologischer Kritik* (Frankfurt and New York: Campus Verlag), pp. 289–301.

Mayer-Ahuja, N. (2013), 'Prekär, Informell – Weiblich? Zur Bedeutung von "Gender" für die Aushöhlung Arbeitspolitischer Standards', in H.-J. Burchardt, S. Peters and N. Weinmann (eds), *Arbeit in Globaler Perspektive: Facetten Informeller Beschäftigung* (Frankfurt and New York: Campus Verlag), pp. 55–78.

Mayer-Ahuja, N. (2017), 'Die Globalität Unsicherer Arbeit als Konzeptionelle Provokation. Zum Zusammenhang Zwischen Informalität im "Globalen Süden" und Prekarität im "Globalen Norden"', *Geschichte Und Gesellschaft*, 43, 264–96.

Mbembe, A., and S. Nuttall (2004), 'Writing the world from an African metropolis', *Public Culture*, 16:3, 347–72, https://doi.org/10.1215/08992363-16-3-347 [accessed 4 October 2022].

Mbembe, A., and J. Roitman (1995), 'Figures of the subject in times of crisis', *Public Culture*, 7:2, 323–52, https://doi.org/10.1215/08992363-7-2-323 [accessed 4 October 2022].

McDowell, L. (2003), *Redundant Masculinities?: Employment Change and White Working Class Youth* (Malden and Oxford: Blackwell Publishing).

McFarlane, C. (2010), 'The comparative city: Knowledge, learning, urbanism', *International Journal of Urban and Regional Research*, 34:4, 725–42, https://doi.org/10.1111/j.1468-2427.2010.00917.x [accessed 4 October 2022].

McFarlane, C. (2011), *Learning the City: Knowledge and Translocal Assemblage* (New Jersey: Wiley & Blackwell).

McFarlane, C. (2012), 'Rethinking informality. Politics, crisis and the city', *Planning Theory & Practice*, 13:1, 89–108.

McGovern, M. (2011), *Making War in Côte d'Ivoire*, New edition (Chicago: University of Chicago Press).

McKinsey (2013), *McKinsey Study: Berlin Can Become Europe's Leading Startup Hub* (Berlin: McKinsey & Company).

Meagher, K. (2005), 'Social capital or analytical liability? Social networks and African informal economies', *Global Networks*, 5:3, 217–38, https://doi.org/10.1111/j.1471-0374.2005.00116.x [accessed 4 October 2022].

Meagher, K. (2007), 'Introduction: Special issue on "informal institutions and development in Africa"', *Afrika Spectrum*, 42:3, 405–18.

Meagher, K. (2010), *Identity Economics: Social Networks and the Informal Economy in Nigeria* (Woodbridge: James Currey).

Meagher, K., and I. Lindell (2013), 'ASR forum: Engaging with African informal economies: Social inclusion or adverse incorporation?', *African Studies Review*, 56:3, 57–76, https://doi.org/10.1017/asr.2013.79 [accessed 4 October 2022].

Médard, J.-F. (1992), 'Le "big man" en Afrique: Esquisse d'analyse du politicien entrepreneur', *L'Année Sociologique (1940/1948-)*, 42, 167–92, https://www.jstor.org/stable/27890139 [accessed 4 October 2022].

Meillassoux, C. (1972), 'From reproduction to production: A Marxist approach to economic anthropology', *Economy and Society*, 1:1, 93–105, https://doi.org/10.1080/03085147200000005 [accessed 4 October 2022].

Meillassoux, C. (1979), *Femmes greniers et capitaux* (Paris: Maspero).

Melamed, J. (2015), 'Racial capitalism', *Critical Ethnic Studies*, 1:1, 76–85, https://doi.org/10.5749/jcritethnstud.1.1.0076 [accessed 4 October 2022].

Merton, R. K. (1976), *Sociological Ambivalence and Other Essays* (New York: Free Press).

Merton, R. K., and E. Barber (1963), 'Sociological ambivalence', in E. A. Tiryakian (ed.)', *Sociological Theory, Values and Sociocultural Change: Essays in Honor of Pitirim A. Sorokin* (London: Free Press of Glencoe), pp. 91–120.

Mezzadra, S. (2012), *Wie Viele Geschichten der Arbeit?: Für eine Theorie des Postkolonialen Kapitalismus* (EIPCP), http://eipcp.net/transversal/0112/mezzadra/de [accessed 4 October 2022].

Mignolo, W. (2007), 'Delinking: The rhetoric of modernity, the logic of coloniality and the grammar of de-coloniality', *Cultural Studies*, 21:2–3, 449–514, https://doi.org/10.1080/09502380601162647 [accessed 4 October 2022].

Mignolo, W. (2013), 'On comparison: Who is comparing what and why?', in R. Felski and S. S. Friedman (eds), *Comparison: Theories, Approaches, Uses* (Baltimore, MD: Johns Hopkins University Press), pp. 99–119.

Le Ministère de la Fonction Publique (2019), 'Nomenclature des concours', https://www.fonctionpublique.gouv.ci/index.php/front-page/navigator/statics/menu/recrutement/nomenclature [accessed 8 August 2019].

Ministère de la promotion de la jeunesse, de l'emploi des jeunes et du service civique (MPJEJSC) (2016), *La Politique Nationale de La Jeunesse et Les Stratégies* (Abidjan: République de la Côte d'Ivoire), http://www.jeunesse.gouv.ci/sites/default/files/politique-nationale-a-la-jeunesse.pdf [accessed 4 October 2022].

Ministère d'Etat, Ministère de l'Emploi, des Affaires Sociales et de la Solidarité (2012), *Document de Politique Nationale de l'Emploi adoptée le 7 juin 2012* (Abidjan: République de la Côte d'Ivoire), https://www.ivoirehandicaptv.net/wp-content/uploads/2019/07/PNE-version-finale.pdf [accessed 4 October 2022].

Miran-Guyon, M. (2017), 'Côte d'Ivoire: The return of the elephant?', *Afrique Contemporaine*, 263–4:3, 11–24.

Misztal, B. A. (2001), 'Normality and Trust in Goffman's Theory of Interaction Order', *Sociological Theory*, 19:3, 312–24, https://doi.org/10.1111/0735-2751.00143 [accessed 4 October 2022].

Moebius S., and A. Wetterer (2011) 'Symbolische Gewalt', *Österreichische Zeitschrift für Soziologie*, 36:4, 1–10, https://doi.org/10.1007/s11614-011-0006-2 [accessed 4 October 2022].

Monteith, W. (2020), 'Re-thinking "work" from the global South', *Futures of Work*, 1 April, https://futuresofwork.co.uk/2020/04/01/re-thinking-work-from-the-global-south/ [accessed 25 September 2021].

Monteith, W., D.-O. Vicol and P. Williams (eds) (2021), *Beyond the Wage: Ordinary Work in Diverse Economies* (Bristol: Bristol University Press).

Mosoetsa, S., J. Stillerman and C. Tilly (2016), 'Precarious labor, south and north: An introduction', *International Labor and Working-Class History*, 89:April, 5–19, https://doi.org/10.1017/S0147547916000028 [accessed 4 October 2022].

Motakef, M. (2015), *Prekarisierung* (Bielefeld: Transcript).

Mullings, B. (1999), 'Insider or outsider, both or neither: Some dilemmas of interviewing in a cross-cultural setting', *Geoforum*, 30:4, 337–50.

Munck, R. (2013), 'The Precariat: A view from the South', *Third World Quarterly*, 34:5, 747–62, https://doi.org/10.1080/01436597.2013.800751 [accessed 4 October 2022].

Münnich, S. (2017), 'Netzwerke, Felder und die Wirtschaftssoziologische "Neoklassik". Zentrale Vertreter und Perspektiven der New Economic Sociology', in A. Maurer (ed.), *Handbuch der Wirtschaftssoziologie* (Wiesbaden: Springer Fachmedien Wiesbaden), pp. 107–25.

Münnich, S., and P. Sachweh (2017), 'Einleitung: Varianten des kapitalistischen Geistes im Wandel? Zum schwierigen Verhältnis von Kapitalismus und Kultur', in P. Sachweh and S. Münnich (eds), *Kapitalismus Als Lebensform* (Wiesbaden: Springer VS), pp. 3–26.

Myers, G. (2020), *Rethinking Urbanism: Lessons from Postcolonialism and the Global South* (Bristol: Bristol University Press).

Nachtwey, O., and T. Seidl (2020), 'The solutionist ethic and the spirit of digital capitalism', *SocArXiv*, https://doi.org/10.31235/osf.io/sgjzq [accessed 4 October 2022].

Neckel, S. (1991), *Status Und Scham: Zur Symbolischen Reproduktion Sozialer Ungleichheit* (Frankfurt and New York: Campus Verlag).

Nee, V. (2005), 'The new institutionalisms in economics and sociology', in N. J. Smelser and R. Swedberg (eds), *The Handbook of Economic Sociology* (New York: Princeton University Press), pp. 49–74.

Negri, A. (2018), *From the Factory to the Metropolis: Essays*, Volume 2 (Cambridge: Polity).

Neilson, B., and N. Rossiter (2008), 'Precarity as a political concept, or, Fordism as exception', *Theory, Culture & Society*, 25:7–8, 51–72, https://doi.org/10.1177/0263276408097796 [accessed 4 October 2022].

Neves, D., and A. du Toit (2012), 'Money and sociality in South Africa's informal economy', *Africa*, 82:1, 131–49, https://doi.org/10.1017/S0001972011000763 [accessed 4 October 2022].

Newell, S. (2006), 'Estranged belongings. A moral economy of theft in Abidjan, Côte d'Ivoire', *Anthropological Theory*, 6:2, 179–203, https://doi.org/10.1177/1463499606065034 [accessed 4 October 2022].

Newell, S. (2009), 'Godrap girls, Draou boys, and the sexual economy of the bluff in Abidjan, Côte d'Ivoire', *ETHNOS*, 74:3, 379–402.

Newell, S. (2012), *The Modernity Bluff: Crime, Consumption, and Citizenship in Côte d'Ivoire* (Chicago: Chicago University Press).

Nguessan, J. (2019), *Panorama des Télécommunications/TIC en Côte d'Ivoire* (Autorité de Régulation des Télécommunications/TIC de Côte d'Ivoire (ARTCI)), https://www.itu.int/en/ITU-D/Regional-Presence/Africa/Documents/ICT%20Indicators%202019/Presentations/session-4-cote-divoire-panorama-des-telecoms-tic-fr.pdf [accessed 8 September 2021].

Nickel, H. M. (2009), 'Die 'Prekarier' –Eine Soziologische Kategorie? Anmerkungen aus einer Geschlechtersoziologischen Perspektive', in R. Castel and K. Dörre (eds), *Prekarität, Abstieg, Ausgrenzung* (Frankfurt and New York: Campus Verlag), pp. 209–18.

Nijman, J. (2007), 'Introduction comparative urbanism', *Urban Geography*, 28:1, 1–6.

North, D. C. (1991), 'Institutions', *Journal of Economic Perspectives*, 5:1, 97–112.

Nuttall, S., and A. Mbembe (eds) (2008), *Johannesburg: The Elusive Metropolis* (Durham, NC: Duke University Press).

OECD (2019), *Self-Employment Rate*, https://data.oecd.org/emp/self-employment-rate.htm [accessed 24 July 2019].

Orange Côte d'Ivoire (2020), *Vous Rapprocher de l'essentiel – Orange* (YouTube), https://www.youtube.com/watch?v=Bvlnd4y17aw [accessed 26 May 2021].

Ouédraogo, S. (ed.) (2010), *Dynamiques et rôles économique et social du secteur informel des TIC en Afrique de l'Ouest et du Centre: Cas du Burkina Faso, du Cameroun et du Sénégal. Rapport final de recherche* (Ottawa: International Development Research Centre CRDI), https://idl-bnc-idrc.dspacedirect.org/bitstream/handle/10625/45871/132346.pdf [accessed 26 May 2022].

Paret, M. (2016), 'Towards a precarity agenda', *Global Labour Journal*, 7:2, 111–22.

Paugam, S. (2000), *Le Salarié de la précarité* (Paris: Presses Universitaires de France).

Peck, J. (2015), 'Cities beyond Compare?', *Regional Studies*, 49:1, 160–82, https://doi.org/10.1080/00343404.2014.980801 [accessed 4 October 2022].

Pelizzari, A. (2008), 'Widerständiges Prekariat? Probleme der Interessensvertretung in fragmentierten Arbeitsmärkten', in R. Eickelpasch, C. Rademacher and P. R. Lobato (eds), *Metamorphosen Des Kapitalismus – Und Seine Kritik* (Wiesbaden: VS Verlag für Sozialwissenschaften), pp. 193–215.

Pfaff, J. (2010), 'A mobile phone: Mobility, materiality and everyday Swahili trading practices', *Cultural Geographies*, 17:3, 341–57, https://doi.org/10.1177/1474474010368606 [accessed 4 October 2022].

Pickvance, C. G. (2001), 'Four varieties of comparative analysis', *Journal of Housing and the Built Environment*, 16:1, 7–28, https://doi.org/10.1023/A:1011533211521 [accessed 4 October 2022].

Piot, C. (1999), *Remotely Global: Village Modernity in West Africa* (Chicago: University of Chicago Press).

Polanyi, K. (1944), *The Great Transformation* (New York: Rinehart).

Polanyi, K. (1957), 'The economy as instituted process', in K. Polanyi, C. Arensberg and H. W. Pearson (eds), *Trade and Market in the Early Empires: Economies in History and Theory* (New York: Free Press), pp. 243–70.

Portes, A. (2006), 'Institutions and development: A conceptual reanalysis', *Population and Development Review*, 32:2, 233–62, https://doi.org/10.1111/j.1728-4457.2006.00117.x [accessed 4 October 2022].

Portes, A. (2010), *Economic Sociology: A Systematic Inquiry* (Princeton, NJ: Princeton University Press).

Portes, A., M. Castells and L. A. Benton (eds) (1989), *The Informal Economy: Studies in Advanced and Less Developed Countries* (Baltimore, MD: Johns Hopkins University Press).

Precarias a la deriva (2004), *Streifzüge durch die Kreisläufe feminisierter prekärer Arbeit*, https://transversal.at/transversal/0704/precarias-a-la-deriva/de [accessed 26 May 2022].

Proteau, L. (2002), *Passions scolaires en Côte d'Ivoire: Ecole, état et société* (Paris: Karthala Editions).

Przyborski, A., and M. Wohlrab-Sahr (2009), *Qualitative Sozialforschung: Ein Arbeitsbuch* (München: Oldenbourg).

Ravenelle, A. J. (2019), *Hustle and Gig: Struggling and Surviving in the Sharing Economy* (Berkeley: University of California Press).

Reckinger, G. (2010), *Perspektive Prekarität: Wege benachteiligter Jugendlicher in den transformierten Arbeitsmarkt* (Konstanz: UVK Verlagsgesellschaft).

Reckwitz, A. (2002), 'Toward a theory of social practices: A development in culturalist theorizing', *European Journal of Social Theory*, 5:2, 243–63, https://doi.org/10.1177/13684310222225432 [accessed 4 October 2022].

Reiners, D. (2010), *Verinnerlichte Prekarität: Jugendliche MigrantInnen am Rande der Arbeitsgesellschaft* (Konstanz: UVK Verlagsgesellschaft).

Rekhviashvili, L. (2015), 'Counterbalancing marketization informally. Institutional reforms and informal economic practices in Georgia (2003–2012)'. Dissertation, Central European University, Budapest.

République de la Côte d'Ivoire (2015), *Enquete sur le niveau de vie des menages en Côte d'Ivoire (ENV 2015)* (Abidjan: Ministère d'Etat, Ministère du Plan et du Developpement).

Richardson, L. (2018), 'Platforms as urban technology?', *Mediapolis: A Journal of Cities and Culture* 3:4, https://www.mediapolisjournal.com/2018/11/platforms-as-urban-technology/ [accessed 22 April 2020].

Ritzer, G. (2015), 'Prosumer capitalism', *Sociological Quarterly*, 56:3, 413–45, https://doi.org/10.1111/tsq.12105 [accessed 4 October 2022].

Ritzer, G., and N. Jurgenson (2010), 'Production, consumption, prosumption: The nature of capitalism in the age of the digital "prosumer"', *Journal of Consumer Culture*, 10:1, 13–36, https://doi.org/10.1177/1469540509354673 [accessed 4 October 2022].

Robinson, J. (2002), 'Global and world cities: A view from off the map', *International Journal of Urban and Regional Research*, 26:3, 531–54, https://doi.org/10.1111/1468-2427.00397 [accessed 4 October 2022].

Robinson, J. (2004), 'In the Tracks of Comparative Urbanism: Difference, Urban Modernity and the Primitive'. *Urban Geography* 25(8):709–23, https://doi.org/10.2747/0272-3638.25.8.709 [accessed 4 October 2022].

Robinson, J. (2006), *Ordinary Cities: Between Modernity and Development*, New edition (London and New York: Routledge).

Robinson, J. (2011), 'Cities in a world of cities: The comparative gesture', *International Journal of Urban and Regional Research*, 35:1, 1–23, https://doi.org/10.1111/j.1468-2427.2010.00982.x [accessed 4 October 2022].

Robinson, J. (2015), 'Thinking cities through elsewhere: Comparative tactics for a more global urban studies', *Progress in Human Geography*, [early view], 1–27, https://doi.org/10.1177/0309132515598025 [accessed 4 October 2022].

Robinson, J. (2016), 'Thinking cities through elsewhere: Comparative tactics for a more global urban studies', *Progress in Human Geography*, 40:1, 3–29, https://doi.org/10.1177/0309132515598025 [accessed 4 October 2022].

Rodgers, S., and S. Moore (2018), 'Platform urbanism: An introduction', *Mediapolis Roundtables*, 4(3), https://www.mediapolisjournal.com/2018/10/platform-urbanism-an-introduction [accessed 1 October 2022].

Rosenblat, A. (2018), *Uberland: How Algorithms are Rewriting the Rules of Work* (Berkeley: University of California Press).

Rossi, U. (2019), 'The common-seekers: Capturing and reclaiming value in the platform metropolis', *Environment and Planning C: Politics and Space*, 37:8, 1418–33, https://doi.org/10.1177/2399654419830975 [accessed 4 October 2022].

Rossi, U. (2020), 'Fake friends: The illusionist revision of Western urbanology at the time of platform capitalism', *Urban Studies*, 57:5, 1105–17, https://doi.org/10.1177/0042098018821581 [accessed 4 October 2022].

Rossi, U., and A. Di Bella (2017), 'Start-up urbanism: New York, Rio de Janeiro and the global urbanization of technology-based economies',

Environment and Planning A, 49:5, 999–1018, https://doi.org/10.1177/0308518X17690153 [accessed 4 October 2022].

Rossiter, N., and B. Neilson (2005), 'From precarity to precariousness and back again: Labour, life and unstable networks', *Fibreculture Journal*, 5, http://five.fibreculturejournal.org/fcj-022-from-precarity-to-precariousness-and-back-again-labour-life-and-unstable-networks/ [accessed 26 May 2022].

Roth, C. (2007), '"Tu ne peux pas rejeter ton enfant !" Contrat entre les générations, sécurité sociale et vieillesse en milieu urbain Burkinabé', *Cahiers d'Etudes Africaines*, 1:185, 93–116.

Roy, A. (2011), 'Conclusion. Postcolonial urbanism: Speed, hysteria, mass dreams', in A. Roy and A. Ong, *Worlding Cities: Asian Experiments and the Art of Being Global* (Chichester and Malden, MA: Wiley-Blackwell), pp. 307–35.

Sadowski, J. (2020), 'The Internet of landlords: Digital platforms and new mechanisms of rentier capitalism', *Antipode*, 52:2, 562–80, https://doi.org/10.1111/anti.12595 [accessed 4 October 2022].

Sahlins, M. D. (1963), 'Poor man, rich man, big-man, chief: Political types in Melanesia and Polynesia', *Comparative Studies in Society and History*, 5:3, 285–303, https://doi.org/10.1017/S0010417500001729 [accessed 4 October 2022].

Sahlins, M. D. (1972), *Stone Age Economics* (New York: Aldine de Gruyter).

Sassen, S. (2001), *The Global City: New York, London, Tokyo* (Princeton, NJ: Princeton University Press).

Sayer, A. (1992), *Method in Social Science: A Realist Approach*, 2nd edition (New York: Routledge).

Sayer, A. (2015), 'Critical realism in geography', in *International Encyclopedia of the Social & Behavioral Sciences* (Amsterdam: Elsevier), pp. 277–80, https://doi.org/10.1016/B978-0-08-097086-8.72010-1 [accessed 4 October 2022].

Scherschel, K., M. Krenn and P. Streckeisen (2012), *Neue Prekarität: Die Folgen aktivierender Arbeitsmarktpolitik – Europäische Länder im Vergleich* (Frankfurt and New York: Campus Verlag).

Schilling, H. (2017), 'Yopougon: Together, but not entirely', *Afrique Contemporaine*, 263–4:3, 121–39.

Schilling, H., T. Blokland and A. Simone (2019), 'Working precarity: Urban youth tactics to make livelihoods in instable conditions in Abidjan, Athens, Berlin and Jakarta', *Sociological Review*, 67:6, 1333–49, https://doi.org/10.1177/0038026119858209 [accessed 4 October 2022].

Schilling, H., and O. Dembélé (2019), 'Jeunes entreprenants de la téléphonie mobile à Abidjan: Du lien social entrepreneurial au service de l'exploitation économique', *Politique Africaine*, 153:1, 181–201, https://doi.org/10.3917/polaf.153.0181 [accessed 4 October 2022].

Schmidt, F. A. (2016), *Arbeitsmärkte in der Plattformökonomie – Zur Funktionsweise und den Herausforderungen von Crowdwork und Gigwork* (Bonn: Friedrich-Ebert-Stiftung).

Scholz, T. (2017), *Uberworked and Underpaid* (Cambridge: Polity).

Schor, J. B. (2020), *After the Gig: How the Sharing Economy Got Hijacked and How to Win it Back* (Berkeley: University of California Press).

Schreyer, J., and J.-F. Schrape (2018), 'Plattformökonomie und Erwerbsarbeit. Auswirkungen algorithmischer Arbeitskoordination – das Beispiel Foodora', Working Paper Forschungsförderung 087 (Düsseldorf: Hans Böckler Stiftung).

SCHUFA (2022), *About us: Company*, https://www.schufa.de/schufa-en/about-us/company/how-schufa-works/ [accessed 25 September 2022].

Scully, B. (2016), 'Precarity north and south: A southern critique of Guy Standing', *Global Labour Journal*, 7:2, 160–7.

Seekings, J. (2008), 'Beyond fluidity. Kinship and households as social projects', Working Paper CSSR, 237, Center for Social Science Research, University of Cape Town.

Sewell, G., and B. Wilkinson (1992), 'Someone to watch over me': Surveillance, discipline and the just-in-time labour process', *Sociology*, 26:2, 271–89, https://doi.org/10.1177/0038038592026002009 [accessed 4 October 2022].

SICOGI (2020), 'Qui sommes nous? > HISTORIQUE', https://sicogi.com/historique/ [accessed 24 September 2021].

Simone, A. M. (2004a), 'People as infrastructure: Intersecting fragments in Johannesburg', *Public Culture*, 16:3, 407–29.

Simone, A. M. (2004b), *For the City Yet to Come: Changing African Life in Four Cities* (Durham: Duke University Press).

Simone, A. M. (2010), *City Life from Jakarta to Dakar: Movements at the Crossroads* (New York and Abingdon: Routledge), http://www.lob.de/cgi-bin/work/suche2?titnr=254951352&flag=citavi [accessed 4 October 2022].

Simone, A. M. (2018), *Improvised Lives: Rhythms of Endurance in an Urban South* (Cambridge: Polity Press).

Simone, A. M. (2019), 'Contests over value: From the informal to the popular', *Urban Studies*, 56:3, 616–19, https://doi.org/10.1177/0042098018810604 [accessed 4 October 2022].

Simone, A. M. (2021), 'Ritornello: "People as infrastructure"', *Urban Geography*, 42:9, 1341–8, https://doi.org/10.1080/02723638.2021.1894397 [accessed 4 October 2022].

Simone, A. M., and E. A. Pieterse (2017), *New Urban Worlds: Inhabiting Dissonant Times* (Cambridge, UK and Medford, MA: Polity).

Skeggs, B. (2004), *Class, Self, Culture* (London: Psychology Press).

Skeggs, B. (2011), 'Imagining personhood differently: Person value and autonomist working-class value practices', *Sociological Review*, 59:3,

496–513, https://doi.org/10.1111/j.1467-954X.2011.02018.x [accessed 4 October 2022].

Skelton, T., and G. Valentine (1998), *Cool Places: Geographies of Youth Cultures* (London and New York: Routledge).

Slavnic, Z. (2010), 'Political economy of informalization', *European Societies*, 12:1, 3–23, https://doi.org/10.1080/14616690903042724 [accessed 4 October 2022].

Smelser, N. J., and R. Swedberg (eds) (2005), *The Handbook of Economic Sociology* (Princeton, NJ: Princeton University Press).

Smith, A., and A. Stenning (2006), 'Beyond household economies: Articulations and spaces of economic practice in postsocialism', *Progress in Human Geography*, 30:2, 190–213.

Smith, D. (1990), *The Conceptual Practices of Power: A Feminist Sociology of Knowledge* (Boston, MA: Northeastern University Press).

Sommer, B. (2010), *Prekarisierung und Ressentiments* (Wiesbaden: VS Verlag für Sozialwissenschaften).

Soto, H. de (1989), *The Other Path: The Invisible Revolution in the Third World* (New York: Harper and Row).

Srnicek, N. (2016), *Platform Capitalism* (Cambridge, UK and Malden, MA: Polity).

Staab, P., and O. Nachtwey (2016), 'Market and labour control in digital capitalism', *TripleC: Communication, Capitalism & Critique. Open Access Journal for a Global Sustainable Information Society*, 14:2, 457–74.

Standing, G. (2002), *Beyond the New Paternalism: Basic Security as Equality* (New York: Verso).

Standing, G. (2011), *The Precariat* (London: Bloomsbury Academic), http://www.bloomsburycollections.com/book/the-precariat-the-new-dangerous-class [accessed 23 June 2015].

Stasik, M., V. Hänsch and D. Mains (2020), 'Temporalities of waiting in Africa', *Critical African Studies*, 12:1, 1–9, https://doi.org/10.1080/21681392.2020.1717361 [accessed 4 October 2022].

Sultana, F. (2007), 'Reflexivity, positionality and participatory ethics: Negotiating fieldwork dilemmas in international research', *ACME: An International Journal for Critical Geographies*, 6:3, 374–85.

Sutter, O. (2013), *Erzählte Prekarität: Autobiografische Verhandlungen von Arbeit und Leben im Postfordismus* (Frankfurt and New York: Campus).

Swaan, A. de (1988), *In Care of the State: Health Care, Education and Welfare in Europe and the USA* (New York: Oxford University Press).

Swedberg, R. (1990), *Economics and Sociology: Redefining their Boundaries: Conversations with Economists and Sociologists* (Princeton, NJ: Princeton University Press).

Sztompka, P. (1999), *Trust: A Sociological Theory* (Cambridge: Cambridge University Press).

Tassinari, A., and V. Maccarrone (2017), 'The mobilisation of gig economy couriers in Italy: Some lessons for the trade union movement', *Transfer: European Review of Labour and Research*, 23:3, 353–7, https://doi.org/10.1177/1024258917713846 [accessed 4 October 2022].

Taylor, R. J., L. M. Chatters, C. B. Hardison and A. Riley (2001), 'Informal social support networks and subjective well-being among African Americans', *Journal of Black Psychology*, 27:4, 439–63, https://doi.org/10.1177/0095798401027004004 [accessed 4 October 2022].

Terranova, T. (2000), 'Free labor: Producing culture for the digital economy', *Social Text*, 18:2, 33–58.

TheJobOfMyLife (2019), 'Questions and answers about the program', http://ausbildungsinteressierte.thejobofmylife.de/en/faq.html [accessed 27 April 2019].

Thelen, T. (2015), 'Care as social organization: Creating, maintaining and dissolving significant relations', *Anthropological Theory*, 15:4, 497–515, https://doi.org/10.1177/1463499615600893 [accessed 4 October 2022].

Thieme, T. A. (2018), 'The hustle economy. Informality, uncertainty and the geographies of getting by', *Progress in Human Geography*, 42:4, 529–48.

Tilly, C. (1999), *Durable Inequality* (Berkeley: University of California Press).

Tilly, C. (2001), 'Relational origins of inequality', *Anthropological Theory*, 1:3, 355–72.

Tilly, C., and C. Tilly (1998), *Work Under Capitalism* (Boulder, CO: Westview Press).

Tonkiss, F. (2015), 'Afterword: Economies of infrastructure', *City*, 19:2–3, 384–91, https://doi.org/10.1080/13604813.2015.1019232 [accessed 4 October 2022].

Touré, M. (2010), 'Logique des contrats et réalité du marché: La filière de la grande distribution des cartes de recharge téléphoniques', *Les Cahiers d'Outre-Mer: Revue de Géographie de Bordeaux*, 63:251, 403–18, https://doi.org/10.4000/com.6074 [accessed 4 October 2022].

Tsing, A. (2009), 'Supply chains and the human condition', *Rethinking Marxism*, 21:2, 148–76, https://doi.org/10.1080/08935690902743088 [accessed 4 October 2022].

UKBAA (2022), 'Different sources of funding', https://ukbaa.org.uk/wp-content/uploads/2020/09/Different-sources-of-funding.pdf [accessed 1 October 2022].

Ullrich, C. (2004), 'Aktivierende Sozialpolitik und individuelle Autonomie', *Soziale Welt*, 55, 145–58, doi.org/10.5771/0038-6073-2004-2-145 [accessed 4 October 2022].

Ungruhe, C., and J. Esson (2017), 'A social negotiation of hope: Male West African Youth, "waithood" and the pursuit of social becoming through football', *Boyhood Studies*, 10:1, 22–43, https://doi.org/10.3167/bhs.2017.100103 [accessed 4 October 2022].

Vallas, S., and J. B. Schor (2020), 'What do platforms do? Understanding the gig economy', *Annual Review of Sociology*, 46:1, 273–94, https://doi.org/10.1146/annurev-soc-121919-054857 [accessed 4 October 2022].

Vigh, H. (2010), 'Youth mobilisation as social navigation. Reflections on the concept of dubriagem', *Cadernos de Estudos Africanos*, 18/19, 140–64, https://doi.org/10.4000/cea.110 [accessed 4 October 2022].

Viti, F. (2013), *Travail et apprentissage en Afrique de l'Ouest: Sénégal, Côte d'Ivoire, Togo* (Paris: Karthala Editions).

Vogel, B. (2009), 'Das Prekariat. Eine Neue Soziale Lage?', in R. Castel and K. Dörre (eds), *Prekarität, Abstieg, Ausgrenzung: Die Soziale Frage Im 21. Jahrhundert* (Frankfurt and New York: Campus), pp. 197–208.

Vuarin, R. (1994), 'L'argent et l'entregent', *Cahier Des Sciences Humaines*, 30:1–2, 255–73.

Vuarin, R. (2000), *Un système africain de protection sociale au temps de la mondialisation, ou, 'Venez m'aider à tuer mon lion…'* (Paris: Harmattan).

Wacquant, L. (2016), 'A concise genealogy and anatomy of habitus', *Te Sociological Review*, 64, 64–72.

Weber, M. (1947), *The Theory of Social and Economic Organization*, trans. A. M. Henderson and T. Parsons (Glencoe, IL: Free Press).

Weber, M. (1972), *Wirtschaft und Gesellschaft: Grundriss der verstehenden Soziologie*, 5, revised edition, Study Edition [reprint] (Tübingen: Mohr-Siebeck).

Wehr, I. (2009), 'Esping-Andersen travels South. Einige kritische Anmerkungen zur vergleichenden Wohlfahrtsregimeforschung', *Peripherie*, 114/115:29, 168–93.

Weiss, B. (2009), *Street Dreams and Hip Hop Barbershops: Global Fantasy in Urban Tanzania* (Bloomington: Indiana University Press).

Wellman, B., and S. Wortley (1990), 'Different strokes from different folks: Community ties and social support', *American Journal of Sociology*, 96:3, 558–88.

White, H. C. (1981), 'Where do markets come from?' *American Journal of Sociology*, 87:3, 517–47, https://doi.org/10.1086/227495 [accessed 4 October 2022].

Williams, C. C., and S. Nadin (2012), 'Work beyond employment: Representations of informal economic activities', *Work, Employment & Society*, 26:2, 1–10, https://doi.org/10.1177/0950017012437006 [accessed 4 October 2022].

Williams, J. C., and V. A. Zelizer (2005), 'To commodify or not to commodify. That is not the question', in M. Ertman and J. C. Williams (eds), *Rethinking Commodification: Cases and Readings in Law and Culture* (New York: NYU Press), pp. 362–82.

Wilz, S. M. (2005), 'Der Arbeitskraftunternehmer – Yeti oder Prototyp? Ein Plädoyer für aktive Grenzgängerei zwischen Arbeits-, Industrie- und Organisationssoziologie', in M. Faust, M. Funder and M. Moldaschl (eds), *Die 'Organisation' Der Arbeit* (München and Mering: Rainer Hampp Verlag), pp. 195–226.

Wood, A. J., M. Graham, V. Lehdonvirta and I. Hjorth (2019), 'Good gig, bad gig: Autonomy and algorithmic control in the global gig economy', *Work, Employment and Society*, 33:1, 56–75, https://doi.org/10.1177/0950017018785616 [accessed 4 October 2022].

Woodcock, J., and M. Graham (2020), *The Gig Economy: A Critical Introduction* (London: Polity Press).

Woodcock, J., and M. R. Johnson (2018), 'Gamification: What it is, and how to fight it', *Sociological Review*, 66:3, 542–58, https://doi.org/10.1177/0038026117728620 [accessed 4 October 2022].

Zelizer, V. A. (1994), *The Social Meaning of Money* (New York: Basic Books).

Zelizer, V. A. (1996), 'Payments and social ties', *Sociological Forum*, 11:3, 481–95, https://doi.org/10.1007/BF02408389 [accessed 4 October 2022].

Zelizer, V. A. (2000), 'The purchase of intimacy', *Law and Social Inquiry*, 25:3, 817–48.

Zelizer, V. A. (2012), 'How I became a relational economic sociologist and what does that mean?', *Politics & Society*, 40:2, 145–74, https://doi.org/10.1177/0032329212441591 [accessed 4 October 2022].

Zimmermann, B. (2006), 'Changes in work and social protection: France, Germany and Europe', *International Social Security Review*, 59:4, 29–45, https://doi.org/10.1111/j.1468-246X.2006.00252.x [accessed 4 October 2022].

Index

EU authorised representative for GPSR:
Easy Access System Europe, Mustamäe tee 50,
10621 Tallinn, Estonia
gpsr.requests@easproject.com

www.ingramcontent.com/pod-product-compliance
Ingram Content Group UK Ltd.
Pitfield, Milton Keynes, MK11 3LW, UK
UKHW021833100926
8556IPUK00004B/322
* 9 7 8 1 5 2 6 1 6 2 0 9 0 *